Heaths and Heathers

Heather garden at Liverpool University Botanic Gardens, Ness.
Burton on the Wirral, Cheshire

Heaths and Heathers

Calluna, Daboecia and Erica

Terry L. Underhill NDH

DAVID & CHARLES : NEWTON ABBOT

ISBN 0 7153 4970 8

First published 1971
Second impression 1972

Set in 11 pt Bembo, 1 pt leaded
and printed in Great Britain
by Latimer Trend & Company Limited Plymouth
for David & Charles (Publishers) Limited
South Devon House   Newton Abbot   Devon

To
My wife, DOROTHY
YVONNE LESSWARE
ROGER M. LEA
MARILYN EVANS
D. McCLINTOCK
P. LIPMAN
and many friends and relations whose lives have
at times been ruled by this book

Contents

List of Illustrations

Plates

9

In Text

Botanical drawings by Marilyn Evans

Introduction

I do not really know why I first took an interest in heaths and heathers, but my love for this group of plants really developed at Liverpool University Botanic Gardens at Ness, in the Wirral, Cheshire, when under the director, Ken Hulme, a two-acre heather garden was being developed on the hillside. During a few days convalescing from a very minor operation, I made detailed lists of the characteristics of *Erica carnea* (syn *E. herbacea*) cultivars in an attempt to try to make a dichotomous key. I must admit that despite noting botanical features and measuring leaves, calyx, corolla, stigma, styles, ovaries, etc, I was left with the conclusion that the cultivars were very mixed up and that the type of key I had in mind would need to be done, if it was at all possible, by a large organisation or perhaps a full-time research student or officer.

Over the last nine years I have browsed through numerous catalogues and books jotting down various odd bits of information, and visited many gardens, all the time adding to my notes on heaths and heathers. I enjoyed the new books of recent years, such as F. J. Chapple's *The Heather Garden*, and D. Fyfe Maxwell's and P. S. Patrick's *The Heather Garden*, as well as that old favourite *Hardy Heaths* by A. T. Johnson. The enlarged catalogue entitled *Hardy Heaths and Heather Garden* by John F. Letts was a new venture which is to be greatly admired; but in all these I found the list of species, cultivars and varieties to be incomplete. I was encouraged to try to write a book that could be looked upon as a reference and I am probably the first to realise its limitations; it does not serve as a means of identification of the numerous cultivars and certainly will not include all the species in existence. I aim to deal with the hardy species, varieties and cultivars in detail and offer enough on the South African and glasshouse heaths to stimulate an interest. It must be left to an enthusiastic research worker, the RHS or The Heather

13

Society eventually to produce a system of identification—I wish them luck.

I encountered many problems: describing the colour of the flowers and foliage which seemed to change with age, soil conditions and prevailing weather; which cultivar or varietal name was the correct one to use and even which was the now recognised specific epithet. My list regretfully will not and cannot be complete as there is nothing at present to stop anybody finding a piece of heath or heather on the moors, or on a plant in their garden, or a seedling, with a characteristic that they like and giving this form a name, irrespective of whether it is worth growing or whether there are other identical forms.

In 1970 the Heather Society was appointed the international registration authority for garden heaths and heathers. This appointment was made by the International Society for Horticultural Sciences' committee for horticultural nomenclature and registration at the International Horticultural Congress in Tel Aviv. In future no new cultivar name will be valid unless registered with the authority, which will deal with *Calluna*, *Daboecia*, *Erica*, *Andromeda* and *Bruckenthalia*.

One

The history and uses of heaths and heathers

The history of heaths goes back to the great Greek and Roman civilisations, when such philosophers as Theophrastus, the favourite pupil of Aristotle, and Pliny the Elder in their books on plants referred to the heaths as *Ereike*. The name *Ereike* included *Calluna* which was separated from *Erica* by Salisbury in 1802.

Ericas and *Callunas* have been used for thousands of years by highland and moorland dwellers who, out of sheer necessity, had to use heather for building material, brooms, beds and even drinks. There was a famous brew of heather ale, though the recipe was lost about the time of the Picts. Heaths and heather were used as grazing for sheep, deer and grouse, the *Calluna* being regarded as far superior for this purpose and therefore known as the 'He heath', whereas *Erica tetralix* and *E. cinerea*, being so much inferior, were known as 'She heath'. The importance of heaths and heather is emphasised by the fact that there have been laws governing the burning of heather since 1401.

Early botanists were interested in heaths and heathers enough to record a white *Calluna vulgaris* as early as 1597. In his *Species Plantanum* (1753) Linnaeus recorded twenty-three species of *Erica*, twelve of which came from the Cape Peninsula of Africa, these probably being introduced into cultivation by traders. Heaths and heathers were now being grown in gardens and from about 1770 the number grown increased rapidly; this was helped by Thunberg and Masson who went plant-hunting in South Africa. By 1823 there were over 400 species in cultivation, and the growing of heathers was looked upon as 'the thing to do', just as recently among horticulturists talking *Rhododendrons* and *Camellias* was the vogue.

H. C. Andrews, in his monograph entitled *Coloured Engravings of Heaths*, which was produced in four volumes between 1802 and 1830, illustrated just over 280 species and, in his five-volume monograph on the genus *Erica*, illustrated over 300 species. Loudon writes that at Edinburgh *Callunas* and *Ericas* were used as an edging, being clipped, instead of box (*Buxus*) because they formed less harbourage for slugs. In 1838 he stated that heaths were often planted out in formal beds from glasshouses or grown in pots or beds inside. It was fashionable to have an Ericetum, which was a conservatory for heathers, or an Ericacetum for Ericaceous plants and shrubs.

The 'lucky white heather' has been known for a long time in Scotland but is relatively new in the south of England; Queen Victoria is reputed to have brought it south from Balmoral, but as white forms of *Calluna* can be found in most counties the tale is probably untrue. It is unusual that the luck associated with the heather is transferable and not just confined to the finder. Some nurseries in Britain grow white heather for the 'luck' market, but in the south-west it is not even *Calluna* that is grown, but one of the tree heaths, *Erica lusitanica*.

At the end of the nineteenth century heaths and heathers went out of fashion but since World War II they have been gaining ground again, and the Heather Society was formed in 1963. This interest is not so much in the Cape heaths but in the hardy species of *Erica*, *Calluna* and *Daboecia*.

There are many varieties and cultivars listed in numerous catalogues. Some it appears, are hardly worth growing, others are so similar to one another as to be scarcely worth separating, whereas some names listed are of plants probably now lost to cultivation. There are fourteen species of *Erica* and *Calluna vulgaris* in Europe, North Asia and the Mediterranean area, and about 605 species of *Erica* in South Africa, all south of the Limpopo River. Baker and Oliver, in their book *Ericas in South Africa* (1967), point out that there are many species of *Erica* left on herbarium sheets for identification, but they suspect that after a full check has been made on all the so-called species, and varietal differences and similarities have been taken into consideration, the number of species should remain constant.

Why grow heaths and heathers?

Not many groups of plants are as diverse and have as many assets as the heaths and heathers (*Erica*, *Calluna* and *Daboecia*). With flowers and

Page 17 (above) Young yellow growths on *Calluna vulgaris* 'Hammondii Aureifolia'; (below) a heather garden on a flat site at the Royal Horticultural Society's gardens, Wisley

Page 18 (*above*) 'Sheep-track' path, Liverpool University Botanic Gardens, Ness; (*below*) trees and shrubs intermingling with and forming a background to part of the heath bank at Liverpool University Botanic Gardens

foliage they can provide us with colour all the year round. Throughout the whole year there are golden-yellow tightly packed leaves on the 4–6in high *Calluna vulgaris* 'Ruth Sparkes', or *C.v.* 'Aurea' and *C.v.* 'Beoley Gold', both of which are about 18in high, or *C.v.* 'Joy Vanstone' which changes from golden tints to rich orange in the winter.

In the spring all the young growths of *C.v.* 'Hammondii Aureifolia' appear just like golden-yellow flowers (plate, p 17) which, as the season progresses, change to pale green and blend in with the dark green foliage. *Erica mediterranea* (syn *E. erigena*) 'Golden Dome' will make a reasonably dense bush of light golden foliage up to 2ft high. If it is ground cover we are after, the golden-bronze *E. carnea* (syn *E. herbacea*) 'Ann Sparkes' reaches a maximum height of 9in, or *E. cinerea* 'Golden Drop' has bronze tints becoming darker as the winter progresses. As unusual cream colour is given by *E. cinerea* 'Snow Cream'. Copper-coloured foliage may be had in *Calluna vulgaris* 'Cuprea'. Silver foliage is given by *E. tetralix* 'Alba Mollis', *C.v.* 'Silver Queen' or *C.v.* 'Hirsuta Typica'.

What could be better in the winter than a group of one of the orange and red-tinted *C. vulgaris* cultivars, such as 'Prostrate Orange' at 6in high, the very popular 'Robert Chapman' with flame colours to a height of 18in, or 'Golden Feather' at a similar height, also having gold to soft orange tints? *C.v.* 'Hammondii Aureifolia' is not the only cultivar to produce coloured foliage in the spring: *C.v.* 'Mrs Pat' has the most delightful pink tips, and a pleasing yellow is given by *E.* × *watsonii* 'Dawn'. *C.v.* 'Gnome' has light-green tips in the spring above its normal dark green foliage and is sometimes used as a substitute for a dwarf conifer in rock gardens. In the right place the dark green foliage of *C.v.* 'Serlei' can look most attractive—it may be used as a foil or background for lighter-foliage cultivars. *C.v.* 'Rosalind' (Crastock Heath Variety) is a very pale green and most gardeners are well aware of the attractive light green of the foliage of *E. carnea* (syn *E. herbacea*) 'Springwood White', and the dark green with purplish tints of *E. carnea* (syn *E. herbacea*) 'Vivellii', two useful ground-cover plants.

Height varies so much in heaths and heathers. The smallest are *Calluna vulgaris* 'Golden Carpet' at 2in, and *C.v.* 'Hirsuta Compacta' and *E. cinerea* 'Mrs Dill' at 3–4in. Most of the *E. tetralix, E. ciliaris, E. cinerea* and *E. carnea* (syn *E. herbacea*) cultivars are between 6 and 9in tall, as are some *Calluna vulgaris* cultivars such as 'Humpty Dumpty' and 'Tom Thumb'. Most of the *Callunas*, like *E. vagans*, will reach 18–24in. Some will reach 30in, for example *C.v.* 'Mair's Variety'.

B

The usual height for most of the E. *mediterranea* (syn E. *erigena*) culti-vars is 3–4ft and E. *australis* can often be found reaching 6ft. E. *lusitanica* and E. × *veitchii* 'Exeter' reach between 6 and 8ft and E. *arborea* be-tween 15 and 20ft—quite a variation. They also vary in habit from creeping to erect or bushy.

A good heather garden could have plants flowering throughout the whole year: E. *carnea* (syn E. *herbacea*) in the winter, E. *mediterranea* (syn E. *erigena*) in the spring, followed by E. *cinerea*, E. *ciliaris* and E. *tetralix* in the summer, E. *vagans* in the early autumn, with *Calluna vulgaris* up until winter when the cycle starts again. There is a considerable range of colour. Admittedly only one yellow-flowered species, E. *pageana*, will survive out of doors in Great Britain, and then only in sheltered localities, but why worry when so many other colours are available to choose from?

There are numerous white *Callunas*, and E. *carnea* (syn E. *herbacea*) has two excellent whites in 'Springwood White' and 'Cecilia M. Beale'. E. *ciliaris* 'Stoborough' is a good summer white and E. *vagans* 'Lyonesse' is very good for the autumn. Taller whites are given in the spring, early summer and winter respectively by E. *australis* 'Mr Robert', E. *arborea* 'Alpina' and E. *lusitanica*. Single pinks are numerous in *Callunas*, and C. *vulgaris* 'County Wicklow' is a good double pink; E. *cinerea* 'C. G. Best' is an excellent pink for the summer. Pink tints are very hard to describe as they vary from pure colours to those with hints of purple, as E. *carnea* (syn E. *herbacea*) 'King George', or deep pink to red as in E. *vagans* 'Mrs D. F. Maxwell'. The purples tend to dominate the pink in such cultivars as C.*v.* 'Minima', E. *cinerea* 'P. S. Patrick' or *Daboecia cantabrica* 'Hookstone Purple'. Lavenders to soft lilacs are numerous and C.*v.* 'Hiemalis' or E. *cinerea* 'Eden Valley' are good plants. Carmine is a description given to the flowers of E. *carnea* (syn E. *herbacea*) 'Eileen Porter', pure red to E. *cinerea* 'Coccinea' and 'Plummer's Seedling', and crimson to such cultivars as C.*v.* 'Golds-worth Crimson' or *Daboecia azorica*. C.*v.* 'Alportii' and E. *carnea* (syn E. *herbacea*) 'Loughrigg' could be described as of a purple tint com-bined with red.

The majority of heath and heather flowers are single and the doubles occur only in one *Erica*, E. *mackaiana* 'Plena', and in *Calluna vulgaris* such as 'Alba Plena' and 'Ruth Sparkes', both white, and 'H. E. Beale' and 'J. H. Hamilton', useful pinks. An examination of the shape of the corolla will reveal a considerable variation. E. *tetralix* 'Mary Grace' has its corolla split into segments. The ovoid-urn corolla is found in E.

carnea (syn *E. herbacea*) 'Springwood White' and 'Springwood Pink'. The urceolate-oval corolla is characteristic of most of the *E. cinerea* varieties and cultivars. *E. ciliaris* has a longer urn-shaped (urceolate) corolla. The corolla is an open bell shape, like a cup, in *E. canaliculata*, globular in *E. vagans* and egg-shaped in *Daboecia cantabrica*. The corollas of *E. lusitanica* and *E. australis* are cylindrical. These flowers may be in spikes as in *Calluna vulgaris*, racemes as with *E. ciliaris*, one-sided racemes as in *E. carnea* (syn *E. herbacea*) or in tapering racemes with leafy growths beyond as with *E. vagans*. The flowers are held in clusters in *E. mackaiana* and *E. tetralix*, in numerous clusters forming a spike as with *E. cinerea* and *E. lusitanica*, or in umbels as in *E. umbellata*.

One or two, particularly *E. arborea* and the rarely seen *E. manipuliflora* (syn *E. verticillata*) have very strongly scented flowers. *E. australis* and *E. lusitanica* have a little scent.

In addition to these attractions, many heaths and heathers are tolerant of bad conditions. Many of the dwarfer kinds, particularly *C. vulgaris*, can be walked upon, and even nibbled by animals such as sheep, without suffering damage. *C. vulgaris* and *E. carnea* (syn *E. herbacea*), particularly, will withstand salt spray and almost all, bar the large bush and tree heaths and the tender *E. pageana*, will withstand gales, ice and snow.

Some are lime-tolerant, while others actually prefer alkaline conditions as is described in Chapter Two. Others, particularly *E. cinerea*, prefer acid conditions and *E. tetralix* and *E. ciliaris* like moist spots.

The plants are also accommodating in being easy to maintain; at most, all that is required is an annual clipping and a top dressing, and some do not even need that. They will flower successfully for many years. Their labour-saving character is probably one of the major reasons for their growing popularity. They can be used, as described in this chapter, for very many purposes and in many different types of horticultural features. The enthusiasm that women have nowadays for flower arrangement, particularly miniature designs, must also contribute to their popularity.

The heather garden

This can be the rugged 'mountain' type with large mounds and rocky outcrops projecting from among the plants, with perhaps a stream wending its way down through, or a 'moorland' heather garden (plate, p 17), which is flatter and with fewer rocks, a softer landscape than the mountain garden.

All paths should be informal and generally follow the contours, like sheep tracks (plate, p 18); on no account must there be any edges to the paths—just plants or rocks at the sides. All planting should be in informal groups, preferably intermingling. Trees can be used but these must be selected with care, as they may grow too large, causing excessive shade, or dominate the area. *Sorbus* and *Betulas* do very well in the moorland garden, along with such shrubs as *Rhododendrons*, *Genistas* and *Cytisus* (plate, p 18); conifers are good but will look better in a mountain heather garden. Great care must be taken in the use of the tree heaths, which can quickly spoil the perspective of a heather garden.

The heather garden at the Liverpool University Botanic Gardens, Ness, which is a clever combination of both mountain and moorland heather gardens, has made great use not only of *Erica*, *Calluna* and *Daboecia* in drifts and around rocky outcrops, in groups under trees, or spilling over paths, but of such natural ground-cover plants as *Acaena*, *Antennaria*, *Thymus*, *Cotula* and *Anthemis nobilis* and its non-flowering form 'Treneague', the shrubby and non-shrubby *Potentilla* and such compact grass species as *Festuca ovina* and *Festuca ovina* 'Glauca'.

Rock garden

Erica carnea (syn *E. herbacea*) is the only truly alpine *Erica*. One could argue that *Erica arborea* 'Alpina' should also be classified as an alpine because of its natural habitat, but only a very large rock garden could accommodate it, although I have seen it successfully used as a back-cloth or screen to a rock garden. Some *Calluna* cultivars such as 'Humpty Dumpty' and 'Gnome' look like miniature conifers and some like 'Mrs Ronald Gray' creep over rocks and make ideal crevice plants. So often it is difficult to find plants that will add colour to a rock garden in autumn and winter, particularly if one is trying to balance the planting to get an all-the-year-round effect.

Carefully planted these can give a rugged boldness to an alpine garden, cascading over rocks or wedged in crevices, creeping over paths where they can be walked upon or flowering around stepping-stones. Provided pruning (removal of flowers) is carried out carefully so that an uneven finish is left, as opposed to a smooth effect, almost any heath or heather will be a valuable addition to a rock or alpine garden.

'Ad lib' planting

With the ever-growing interest in heaths and heathers, more and more varieties and cultivars of innumerable species and hybrids have come on the market and the enthusaist is tempted to build a large collection instead of having large drifts of only one or two types.

This has created its own problems, a solution of which is the system of *ad lib* planting where single plants of various varieties or cultivars are grown *en masse*. Little attention is paid to colour clash and the only governing rule appears to be not to have too marked a difference in height of associated plants. The effect of such a clash of many colours is stimulating and is far more relaxing to the eye in the garden than one would imagine. This system of layout and design had to be used as I built up my collection of plants.

Ground cover

While heaths and heathers will rapidly cover large areas of land in a short time, they will not smother and kill weeds. As for other ground-cover plants, the new site must be well cleaned of perennial and annual weeds before planting. After planting, then a season or so of weed control, it is usual for the ground to be completely covered over, thereby preventing the germination of fresh weed seeds, unless the planting distances were too great.

The most commonly used species is *Erica carnea* (syn *E. herbacea*) and particularly the cultivar 'Springwood White' (plate, p 35). Needing little maintenance, it is fast growing, stands half shade and is tolerant of alkaline conditions. *Calluna*, *Daboecia* and *Erica* (all bar the large shrub and tree *Ericas*) make good ground-cover plants although obviously the more rampant growers are the most commonly used. Unfortunately, with the exception of *E. carnea* (syn *E. herbacea*), heaths and heathers are intolerant of heavy shade.

Shrub borders

Far too many professional horticulturists and amateur gardeners fail to realise the potential of heaths and heathers in a shrub border. So often their imagination goes only as far as *Erica*, *Calluna* and *Daboecia* in a heather garden or on the edge of a rock garden, or *Erica carnea* (syn *E.*

herbacea) as a ground cover for some of the other shrubs. The glorious scent, the graceful habit and the abundance of flowers of *Erica arborea* 'Alpina' (plate, p 35) or the range of mauves on *Erica mediterranea* (syn *E. erigena*) must rank them as ideal material for any choice shrub border. If it is a mixed border with shrubs and herbaceous material, *Ericas*, *Callunas* or *Daboecias* will fit excellently in a planting scheme. A good solid group of one of the shrub heaths can make an ideal backbone to an island planting of basically herbaceous material.

Peat walls and raised peat beds

Such is the determination of some gardeners that they will go to great lengths to grow any species, variety or cultivar of plant that they like, irrespective of the suitability of the ground or climate they can offer. Often on highly alkaline (limy) soil an enthusiastic gardener wishes to grow at least one plant of *Erica cinerea* or *E. tetralix*, or one of the winter-foliage *Callunas*, and therefore builds a raised bed of acid soil, using peat blocks as a wall. Provided methods of irrigation are incorporated or are close at hand, exceptionally good results can be had. Plants should be incorporated as the supporting wall is being built and a compost of almost pure peat used as a 'cement'. It is best to put in well-rooted cuttings rather than large plants, provided great care is taken to see that they do not dry out in the early stages of growth.

In one garden I know, a raised peat bed with many choice Ericaceous plants, and large splashes of colour provided by one or two outstanding cultivars of *Erica* and *Calluna*, has made a most useful feature.

Paving, patios and courtyards

Erica and *Calluna* by their basic leaf shape are adapted for a frugal living and are well suited to growing in the little gaps left between the stones of paved areas. So often the gardens of cottages and converted farmhouses have little courtyards or patios with small holes and spots where heaths and heathers would thrive and add a useful contrast to the other plants.

Bedding

I have only once seen *Erica* and *Calluna* used as a substitute for bedding plants and this was at the Somerset Farm Institute at Cannington, where some students had substituted for the normal wallflowers, forget-me-nots and tulips a display of pot-grown *Ericas* and *Callunas*. Skilful use had been made of contrast in foliage colour and heights and an edging had been made of winter-flowering *Erica carnea* (syn *E. herbacea*) cultivars. The whole effect was stimulating and in the winter sunlight looked most effective. Considering how dreary many people's flower-beds look in the winter, there must be a future for this sort of imaginative bedding. Most of the plants were still in their pots and in the spring would have been removed to the plunge beds and frames in the nursery.

Sometimes the little bed at the foot of a tree or shrub (plate, p 35) is made into an island planting where the carpet-forming *Ericas* and *Callunas* are used, the trees and shrubs often benefitting from the cool root-run given by the plants. Labour costs are reduced as the plants will keep down weeds, while at the same time adding the attraction of flowers and foliage. Care has to be taken in plant selection when planting under trees, as most *Ericas* and *Callunas* will not tolerate any shade or drips. *Erica carnea* (syn *E. herbacea*) is most suited to these conditions and has the additional advantage that the carpet of plants will not suffer when the fallen leaves are removed with a wire rake, whereas most *Ericas* and many *Callunas* will get damaged and broken.

Winter effect

While coloured-foliage heaths and heathers may very well be used as a substitute for bedding plants in winter, or to add extra colour to a heather garden, they may also be used as focal points of colour in the garden, particularly many of the recently introduced *Callunas* whose foliage turns to bright red in late autumn/early winter. However the colour is usually only on the side of the plant, the stems and leaves facing south to south-west; these plantings therefore should be made directly north to north-east from the normal point of viewing, so that one looks at the colour face-on and not from the side.

Edges and hedges

Heaths and heathers quickly attain their maximum size and some of them are ideal as small hedges. They do not require much clipping and are usually prolific bloomers. *Erica vagans* and *E. mediterranea* (syn *E. erigena*) appear to be the most popular heath for hedges, and *E.* × *darleyensis* or *E. carnea* (syn *E. herbacea*) for edges to paths or borders.

Cut flowers

Heaths and heathers are widely used in flower arrangements. Their wide variations in leaf colour, shape of twig and branch, length of inflorescence and time of flowering, combined with a most wonderful range of tints and hues, make them very popular, whether on their own or as part of a mixed arrangement. For sprays and bouquets they are frequently used, and the little inflorescences are favoured in miniature flower arrangements. Sometimes they are used as a foil for a couple of large flowers: such as *Helleborus orientalis* coming out from a bed of *Erica carnea* (syn *E. herbacea*) 'Vivellii', or *Gentiana sino-ornata* among the pink-purple flowers of *E. vagans* 'Mrs D. F. Maxwell'. As foliage plants they are very good, particularly the larger bush and tree heaths.

All fresh material should be picked just before it is at its best to get the fullest life from it. If picked when at its peak it would last only a couple of days and not keep its form when dying. As it is, after about one week the leaves start to lose their colour and the flowers turn russet. Woody material should be split and crushed, placed in hot water (just bearable for one's hands) for half an hour and then stood in cold water in cool, airy conditions until it is to be used.

It is even more common to use dried heaths and heathers for their flowers and foliage in winter flower arrangements. Many calendars or pictures of dry flowers make use of heathers. They are nowadays a major part of a current flower-decoration idea: a small arrangement made in a large clear-glass jar, such as that used for bath salts, its top sealed. I am told that after one year everything is still in the same condition as when first arranged. The secret of success with dried heathers lies in the way in which they are dried. Bunches can be made of good sprigs, hung upside-down to dry in a cool, dry atmosphere. Or their stems may be prepared and then put in a solution of one part glycerine to two parts of warm water. The leaves will turn from golden-brown to brown, but will be less liable to drop. Although the flowers of *Ericas* and *Callunas* turn to russet shades and persist, very careful handling is needed after they have been dried for twelve months.

At Kernock in Cornwall there is a 25 acre white-heather farm where the original rooted cutting, planted in the 1920s from a button-hole sprig of the Portuguese *Erica lusitanica*, is now 8ft high and about 12ft in circumference. It was about eight years after planting the original seedlings before the heather could be harvested. Heather is not a flower that can be sold in vast quantities to one buyer, therefore needing a large number of small outlets. Nevertheless over 7,000 boxes, each containing a minimum of 12 bunches, are sent annually from the Cornish nursery all over Britain including Scotland, and they are regularly sent to Ireland and Canada. Because of its general freedom from pests and diseases the white heather does not carry strict health regulations, which eases its export.

Pasturage

It is well known how the hill farmers rely upon heaths and heathers for sheep grazing. The main species grazed are *Calluna vulgaris*—'He heath'—and *Erica cinerea*—'She heath'. Deer, goats, and cattle can all graze reasonably satisfactorily on the young tips and it is common in the winter on Dartmoor, as on other moors, to see sheep, cows and ponies scratching the snow away to get at the young growths. Mutton from sheep grazed on the moors is reputed to have a good flavour. Many a gamekeeper speaks highly of sheep on the northern grouse moors, as their tracks through the heather make ideal roads for the young game to move about along. The main diet of the grouse is heather tips; as they follow the grazing animals around, moving in as soon as the snow is moved and the herbage exposed, the birds can be fairly easily spotted.

Litter for animals

Where heather can be cut in profusion it is sometimes used as a general bedding and litter material for cattle, particularly young bullocks, although its absorbent powers are limited and straw or similar material has to be added.

Tracks and footpaths

Due to the twiggy nature of *Calluna vulgaris*, its abundance on moors and its ability to stand for some time in wet conditions before rotting, it has been used frequently as a base for a footpath or track in slightly boggy areas. Repeated dressings of heather walked and trampled in prevent the traveller, his horse or light vehicle from sinking.

Drainage

Field drains may be made by filling the base of a trench with the tops of old heather plants, the trench then being filled in. It is surprising how long such a land drain will work, though this depends very much on the type of soil, as the biggest problem is silting up.

Packing

Where industry is sited near the edge of a moor, as is the case in Derbyshire, it is not surprising that heather should replace straw as a packing material for such heavy items as pipes, sanitary equipment, etc. It is cut with large scythes (hand or machine), and then bundled prior to use.

Prevention of soil erosion

The popularity of the seaside and the ever-increasing use by the public of sand-dunes for shelter from sea breezes has discouraged the growth of Marram grass and caused the dunes in many places to disintegrate and shift with the winds. The laying of lines of twiggy material across the sand areas slows up the sand movement and encourages fresh dunes. Brushwood is often used but, where available, heather plants with their tough twiggy nature quickly encourage fresh dunes to form and, if these are replanted with Marram, new areas can be stabilised.

This method of checking sand drift is often used in Holland. *Calluna* is also used for stabilising banks of canals in some districts by binding together the soil.

Houses, walls and buildings

For economic reasons the moorland and highland dwellers were once compelled to use the materials close at hand for as many purposes as they could find. Heather sods—that is, clumps of roots with straggly bits of stems attached—were used as bricks for walls, with peat and soil as a cement to bond them. Projecting stems and roots were used to hold a protective covering of mud. Where a roof was required, whether to protect the top of the wall or cover a shed, outbuilding or house, bundles of heather approximately 14in long and 3–4in round were fixed to a pole framework, the base of the stems pointing upwards and the flowers to the outside. They were packed very tightly together to give a reasonably water-proofed and certainly hard-wearing thatch. The thatch was then clipped into shape having been fixed down by branches, willow wands or heather ropes.

In the eastern central Highlands of Scotland the crofters had buildings with strong walls of rock and peat blocks, strengthened with poles, and a strong roof framework of poles on top. On to these heather divots with scalloped edges were laid, like giant tiles, and the gaps between them filled with tough grass or straw to make the whole thing water-tight. A fringe of heather was put at the edge to stop water dripping down the walls of the building. Sometimes the divots were thinner and were covered by a normal heather thatch.

There is a Highland story which says that the traditional tune, the Pibroch, was played by the McDonalds of Glen Gary as they marched around the church of Kilchrist, with its similar timber and heather thatch which they had set on fire, while the congregation consisting of the McKenzie clan screamed as they burned inside.

Nowadays where heather is used for thatch the roof is usually water-proofed underneath with more modern materials. The advantage of a heather thatch is that it is not attacked by birds so much as the reed and straw thatches. On Skye and other Hebridean islands, many buildings with heather walls and roofs have stood for centuries.

Walls, screens, hurdles

Clods of peaty soil held together by heather roots are cut and may be used for building walls and banks, or a row of stakes may be inter-twined with large heather plants to make a useful screen. Hurdles may be made with the long supple twigs from the taller *Callunas*. In horse-racing many of the fences and jumps are made of stakes intertwined with heather, although there is a tendency nowadays to use other material such as gorse.

Roofing pegs

At one time pieces of heather stem were used as pegs for fixing slates to roofs.

Beds

Having built his home of heather the hill shepherd would feel tired and would have lain down on his heather bed. A log framework on the ground was carefully packed with clumps of heather. The growing tips all pointed upwards, while the roots pointed downwards and outwards, the best parts therefore going into the centre of the bed. They are supposed to be very comfortable, but my effort once as an unskilled backwoodsman when camping in making a heather bed was not very successful and I quickly reverted to the comfortable, flat but hard ground. However we had a wonderful fire to cook the breakfast on in the morning, when I kindled and fed the flames with the heather and logs.

Fuel

The crofters with their peat fires and ovens could not fail to burn a certain amount of heath and heather when they removed the top spit of peat from the moors and dried and stacked it before use. The thin brushwood collected from *Callunas* or *Ericas* when dried makes ideal tinder for starting fires. Many heather farmers and fire officers will know that in the heather districts the material on the plants in the open is highly inflammable, and vast areas can easily be set ablaze through carelessness.

For some reason it was once the custom to burn branches of *Erica tetralix* on the eve of All Saints' Day.

Medicine

The shoots of *Erica cinerea* were once used as an astringent. It is probable that some of the old herbalists still use it in their mixtures.

Dyeing material

For many years back crofters have boiled the shoots and young stems of *Calluna vulgaris* with alum and then cooled and filtered it. Materials boiled in the filtrate would, after a short period of time, assume golden tints when dry. Sometimes these tints would have an orange hue.

The age of heather makes a difference as to the resultant colour. For green, use young heather tips that have not flowered. Boil for 2hr, remove the heather and then boil for a further ½hr with a mordant such as alum (chrome, iron and tin may be used to fix the colour to the fibre, so that it will not bleed or fade away, but these three will affect the colour).

Yellow results from the use of the full flower in boiling for 1 hr then, after removal of the heather, boiling for a further ½hr with alum.

For purple, the old heather tops are boiled with the material for 2hr, then the tops are removed and boiled for a further ½hr with 1oz of alum to each 1lb of material, usually wool.

Brown results when dead flowers and tips are boiled for 2hr and then a further ½hr with alum.

The fascination of the use of *Calluna* in particular for dyeing is the glorious variability of greens and yellows, purples and browns that one can get. Probably the major setback is that it is not easy to achieve at a second boiling the same tint as at a previous boiling, although the ingredients might very well appear the same. Oak-bark was often blended to give other colours. This system of dyeing material is still used, and is now having a new lease of life as many people take up this fascinating hobby with home-made vegetable dyes.

Tanning of leather

Common heather was apparently used at various times for the tanning of leather, though literary references to this practice are difficult to trace. However a late seventeenth-century traveller in Galloway described this custom of using heather instead of oak-bark as prevalent in that province.

Baskets

Craftsmen of bygone years were very adept at employing the materials close at hand wherever possible for any items or crafts that could use them, and in some areas fishing baskets were made by using long twigs and stems of heather woven or tied together.

Heather ropes

The gad rope (from the Gaelic for rope, *gaid*), made by the islanders and villagers of the west coast of Scotland, and very strong, consisted of tough stems twisted by hand. Where ropes were needed for the plough, roots were used which, while less pliable, were ideal for heavy duty.

Pipes

Many men are very proud of their briar pipes and are probably totally unaware that in this case the word 'briar' does not mean the rose briar but is the poor English translation of the French *bruyère* (*Erica arborea*). The roots of *Erica arborea* are dug out of boggy ground in the Mediterranean region, particularly in southern France, Italy, Sicily and Corsica where the main briar-pipe industry is based, although the majority of the finishing work is carried out in Great Britain. The knotty roots are kept in moist sheds until required and are then cut into short lengths while still green and boiled from eight to ten hours, which prevents them from cracking. The lengths of root are then hollowed with saws. It is said that a number of years ago poor Italian peasants who cut and drilled the pipewood received compensation for sawn-off fingers from the Italian government and many a peasant heavily in debt is supposed to have removed the end of a finger. When polished and finished *bruyère* pipewood is a pleasant reddish brown and does not burn easily.

Brushes and besoms

Erica scoparia is known as the 'Besom heath', but in this country it was *Calluna vulgaris* which was most used for brushes and besoms. Old wood is far too brittle and the long young wiry wood is used. Bundles of stiff twigs were often joined together and used as pot scrubbers; such brushes were called *renges*.

Drinks

Legend has it that the proper heather drinks which our ancestors so cherished were lost at the time of the Picts. Nowadays we have only heather ale which, while by no means as potent, still makes a most welcome beverage.

As many people have found out the hard way, home-made wines and beers can be very potent and heather ale is no exception. To make 2gal of heather ale one needs to gather enough heather-flower spikes in bloom to fill a 1gal container. The flower heads are covered with water and boiled for approximately 1hr. This is then strained into a container that will take just over 2gal. 1oz of ginger, four or five cloves and ½oz of hops are boiled for nearly 20min in 2pt of water. This is then strained and 1lb of sugar, plus 1lb of malt, are added and boiled for a few minutes. It is then covered and allowed to cool to about 75° to 80° F, when 1 teaspoonful of yeast is added. This is added to the original 1gal of water that the heather shoots were boiled in. Cooled water, that has been previously boiled, is added to make a total of 2 gal of liquid. After two or three days of fermentation the top of the fermenting liquid is skimmed off and the remaining liquid is siphoned into sterilised bottles. The tops are screwed down and in three to twenty-one days time the ale is fit for drinking. Great care should be taken when decanting from the bottle as there will be a small deposit (lees) left at the bottom which it is not advisable to drink, being rather potent. I am told that a large glass of heather ale and a double whisky shortly before going to bed will necessitate the use of an alarm clock in the morning!

Honey

Heather honey—honey produced by bees from heather—is much sought after nowadays for its strong characteristic flavour. It is somewhat glutinous and jelly-like and it never granulates like other honeys, but instead tends to retain many tiny air bubbles which it acquires during the process of extraction. On the moors from July to October one can usually find large numbers of hives brought especially for the heather honey, but at other times of the year these hives may be used in orchards, etc.

The amount of nectar secreted by heather depends very much on the soil and prevailing weather conditions. Some years there will be a good flow of nectar and therefore a good honey year; other years it is very poor. It is said that the flow can be stopped by a thundery day and will not commence until new flowers open.

Erica carnea (syn *E. herbacea*) in its natural habitat is good for bees, and at Dartington the bees have always made a good start to the season on the nearby banks of this heath and *E.* × *darleyensis*.

Sometimes bees will cut a hole in the corolla to get at the nectar, particularly in *Daboecia*.

Pot plants

The hardy and Cape heaths are ideal plants for pot culture (plate, page 54), needing very little attention and giving a large number of flowers in proportion to the leaves. This subject is dealt with more fully in 'Heathers in the Glasshouse', Chapter Three.

Page 35 (*above*) *Erica carnea* (*herbacea*) 'Springwood White' used as a ground cover at the Royal Horticultural Society's gardens, Wisley; (*below*) *Erica arborea* 'Alpina' used in a shrub border

Page 36 (*above*) Young *Callunas* being planted in a nursery bed and firmed with the fingers; (*below*) natural-looking path and conifers growing on the heath bank at Liverpool University Botanic Gardens

Two
Planting and cutivation

Soil

A great deal is written in many books on a suitable soil for *Ericas*, *Callunas* and *Daboecias*, much of which is unnecessarily long-winded, as these three genera are very tolerant of a wide range of soils, provided the pH—acidity or alkalinity—is to their liking. But first a few words about pH. Soil chemists, scientists and keen horticulturists have found it essential to have a recognised system of grading soils according to their acidity and alkalinity. By weighing the hydrogen ions in a gram of soil and expressing this by the use of logarithms, a theoretical scale ranging from 0 to 14 has been devised called the pH scale. On this scale 7 is neutral and from 7 to 14 is progressively alkaline (a soil of pH 8·5 to 9 would be regarded as very alkaline), while a soil from 7 to 1 is acid. Peats on some moors have been recorded with a pH of 4, so acidic that virtually nothing will grow on them. Perhaps one should point out at this stage that while the amount of lime in the soil determines the acidity or alkalinity, the pH scale does not indicate the amount of lime that is present. Another point to remember is that calcium (lime) is an essential element for plant growth. Parts of cells, particularly in leaves, contain forms of calcium and even the most acid soils must contain some calcium to support plants. It is possible to buy small soil-testing outfits to determine the pH of your garden soil.

Some plants are indicative of alkaline soils, such as Yew and Beech growing wild and Old Man's Beard (*Clematis vitalba*) rambling over shrubs. Others are indicative of acid conditions such as *Calluna vulgaris*, *Erica cinerea* and *Rumex acetosella*.

The species of heaths and heathers can be divided into three basic groups according to the types of soil they will grow in: (a) lime-lovers and those tolerant of lime; (b) neutral-tolerant kinds with a slight acceptance of alkalinity and complete acceptance of acidity; and (c) those which must have acid conditions. These groups contain:

(a) *Erica arborea*
    E. australis
    E. mediterranea
        (syn *E. erigena*)
    E. carnea (syn *E. herbacea*)
    E. lusitanica
    E. manipuliflora
        (syn *E. verticillata*)
    E. multiflora
    E. terminalis
    E. umbellata
    E. × *darleyensis*
    E. × *veitchii* 'Exeter'

(b) *Erica vagans*
(c) *Calluna vulgaris*
    Daboecia azorica
    D. cantabrica
    Erica canaliculata
    E. ciliaris
    E. cinerea
    E. mackaiana
    E. pageana
    E. scoparia
    E. tetralix
    E. × *watsonii*
    E. × *williamsii*

It is believed that the reason why some heaths and heathers will not thrive in alkaline soils is that the symbiotic partnership of the mycelium of certain fungi or Mycorrhiza with the roots of the heaths is destroyed, as the fungi prefer in some cases acid conditions. There are two basic types of Mycorrhiza: the exogenous group which forms a thin layer on the exterior of the short rootlets which are generally without root hairs, and the endogenous group which penetrate to the cortical tissue of the roots which may be furnished with root hairs. Their classification is hard as these fungi do not produce spores when in association with plants and only do so in cultures.

The fungi generally live parasitically on their host and in return attack humus (organic) and mineral resources of the soil and pass these to the host plant. *Callunas* and *Ericas* are capable of normal nutrition in average soils, but become mycotrophic in soils unfavourable to the direct absorption of nutrients—such as on a heather moor, where the soil is wholly humus, under trees where nitrates are rarely found, or where the light is too low for much assimilation of foods.

Plants generally rely upon the transportation system—whereby water is absorbed by the roots and carried throughout the plant—as a way for food to enter the plant. The mycorrhizal fungi in Xerophytes —plants adapted to living in dry conditions—where the transportation is of necessity low, become more evident and necessary if the plant is to survive. It appears that Mycorrhiza have a greater ability to extract water and nutrients from the soil. Mycorrhiza are found throughout most of the tissue of *Ericas* and even on the seed coats (testa). The seeds of *Calluna vulgaris* when shed carry threads of the Mycorrhiza on the testa to try to ensure that the seedling and resultant new plant automatically has Mycorrhiza present, and therefore will grow away without a check. To ensure that this association took place, many gardeners of the past mixed soil from among growing *Ericas* and *Callunas* in their seed and potting composts, nursery beds, or fresh areas to be planted. Some people believe that inorganic fertilisers destroy the Mycorrhiza and therefore the plants will suffer, but there is no evidence to support this theory.

Some heaths, such as *Erica tetralix* and *Daboecia cantabrica*, withstand very wet conditions, but on the whole under cultivation a well-drained but moisture-retentive soil suits all species, varieties and cultivars of the three genera. It is important that very rich soils are avoided so that the plants can grow strong and sturdy and provide well-matured wood, and not have soft and sappy growth that is easily damaged. All except naturally peaty soils will benefit, after cultivation, with good dressings of peat or rotting leafmould. Heavy clays or loams should be deeply dug and lightened with peat and sand. On pure sand drying-out is a problem and the incorporation of reasonable quantities of organic matter is needed to help retain moisture. The best peat for incorporation is sedge peat, which is capable of retaining a higher amount of moisture than a sphagnum peat, which will also break down too quickly.

As the roots of heaths and heathers are so delicate, it is very easy to suffocate their roots by planting too deep in heavy soil, and in clays or heavy loams planting must be almost on, or very near the surface. It is still possible to grow heaths and heathers on such heavy soils, but the clay does form a barrier to the fine roots, which cannot penetrate or traverse through the neighbouring soil. Sand is the opposite, being very good, but because of drying-out planting is often deeper.

Where it is thought that the plants might dry out due to being in a very dry spot, or in well-drained soil, then the incorporation of liberal amounts of organic matter, such as leafmould, peat or garden compost, will assist matters. Excellent results have been obtained by burying upturned turves, at a depth of 12–18in. Better plants are generally produced in the poorer types of soil, as opposed to the rich fertile loams. Care must be taken in the use of old vegetable-garden soil which often has a very high pH due to liming over many years.

Before planting, all areas of soil should, after being cleaned of weeds,

especially perennials, be well dug and peat, leafmould, sand or other
soil ameliorants added. If it is possible, leave the area fallow for one
season, during which time any perennial weeds which appear can be
removed and annual weeds hoed off or treated with paraquat weedkiller. A light firming is needed, particularly if the general cultivation
has been done with a rotary cultivator when, after good supplies of
organic matter have been added, the soil will be somewhat fluffy in
texture. It is not necessary to remove large stones from the soil, as these
help to conserve moisture and the young plants will greatly benefit by
getting their roots underneath them.

It is possible to have lime-hating heaths and heathers growing in what
one believes to be alkaline soil without the soil being treated with
Epsom salt or sequestrols, because the constant percolation of rain-
water which itself is slightly acid (from the combination of carbon
dioxide in the atmosphere with the water to give weak carbonic acid),
washes down the lime and can leave a neutral or slightly acid soil. The
acidity is increased when organic matter is allowed to build up on the
surface and so under these circumstances great care should be taken
when cultivating not to bring alkaline soil up to the surface; otherwise
the plants will quickly become stunted and chlorotic.

Likewise it would be folly in such soils to water lime-haters with
hard (alkaline) water. I have seen plantings of lime-intolerant *Ericas*
spoilt by top-dressings of well-rotted leafmould because the leaves
were gathered from paths in other parts of the garden and estate that
were dressed with limestone chippings. This then may serve as a warn-
ing that any organic matter that is to be incorporated in the ground
should be checked for its pH value, and the material with a high pH,
that is 7 and over (alkaline) should not be used on ground to be planted
with lime-haters. Beech leafmould can, in limestone or chalky areas, be
high in calcium, and compost that has been treated with lime and an
activator, whether it be an organic or chemical substance, will often be
too alkaline to be used.

It is usual to incorporate well-rotted leafmould and/or peat. A liberal
dressing of peat worked into the surface before planting, and then a
thinner layer of $\frac{1}{2}-1\frac{1}{2}$in on the surface while planting is very beneficial
if it can be afforded. The peat must be moist, as if it is dust-dry before-
hand it will be very difficult to moisten once it is on the ground. This
peat not only gives a good media, which plants can root into, but also
helps moisture retention and in the early stages helps the young plants
to resist root disturbance in the soil due to frost.

Buying plants

There are some nurseries in this country specialising in *Ericas*, *Callunas*, *Daboecias* and other allied plants with a very long list of species, varieties and cultivars. For this reason one is often tempted to go to these nurseries when needing plants, but often many of the outstanding plants are grown by the general and smaller nurseries and to just as high a standard as by the specialist.

Anyone wishing to purchase plants would be well advised to visit the nursery, see the plants growing and make their own observations and judgement as to the standard of cultivation and quality of plants in relation to price. Good nurseries will have horticulturists available who will be able to discuss the merits of their plants and give advice on their treatment.

Plants should be strong and 'healthy looking', bushy not leggy, and true to type. To avoid disappointment, order, or visit and order, well in advance and check your consignment as soon as possible after arrival. The plants should not be dry at the roots; if they are, check on the length of delivery time and contact the nursery at once.

Obviously it is in the plants' and the purchaser's interest to plant them in their permanent position as soon as possible. If you are unable to plant on arrival then unpack them carefully and heel them in a sheltered and shaded place outside, or if it is frosty store them in a cool, frost-free shed.

Planting

The roots of heaths and heathers are very delicate and are very prone to damage from drying out. Most plants will suffer a considerable check if damage occurs to their fine roots, so it is imperative that material for planting is moist and that the soil is not allowed to dry out, particularly in the early stages. Never plant these delicately rooted subjects when the soil is wet and sticky or dust-dry. Nowadays many amateur and commercial growers make use of peat composition pots. One often hears complaints from people that the plants looked well in them when planted out, but then failed to grow properly. This is usually due to the top edge of the peat pots not being removed when planting, with the result that it acts as a wick and draws moisture from lower down in the soil which evaporates on the surface. If this is not attended to within a very short space of time, despite being well soaked before and after planting, they can dry out to such a degree that permanent damage is caused.

Plants should be lifted carefully from a nursery bed, particularly *Erica cinerea*, the roots of which do not seem capable of holding the soil together and therefore suffer badly in transplanting. Because of this rooted cuttings are better for planting out.

Planting is best done with a spade for larger plants and a trowel for smaller ones and they are planted with the lower foliage just resting on the surface of the soil. This will avoid a bare-stemmed look. Although I would advise slightly deeper planting if the plants are at all leggy, this must not be taken to extremes, particularly if the soil is heavy, as like other Ericaceous plants heaths and heathers tend to be shallow rooters. Planting can be done at almost any time of the year, but the usual times are April to May or September to October; the earlier time is more suited to heavy soils, the latter being generally better, if possible, when plants can still be established before winter sets in.

The early-autumn planting in a warm soil encourages early root growth, and it is usual that plants put in during October will have rooted-in by winter. Plants put in during the spring may very easily dry out before rooting has properly taken place. *Erica cinerea* and *E. carnea* (syn *E. herbacea*) will like dryer spots, *E. tetralix*, *E. ciliaris* and *Daboecia* the cooler and more moist positions.

Firming is another necessity, but by firming it is not suggested that plants are rammed home with the heel. Firming with the fingers (plate, p 36) (not even a trowel handle) is best because of the delicate roots the plants have. A common fault is trying to put plants into too small a hole, thereby being tempted to ram the roots into the hole; if the gardener succeeds the plants will have damaged roots, and if not the roots will be on the surface and very prone to drying out.

'At what distance apart should I plant my heaths and heathers?' is a constant cry from gardeners and is yet another question that it is nigh on impossible to answer dogmatically. It obviously would depend on the size of the plant at the time of planting and its ultimate height and width. Many people advocate that the distance apart should be the same as the plant's ultimate height. This often leaves a uniform area of humps and also it can take many years before the allotted space is covered, meaning a great deal of labour spent on weeding and other surface cultivations. I prefer to use a considerably higher density of plants to get rapid cover. Admittedly, unless the plants are clipped at various heights and larger distances are occasionally left between plants, the planted area can have a very flat-topped and uninteresting appearance.

The distances often recommended are 9–18in apart each way for *Erica tetralix*, 12–18in for *E. ciliaris* and *E. cinerea*, 15–24in for *E. carnea* (syn *E. herbacea*), 18–24in for *E. vagans*, and 2½–6ft for *Calluna vulgaris*, the larger heaths and tree heaths. I have heard it suggested that *Daboecia* should be planted from 2½ to 3ft apart. This is very optimistic since it would take four to six years for the plants to meet, if they ever did.

Distances, as mentioned earlier, can also depend on the size of material. So often people will plant two or three-year-old plants, but I much prefer well-rooted and established cuttings that have been stopped once and are breaking well. These are dibbled into the allotted areas sometimes as close as 7 or 8in, particularly with *Erica carnea* (syn *E. herbacea*), *E. cinerea* and *E. tetralix*. A large amount of the planting carried out by the staff of Liverpool University Botanic Gardens at Ness, under its director, J. K. Hulme, was by this rooted-cutting method and anyone who has been fortunate enough to see the results of this work must surely agree with the method (plates, pp 18, 36, 53).

If freshly-rooted material is not going to be planted in its final position for a year or more, it will need to be 'grown on' in pots or deep boxes (never less than 2½in deep, because of drying out), but better still in nursery beds. These are generally 4ft in width, for ease of working, and the plants are each put in a 5–6in square.

We know that seedlings like a little shade, and so young plants will receive similar benefits when shielded from the main force of the sun. In nursery beds the shade can be provided by a wooden framework and brushwood, although hessian or slats of wood in wire netting rolled out on this framework is a better method. Use windbreaks wherever possible to shield both young and freshly planted material from strong winds, particularly cold or salt-laden winds near the coasts.

Many of the books on heaths and heathers discuss at great lengths the planting of a heath garden, formal or informal, and give detailed schemes for planting. There is a well-known saying 'one man's meat is another man's poison' and so it is with heaths and heathers. A combination that one person finds pleasing may be rather distasteful to another. I would be the first to admit that some combinations can be more appealing than others and also that some plants such as *E. cinerea* 'Coccinea' with very dark red flowers, *E. vagans* 'Mrs D. F. Maxwell' with deep cerise flowers, or *Calluna vulgaris* 'Goldsworth Crimson' and

'C. W. Nix', both very deep crimson, are often difficult to place in a planting scheme. Nature is not often guilty of clashing colours.

Watering

When full-scale irrigation or watering is carried out on freshly planted heaths and heathers and is repeated whenever necessary throughout the subsequent couple of growing seasons, the beneficial effect is most marked. This practice was adopted at Ness (Liverpool University Botanic Gardens) and proved most successful. One problem that did arise was that on a very light sandy soil to which granular peat had been added if it became too dry on the surface, there was a tendency for the water applied from the irrigators to run off the surface instead of being absorbed into the soil for the plants to use. In the early stages when the soil is visible between the plants, the water-droplet size from the spray nozzles of the irrigators must not be too large as this would cause damage to the soil structure. Once there is a complete coverage of foliage this problem does not arise.

It must be remembered that in nature *Callunas* with their small, closely packed scale-like leaves and *Ericas*, the majority of which have revolute margins to their leaves, are well adapted for frugal living in soils reasonably low in moisture.

People who propagate and grow the lime-hating heaths and heathers in alkaline districts in special beds of lime-free soil must, if they wish to maintain healthy plants, use lime-free water. This does not become so important for established plants in the open but is most essential in a propagation unit.

During the drought period and other dry spells in 1969 many amateurs in districts of hard (alkaline) water experienced difficulties in keeping some of their heaths and heathers alive. It was not long before their supplies of rain-water in the tub by their glasshouse, if they were lucky enough to have them to begin with, ran dry. Just the occasional irrigation with hard water had to be made, but it was essential to keep these to a minimum.

Feeding and mulching

There are considerable differences of opinion regarding the feeding of heaths and heathers. There is one school of thought that is adamant that only bulky organic matter and organic fertilisers should be applied, while another school has, I feel, a far more reasonable approach and accepts the view that these can well be supplemented by inorganic fertilisers if applied correctly.

Organic matter, such as sedge or moss peat, well-rotted bracken or leafmould, is usually incorporated at planting time and then more is applied, if possible, as a mulch. This annual dressing, when it breaks down, will have many beneficial properties, such as encouraging surface rooting and natural layering. The roots are kept cool and the layer of organic matter is of a spongy texture that will conserve moisture. Provided it is weed free, it is a great asset for weed control. It is for this reason that, while useful, ordinary garden compost should not be used as a mulch, unless it can be guaranteed free from weed seeds. Another point to remember is that garden compost in which lime is added to assist the breakdown usually results in an alkaline compost that would react violently with the acid-loving heaths.

Leaf soil has been used as a feeding mulch with great success. Often the leaves that are put into the leaf pile in many gardens have been swept up from paths and drives, and my experience has been that when these leaves rot down to fine dust the soil that had been gathered when sweeping made the leaf soil sticky and reduced its beneficial properties. Considerable success has been achieved with the use of sawdust, but this must be well-rotted before being applied as a mulch.

Hoof and horn, dried blood and seaweed manure are often applied as an early-spring feed—usually in smaller quantities when an autumn top-dressing of organic matter has been applied. There is no real standard rate of application and it really depends on the vigour that the plants are showing. An average rate of application would probably be about $\frac{3}{4}$ to 1oz per square yard.

Many people refuse to use inorganic fertilisers on their heaths and heathers once they are growing in the garden, saying that the delicate roots will be damaged by the 'crude' chemicals. What I find so interesting is that these same people will happily pot up freely-rooted cuttings into John Innes potting compost acid mixture which will contain the nitrogen in the hoof and horn but the phosphates and potash in the inorganic superphosphate and sulphate of potash respectively. If any roots were going to be damaged by these inorganic chemicals one would expect the damage to occur with these delicately rooted cuttings. This does not appear to be the case. Anyone who has seen the heather bank at Liverpool University Botanic Gardens must have been impressed by the health and vigour of these members of the family

Ericaceae growing on a steep sandy hillside. As well as normal dressings of peat at planting times they were given liberal amounts of John Innes base fertiliser and in subsequent years were top-dressed at the rate of 2oz per square yard with it. The only stipulation that was made when we applied the top-dressing was that the irrigators were put on to wash it into the soil. When the same procedure of irrigation after fertiliser application is carried out by the amateur, dressings at 2oz per square yard of a fertiliser made up of equal parts by weight of sulphate of ammonia, triple superphosphate and sulphate of potash will be of great benefit to the plants and cause no undesirable side effects. I have heard recently of the use of Magamp, a granular fertiliser which slowly releases its food over a couple of years and which is being used increasingly by horticulturists for the compost of containerised plants.

Many amateurs manage to grow excellent beds of heaths and heathers without feeding with fertilisers. The only attention they get is the occasional top-dressing of peat. These plantings seem to grow and flower reasonably well, but there is nevertheless a possibility that the occasional feeding with fertilisers would give them a slightly special look.

Sequestrols

Sequestrols or iron chelates were introduced about 1961 and now have added magnesium and manganese. These compounds will usually cure the chlorosis of plants—yellowing of leaves—caused by deficiencies of iron, magnesium or manganese, which usually occur in alkaline soils —particularly iron deficiency where the iron salts are usually locked up as insoluble compounds and are therefore unavailable to the plants.

Sequestrols are usually most effective on soils that are neutral or just alkaline, or in acid soils where the plants for one reason or another have an anaemic appearance. On very alkaline soils applications are needed at least twice a year. This does not necessarily mean that lime-haters may be grown in highly alkaline soils if regular applications of iron chelates are given: a trial was carried out at Cambridge which resulted in *Erica cinerea, E. tetralix* and some *Rhododendrons* just staying alive for a couple of years without growing appreciably.

The best time for application of sequestrol is just before the spring flush of growth commences, which is March to April, and preferably during a rainy spell. It is dissolved at the rate of half to one level teaspoonful to each pint of water and then applied to the plants according to size, soil, age and state of chlorosis.

With new plantings it is a good practice to water the hole with diluted iron chelate prior to planting.

Maintenance

It is the all-the-year-round effect and the ease of maintenance that is accounting for the popularity of heaths and heathers. However some heaths are easier to maintain than others. *Erica carnea* (syn *E. herbacea*) needs a trim only once every two or three years. Having basically supple (not brittle) stems that do not damage easily when walked upon occasionally, this plant can be easily raked or brushed over to remove leaves or twigs in the autumn or winter.

Erica vagans and *E. terminalis* are so brittle, particularly the latter, that raking and brushing will cause considerable damage.

It is often necessary to go over some *Ericas* a couple of times a year, not only to prune and trim off the dead flowers, but to trim or repair damage caused by snow or wind. *E. terminalis* is very prone to weather damage and so are many of the taller heaths, particularly to snow. *Erica arborea* 'Alpina' is an exception, standing heavy falls of snow very well. My experience has shown *Erica mediterranea* (syn *E. erigena*) to suffer badly during even slight falls of snow, particularly when mature, the plants being splayed from the centre outwards and never regaining their original shape. Some low-growing *Callunas*, such as 'J. H. Hamilton', can be given fairly heavy wear from being walked upon and will still survive and flower.

When choosing species, varieties or cultivars for additions to an existing garden or when planting a new area always bear in mind their adaptability to traffic, weather and maintenance, as well as the colour, height, time of flowering, etc.

Pruning

Shrubs may be pruned for a number of reasons: (1) formative pruning; (2) to produce flowering wood; (3) to control shape or size; (4) to remove old and unwanted flowers; (5) to remove dead, diseased or misplaced material. *Ericas*, *Callunas* and *Daboecias* are no exception and, as shrubs, may well be pruned for all of these reasons.

Rooted cuttings, when well rooted in the propagating medium or when established after potting or lining out, have their tops nipped out or clipped off with shears, depending on the number to be treated, so as to encourage bushy young plants. This is the simplest type of formative pruning. With some of the taller heaths, such as *Erica arborea, E. × veitchii* 'Exeter', *E. lusitanica, E. australis*, etc, it is often desirable to remove a third to half of the previous season's growth after flowering for three or four years to encourage very strong bushy plants, and then allow them to form their natural habit of large blooms or sprays of blooms and leaves. This is a more sophisticated type of formative pruning.

All heaths and heathers very readily produce flowers but will sometimes have masses of tiny little spikes or clusters instead of a reasonable number of large inflorescences (plate, p 53). When this situation arises, feeding is not the only answer, and hard judicious pruning is what is needed. *Erica mediterranea* (syn *E. erigena*) may be cut right back into the hard wood when it will sprout again even from the base. Many beds of *Callunas* have been revitalised by reasonably hard pruning, particularly *Calluna vulgaris* 'H. E. Beale'. *Callunas* should be pruned with some care as generally they will not sprout from really old wood, two- or three-year-old wood being about the oldest that they will usually sprout from. The summer hybrid *Ericas*, such as *E. × watsonii* 'Gwen', are trimmed or are pruned hard in alternate years to maintain the strong young shoots with their attractive early colour and good clusters of flowers.

I detest the habit of clipping beds of heaths and heathers so evenly that they look as if they have been mown. A far more natural undulating effect as seen in the wild (plate, p 72), with shoots of varying heights all over the plants, is much more suitable. The plants should give an interesting yet even effect, and one should avoid the regular hummocks that arise when planting at wide spacings and allowing each plant to develop to its natural size. This hummock effect appears unnatural, like the flat effect that many people give their plantings.

The uneven effect can be given to heathers when being trimmed by using secateurs and cutting at heights varying from 1 to 3in. This is very nice in theory, but almost impossible in practice with a large planting, when shears must be used. Instead of using them in the normal way they should be turned upside down and clipped into the bush. It is necessary to clip annually most of our heaths and heathers, particularly all those which are 3ft or less in height. On the length of stem where the flower spike was borne no new shoots will form; all new shoots will arise from the base of the flowering spike or a continuation of the tip, as is the case with *Erica vagans* and *Calluna vulgaris*.

To stop the plants becoming leggy, encourage new shoots to sprout from the base of the flower stem, and to clean the plant ready for the next season's display, the dead flowers are clipped off. I would recommend removing the dead flower spikes of *Erica ciliaris* and *E. tetralix* in early spring; not that their flowers are of particular beauty during the winter but they add some protection to the plant, particularly with *E. ciliaris*. With *E. cinerea*, *E. vagans* and *Calluna vulgaris* the various russet tints in the dead flowers are a great attraction, particularly in the winter sunlight. The spring-flowering *Ericas* such as *E. × darleyensis* and *E. mediterranea* (syn *E. erigena*) are clipped in June, which is really soon after they have finished flowering and before the new growths have become any appreciable length. The summer and autumn flowering cultivars are, as mentioned earlier, usually left until March and the winter-flowering heath *E. carnea* (syn *E. herbacea*) is trimmed every second or third year in April.

It is fortunate that one does not often have to prune one's plants to remove pest or disease-ridden material. One does occasionally have to remove dead material, due more to mechanical damage—the wind, animals and snow—than dieback. Occasionally with the larger *Ericas*, particularly *E. australis*, *E. arborea* and *E. lusitanica*, a shoot will grow almost at the expense of all the others and will need to be trimmed or removed. I have found that *Erica arborea* 'Alpina' will often produce one or two very long side growths which, unless severely cut back, will bend down and split open the plant or overrun its allotted space (plate, p 35).

Trimming is usually done with shears and pruning with secateurs, although some gardeners become experts with a pruning knife and will always use this in preference to secateurs. Occasionally one does come across a stem which is too large for secateurs without the risk of straining them. A small pruning saw would then be needed.

I would like to re-emphasise the importance while trimming or pruning heaths and heathers of keeping as near the natural shape of the plant as possible.

Mechanical weed control

With heaths and heathers it is imperative that new ground should be cleared of all weeds, both annual and perennial, prior to planting. *Ericas* and *Callunas* might be regarded as good ground-cover plants, but this does not mean that they will smother and destroy existing weeds—far from it. Couch grass, docks, bracken, etc, will, if given half a chance, overrun and destroy fresh plantings of heaths and heathers. If the ground is clean the new plants will, soil and climate permitting, cover the ground and make the germination of fresh weed seeds almost impossible. Until then it will be necessary to carry out some form of weed control. The same systems of weed control will be needed in nursery beds.

HAND WEEDING

This is mainly confined to nursery areas and small plantings. Care must be taken to hold freshly planted specimens down when pulling out well-rooted weeds close to them, as the heath could so easily be pulled out of the ground and suffer a considerable setback. A hand fork is often useful to loosen the ground, or turn over a thin layer of soil where minute weed seedlings exist. Particular attention should be paid when using a hand fork not to loosen the root ball of the heath or heather, unduly damage its delicate roots or pile up soil into the crown of the plant.

HOEING

Provided no germinating perennial weed seeds are allowed to form a rootstock, an area can be kept clean with a hoe. One can use a Dutch hoe, a swan-necked type or a double-sided hoe. It is all a matter of personal choice. The weather must be hot and dry when hoeing so that the weeds will be quickly dessicated and therefore unable to rejuvenate when it rains. It is necessary prior to hoeing to remove seeding weeds or those, such as large groundsel plants, which will still flower and produce viable seeds for days after being hoed off. Care must be taken not to loosen or chop off bits of the plants and to hand weed around them where necessary in areas where a hoe cannot penetrate.

MULCHING

Minute weed seedlings may be killed by a 1in mulch or layer of granulated peat. It is best to apply this on already clean ground and then if any fresh weeds germinate in the mulch these can easily be pulled out of the peat. As anyone will know who has weeded plants with a good peat mulch, this is a far more pleasant task than pulling weeds from ordinary garden soil.

Chemical weed control

This is still in its early stages of development, although many nurseries, large gardens and estates practise chemical weed control among heaths and heathers with success.

One major point that is not known to date is the effect of some of these weed-control chemicals on the eventual rate of growth; whereas 'Chemical A' might very well scorch a certain cultivar and 'Chemical B' does not show any physical damage to that cultivar, the plant treated with 'Chemical A' might very well recover and grow more quickly than that treated with 'Chemical B'.

Simazine: This is often used at rates of 1¼lb of the active ingredient per acre on young lined-out plants that have been planted for a month or more. It is usually applied in a split dose of ¾lb the first time and ½lb a month later. As with other chemical weed controls it is necessary to reduce the soil to a fine tilth. The solution is applied with a sprayer or fine-rosed watering can.

Venzar (Lenacil): Applied at the rate of 2lb active ingredient per acre, this appears to be safer than simazine. It is not a very soluble weedkiller and while it can usually be applied safely at all stages of plant growth, including newly lined-out cuttings, damage, including death, can occur to plants when areas treated with venzar are subjected to periods of heavy rain.

Herbon Red (CIPC): This chemical plus fenuron has been applied in early winter on dirty beds.

Dalapon: Applied at 4lb per acre, this has had considerable success in controlling couch grass in old-established *Ericas*.

Dichlorbenil: Applied before weed emergence up to March at 70lb Casoran granules per acre.

Trifluralin; At 20fl oz per acre incorporated into the soil, this is used in the USA prior to planting.

It is essential that the exact dosage per acre and manufacturer's instructions are followed, or considerable damage can occur. In soils where considerable applications of peat have been made, great care should be taken to make certain it is safe to apply the chemical. It is advisable to try the chemical on a small area before risking it on one's whole collection of plants. Where peat mulching is used the effect of the weedkiller may be impaired.

Heather burning

The young tips of heathers are useful as food, particularly during the winter and spring, for cattle, ponies, sheep, lambs, deer and grouse (of which it is the main diet). To obtain fresh supplies the heather can either be cut and carted away, which is a laborious and time-consuming job, or burnt. On Dartmoor this practice of burning is called 'swaling'. There in the winter one can observe sheep digging down through the snow to find the supply of shoots for food, and as soon as they vacate the plants the birds move in. Good strong heather is of use to the gamekeeper, as the young birds can shelter under the plants or move about in sheep tracks to keep dry. Hill sheep farmers are also well aware of the beneficial effect that heather has in cleaning and keeping in good order the feet of the sheep.

The heather is usually burnt when it is 9–15in tall. After burning, new seedlings will quickly arise which, after a year, will provide good food. Burning is usually carried out on a five- to seven-year cycle. The Statutory Instrument of 1949, No 386, the Heather or Grass Burning (England and Wales) Regulations, which were made in pursuance of Section 20 of the Hill Farming Act, 1946, set out certain conditions governing the burning of heather or grass. It should be done only between 31 March and 1 September and a licence must be obtained from the Ministry of Agriculture. A special licence may be granted out of this period on special application. It should be carried out between sunrise and sunset. Sufficient staff should be at hand to deal with it and keep the burning under control. Suitable control equipment must be available and adjacent land must be protected. Forty-eight hours' notice must be given to interested parties in writing, giving the date, time, place, reasons and extent of the land to be burnt.

Pests and diseases

There are a number of pests and diseases that attack heaths and heathers, but growers, whether commercial or amateur, should not be alarmed as attacks are rare compared with most other garden plants and heaths and heathers are for all intents and purposes free of pests and diseases.

Page 53 (*above*) Part of the heath bank at Liverpool University Botanic Gardens; (*below*) *Calluna vulgaris* 'H. E. Beale' showing a large number of small inflorescences

Page 54 (above) Erica mediterranea (erigena) 'Rosea' in winter; (below) Erica hyemalis

Pests

HEATHER BEETLE—LOCHMACA SATURALIS

This pest can be especially bad on *Callunas*, rarely attacking *Erica cinerea* and *E. tetralix*. The adult beetle and the larvae reduce the number of shoots on a plant by destroying the terminal buds and tender leaves, which are the staple diet of grouse; hence the seriousness of this pest on grouse moors in Holland, England and Germany. Sheep grazing will suffer and the resultant reduction of flowers can affect honey yield. The adult beetle appears in August and September, is ¼in long, olive-brown with a black head and body and granulated wing cases. It hibernates at the end of September in the peat and sphagnum beneath plants. The grubs are $\frac{1}{12}$ in long, slightly curved and pale green, later deepening to greyish-brown with dark blotches of variable sizes on the sides of the body. They have three pairs of very short legs. When fully fed in July the grubs descend to the ground and pupate. Grubs are eaten by the black game in Scotland, also by partridge, pheasants and starlings, but not by grouse, which ironically enough suffer from the damage caused by this beetle. The adult beetle and its larvae appear to encourage a root rot to set in, the first symptom of which is brown foliage—as if damaged by a hard winter. This damage is increased under drought conditions.

Control is either by dusting with derris or nicotine in July and August—care being taken that no derris can find its way into water that may contain fish—or by burning plants in August.

DIEBACK BEETLE—HALTICA ERICETI

Little blue-green beetles and black grubs swarm all over the plants and eat flowers and young tips of the shoots. *Erica* × *watsonii* 'H. Maxwell' appears to be the most susceptible to this pest. Good control can be had by applying malathion dust or liquid.

GALL MIDGE—WACHLLIELLA ERICINA

This pest lays its eggs in June in the south of England in the growing point of the stem and therefore causes a terminal gall to develop. Each gall contains a reddish larva which remains in the gall until the following May, when it pupates and the adult emerges to start the cycle again. It was little known in the late 1940s, but is now on the increase and has to date been confined to *Erica carnea* (syn *E. herbacea*) cultivars. It

D

appears to prefer 'Springwood White' and 'Springwood Pink' but has been recorded on 'Pink Pearl', 'Atro-Rubra', 'King George' and 'Vivellii'. Control consists of destroying affected plants during the autumn and winter.

MISCELLANEOUS

Rabbits will sometimes chew young plants, but eventually in a normal planting there is too much material of a nature that is not their 'favourite vegetable'. Once established, damage to the shoots by eating is not a particular worry. However in some gardens the burrowing underneath by rabbits, or worse still by moles, particularly under young plants, can cause considerable losses, especially from drying out in dry seasons.

In small gardens and ornamental areas where the public have general access with their dogs, considerable damage can be done by urine. When the incident is actually seen occurring, the plant can be saved from damage by being doused with a bucket of water. However this is really impractical in public areas, where one just has to accept that certain plants will be severely damaged and sometimes killed.

Diseases

DIEBACK—MARASMIUS ANDROSACEUS

This fungus causes dieback and sometimes death of the plant, although it occurs usually only on old shoots so that it seldom causes significant damage. The rhizomorphs are almost like horsehair and bear cream or pale brown toadstool-like fruiting bodies 10mm across. It is more common in Scotland than elsewhere in the British Isles and more to the west than the east. Where attacks occur in the garden, a mild disinfectant will quickly clean up the ground after removal of infected plants.

PHYLLOSTICTA ERICAE

This disease is suspected of causing trouble on *Erica carnea* (syn *E. herbacea*) in Germany and has caused leaf browning on plants in Great Britain.

CLADOSPORIUM HERBANUM

This has occurred more than once in Cornwall on *Erica lusitanica* where it causes sooty mould on the foliage.

STENPHYLIUM ERIOCTONUM

This causes a sooty mould on *Calluna vulgaris* which can result in leaf fall and dieback, particularly with plants on the continent. It does occur on leaves in glasshouses.

PHYTOPHTHORA CACTORUM—PHYTOPHTHORA CINNAMOMI

This disease attacks and kills glasshouse heaths and particularly those grown in pots where the compost can be a very favourable media for growth of the fungi. It is encouraged by the use of rain-water from tubs outside, these often being a source of heavy contamination. It has been suggested that beech is susceptible to Phytophthora and therefore compost containing such leafmould should be avoided. Clean water and soil sterilisation reduce the chances of attack considerably. Phytophthora cinnamomi—Erica Wilt—has spores resistant up to five years and can attack poorly grown plants particularly in areas of poor drainage with excessive moisture. Tips of plants turn over, the leaves turning brown before dropping off. It is often associated with root-rot. Has been reported on *Calluna vulgaris* 'Cuprea' and 'F. J. Chapple', and *Erica carnea (herbacea), cinerea, mediterranea, vagans* and × *darleyensis*. Control consists of good cultivation, folia feeding, and watering the soil with 2% formalin.

HONEY FUNGUS—ARMILLARIA MELLEA

Attacks by this devastating fungus with its black rhizomorphs somewhat resembling boot laces and its honey-yellow toadstools are rare on heaths and heathers, although many trees and shrubs are very susceptible. One method of control is to pull up and burn the plants, remove infected soil and replace it with fresh earth.

WITHER TIP

Withering of tips occurs on plants in forests in cold weather and it is a physiological environmental disorder.

DODDER—CUSCUTA EPITHYMUM

This parasitic plant is more abundant than *C. europaea*. It is found on *Calluna vulgaris* as well as gorse and other moorland shrubs. Control consists of burning infected plants and areas when the Dodder is in flower and before it has seeded.

Three

Heathers in the glasshouse

The title of this chapter is rather misleading, for although all the plants to be described in the next few pages will grow under glass, a number of them will also grow outside. A considerable number of the tender ones are grown in very sheltered parts of gardens in the south and west of England.

I well remember a visit to Kew many years ago when I was still a schoolboy keen on plants, but yet to realise that horticulture was to be my vocation. I somehow managed to dodge senior officials responsible for the glasshouses and nursery, and then found a friendly gardener who allowed me to look around this area that so many other keen gardeners must have wished to see. Among the rather motley collection of glasshouses was one noticeable for its smallness, and if my memory serves me correctly, shaded with some light-green emulsion; inside was a varied collection of both young and established plants. One of the workers told me that this was the Cape Heath house, that the plants were very hard to grow and, for this reason, a special house was needed for the botanical collection at the gardens, complete with artificial illumination and a mist unit. I must point out in fairness to Kew that I have not in recent years checked on the authenticity of this information about the house and its contents; at that stage in my life I did not really know what a Cape Heath was. However the incident does show that Cape Heaths have a reputation for requiring special houses with expensive equipment, and for having a high death-rate. But this reputation is undeserved. To those fortunate people who saw the collection looked after by the late Dr Ronald Gray, one need not emphasise how unnecessary expensive equipment is to grow Cape Heaths. There, in his garden, was a collection of glasshouses with just enough heat to keep out the frost and, inside, a most outstanding collection of species.

What are these Cape Heaths and how do they differ from the other heaths and heathers which we grow in our gardens? As the name suggests, they come from South Africa or, to be exact, 605 species (to date) come from the part of Africa south of the Limpopo River, probably the area with the highest density of species of one genus anywhere in the world. There are nine other similar species from South Malawi and the Eastern Highlands of Rhodesia and a further two spread through parts of Ethiopia, Kenya, Uganda, Tanzania and the Congo. The bulk of the 605 are found between Port Elizabeth, Cape Town and Vanrhynsdorp. Many come from the districts of Caledon Paarl, Worcester and Ceres which have over 100in of rain a year; in one area 175in per annum has been recorded. Many of the mountain species can occasionally be covered by a fall of snow with little harmful effect and a large majority of them will stand 6 to 8° F of frost.

The growth of these plants, in their natural habitat, takes place in the winter and early spring, as there are usually large amounts of water available and conditions are relatively cool; only a few flower at this time. Most flower in mid-spring and early summer when conditions become hot and dry. In South Africa, February is usually the hottest and dryest month, whereas July is the coolest and wettest. The soil conditions are usually moist and there are some species that grow in marshy conditions, or even stand in water, but there are no proper aquatics or salt-marsh lovers in this group of plants. Most of them like acid conditions, the pH in places being as low as four or even three. Many of them grow in the limestone hills, but this is probably misleading as there are pockets of acid soil there. Some grow on the north face and others the south-facing mountain slopes; others on shady, moist, rocky ledges. It is because of this variability in natural conditions that the myth of their difficulty of cultivation has grown up, but any observant gardener should quickly be able to master their cultivation.

They are a beautiful group of plants, very diverse in appearance; some have flowers similar to our common tree heaths, others produce blooms similar to *Daphne* or *Sempervivum*. Yet others have long tubular flowers (plate, p 71) vaguely resembling *Manettia* or *Cuphea ignea* (Mexican Cigar plant). Their habit of growth is equally variable.

The variability in botanical features presents problems in their classification. Guthrie and Bolus, two outstanding South African botanists, wrote in *Florus Capensis* (1905), 'The genus is remarkable for an unusual degree of variability in the form of almost all its organs. It is therefore difficult to arrange into satisfactory groups. Many species are obviously allied to others in very different sections, and in most sections and sub-genera, it is necessary to note exceptions to the general botanical characteristics.' They were well aware of the impossibility of the task; nevertheless it is their system involving 41 sections that is still used in the classification.

The first recognised public description of a Cape Heath was in 1601 when Clusius in *Rariorum Plantarum Historia* described, and then very diagrammatically drew, a plant believed to be *Erica viridipurpurea*. Now, more than three and a half centuries later, very few people know much about this group of plants and many would probably be surprised to know that the *Ericas* bought as flowering pot-plants at Christmas, particularly *E. gracilis* and *E. hyemalis* (plate, p 54), are Cape Heaths.

It is probably best to describe their propagation before giving details of their general cultivation. They can be grown from seed; one of the commonest species raised in this way is *E. oatesii*. The method of dealing with the seed of the Cape Heaths is almost identical to that of hardy heaths, as described in Chapter Four, on Propagation, except that even more care must be taken to avoid the conditions that might cause damping off.

Cuttings are the usual method and for the producer of Cape Heaths as pot-plants there are only two periods for propagation: November to February for plants that are not intended to flower until two or more years old, or late August and early September for the small fifteen to eighteen-month-old plants. Where stock is to be increased without aiming for a pot-plant market, cuttings are usually taken in spring.

The usual method is to take the tips of lateral growths when still young, but not unduly soft. They should be approximately 1in long and are often trimmed at the base with a razorblade. I have found this practice to be totally unnecessary, but have found the removal of the bottom third of the leaves, by carefully pulling upwards so as not to damage the tissues of the stem, not just an advantage but a necessity if a good percentage of rooting is wanted.

These cuttings must be inserted only as deep as is necessary to hold them up in a well-drained mixture of peat and sand. I have had excellent results using equal parts sphagnum peat and $\frac{1}{8}$in grist sand. Recently I have had even better results using $\frac{1}{8}$–$\frac{1}{4}$in Perlite, purchased as 'Loam-a-Lite', mixed in equal amounts with sphagnum peat. This helps the cuttings to stay erect when inserted very shallowly. It is so easy to mix these cuttings that where a large collection is being propagated a separate container for each species is to be preferred. Nevertheless one can get as many as forty cuttings in a 5in pot.

The container with its cuttings, having been watered well, can either be placed in a closed propagating frame in good light or, better still, in a mist unit where good rooting will take place in four to six weeks. As soon as they are well rooted, acclimatise the cuttings to the open glasshouse bench for a few days and then pinch back all the cuttings hard to about ½in to encourage them to break well from the base.

Only when they are breaking should they be given their first potting. It is usual to use a 2½in pot. I have had excellent results by discarding the old clay pot and using one of the cleaner plastics. There seems to be a considerable difference of opinion as to the compost they should be put in. Some nurserymen have their own special mixture. Well-flowered plants are known to have been sold growing in almost pure boiler ash. For compost, see Propagating Media and Potting Composts in Chapter Four.

I mentioned earlier the comparative ease with which the late Dr Ronald Gray grew his plants, but it certainly was not with ease that he mixed his compost. He grew excellent plants, but I believe he could have done just as well by using a simpler mixture than the following: two parts Irish moss peat; two parts sedge peat; one part coarse garden soil; and to each bushel he added three heaped teaspoonfuls of dried blood, two heaped teaspoonfuls of flowers of sulphur, two heaped teaspoonfuls of chelated iron, two heaped teaspoonfuls of Solufeed and one and a half teaspoonfuls of superphosphate. I use acid John Innes potting compost, and I have no complaints. My plants are mostly grown throughout the whole of their lives by youngsters during their first two years in horticulture, and despite their initial lack of skill in watering this loamy compost, the use of plastic pots has given excellent results.

The freshly potted plants need only be firmed well if a high proportion of peat is used in the compost, as in normal circumstances the watering-in after potting will firm them enough. They are then stood, pot thick (grouped touching each other), in a temperature of between 55° and 60° F for a couple of weeks, the temperature later being dropped to 50° F.

In these first few weeks they are protected from direct strong winter sunlight. Growth is almost negligible until about early May with cuttings taken in the period November to February, and then, as soon as the growths are long enough, they are pinched again to produce even bushier plants. These plants will prefer the cooler conditions of a cold frame during the summer, but as they are still so small this should only be done when one can guarantee that they will not be neglected as they only have to dry out once and they become useless. Throughout the growing season it might be necessary to pinch some shoots once or twice more, but late September is the last time for stopping, when the plants should be brought back into the safety of a frost-free glasshouse. About December or January they are put into their final pots, from $3\frac{1}{2}$ to 5in.

During the following growing season they must have ample moisture and coolish conditions, so that at the end of May they are stood outside on ash beds. From then until early August they are regularly fed every ten to fourteen days with a solution of sulphate of ammonia, $\frac{1}{2}$oz dissolved in 1gal of water. It is advisable to syringe the plants after feeding to avoid any damage to the foliage by the sulphate of ammonia. In areas of high chemical content in the water and/or a high lime content, it is advisable to use rain-water to avoid marking the foliage unduly or causing death by building up the alkalinity of the soil. If feeding is continued after early August the formation of flower buds is generally inhibited.

By early September, the plants should be fully developed, bud initiation now having taken place, and they are taken into a glasshouse. It is now important to keep the temperature at about 45° F, as higher temperatures cause early flowers and extension growth which tends to mar their beauty, and also give somewhat poorer flower colour. This timetable is almost the same for the spring-rooted cuttings. Those rooted in late August and early September are also pinched once before potting and, if they have three to four resulting side growths, they are not stopped again.

They are stood outside at the end of May and treated the same as two-year-old or older plants. It must be pointed out at this stage that many species cannot be relied upon to flower after such a short time.

A number of go-ahead nurserymen are introducing some of the more exotic and less-tried Cape Heaths as pot-plants, such as the yellow-flowered *E. pageana* (plate, p 71) and the cream and red waxen-tubed *E. glandulosa* (plate, p 71) as well as *E. gracilis* 'Alba', known as *Erica nivalis* in the trade, and *E. hyemalis* (plate, p 54) and *E. mammosa*.

Two-year-old or older plants may be pruned immediately after flowering, and any strong shoots may be nipped back to keep the plant in shape. Potting is usually carried out immediately after flowering, before the general growth commences.

Cape Heaths make excellent cool-glasshouse plants but do not make good house plants. They do not like the low light conditions found in the majority of houses, coupled with a dry atmosphere; the high and fluctuating room temperatures encourage weak secondary growths. So many amateurs try in vain to keep these plants growing in the house while still in flower and can neither propagate them nor grow them on for another year. Certainly I can remember for many years being most unsuccessful with my attempts at growing *E. hyemalis* on the kitchen windowsill, in the days when the death of such a plant, purchased with my meagre pocket money, was indeed a tragedy. As soon as I started growing such purchases in the more suitable environment of a glasshouse I had success. The only chance for Cape Heaths to survive as house plants is to keep them for a very short period, when in full bloom, in a bright window but not in direct sunlight. Then they must be returned to a glasshouse if they are to be grown for another year.

The hardy heaths and heathers can be used most successfully in a cold glasshouse. I can recall once seeing a delightful corner of an unheated glasshouse where snowdrops, crocuses and daffodils were shown to perfection with a foil of *E. carnea* (syn *E. herbacea*) cultivars in 5 and 6in pots and a background of some of the larger heaths, such as *E. lusitanica* in pans and large pots. I would presume that as soon as they had finished flowering they would be plunged up to their rims in weathered sand, peat or similar material outdoors, and regularly fed and watered until another year. There is no reason why a coloured-foliage *Calluna* should not be similarly used.

Four
Propagation

Heaths and heathers must be one of the easiest groups of plants to propagate. They can be propagated by seed, as they do so very easily in the wild. This is most noticeable when vast areas of heather are burnt on the grouse moors, and numerous seedlings sprout up so that the whole area is a mass of young green leaves, ideal material for grouse to feed upon. Apart from propagation by seed, there is layering; the old method of division still practised by many amateurs; and propagation by cuttings, which is without doubt the most popular, easiest and most economical way both in terms of labour and materials. All of the methods are very easy and this is probably another of the reasons why heaths and heathers are enjoying a rapid increase in popularity.

SEED

One of the biggest disadvantages of propagation by seed is that varieties, or to use the correct term, cultivars, do not come true from seed. Although it is by seed that many new forms arise, there are no cultivars of heaths and heathers that are at present known to come 100 per cent true from seed. Another difficulty is the problem in obtaining seed. This can be overcome easily if one is observant and regularly checks up on the plants after flowering. *Erica carnea* (syn *E. herbacea*) and *E. mediterranea* (syn *E. erigena*) and their respective hybrids will very easily drop their seed when ripe whereas most of the others hold their seeds reasonably well until shaken by the wind. One fine day can see all the seed that hitherto looked unripe lost when the capsules dehisce. The generally accepted way to obtain seed is, as soon as the seed looks ripe—when the capsules are full and developed—to cut the stems and dry them in a warm oven at approximately 100° F (42·1° C), or if the seed is obviously ripe the seed heads are kept in a fine muslin bag. When the seed is dry, which ever method has been adopted, the contents of the capsules are knocked out into a fine sieve and cleaned. It is advisable to sow the seed as soon as possible, but if it needs to be stored then it must be in a dry, cool place, the seed being kept in a small paper envelope. The importance of labelling the seed packets cannot be stressed too much as so often our memory fails us when we are confronted a month or so after collection with half a dozen or more packets of seeds.

The seeds of *Ericas* and *Callunas* vary somewhat in texture and colour depending on species, variety or cultivar, but generally the seed is very fine, *E. tetralix* being one of the finest. It is most essential that fresh seed is sown as fine seed rapidly loses its viability.

One can make a calendar for the collection of seed. January is the time for the last of the *Callunas*. May and June for *E. carnea* (syn *E. herbacea*). July for *E.* × *darleyensis* and related cultivars, as well as *E. mediterranea* (syn *E. erigena*). August is the usual month for the tree heaths, such as *E. arborea*, *E. lusitanica*, *E.* × *veitchii* 'Exeter' and *E. australis*. October is the time for the early-summer flowering heaths, such as *E. cinerea* and *E. tetralix*. November for the late-summer flowerers, namely *E. ciliaris* and *E. terminalis* and sometimes the beginning of *E. vagans*. December for the majority of the *E. vagans* and *Calluna vulgaris*. Once one has obtained seed, there remains the question of what to do with it. Growing plants from seed is a very slow process as opposed to other methods of propagation and to many people the time lag between seed sowing and flowering is too long.

Seed may be sown in any soil container that will allow very good drainage. It is advisable to put broken flower pots or crocks in the bottom of each container, with roughage on the top of it. By roughage I mean coarse loam fibre, dried bracken or similar material, not peat or leafmould as these will so easily clog and hinder the drainage, and leafmould could introduce harmful organisms. A piece of perforated zinc placed over the drainage holes will keep out worms. Worms can cause havoc by burrowing up and down in the pot, making casts that bury the seeds too deeply, and the fine soil they produce can block up the drainage holes. On top of this drainage material place 2–3in of peaty soil. There are many recommendations involving the use of soil from the close proximity of established heaths and heathers. This derives from the belief that mycorrhizal activity is essential for the development of heaths and heathers, particularly from seed; this matter of the plant Mycorrhiza is dealt with in Chapter Two, page 38. There is a possibility that collected soil will already contain seeds of other plants, thereby causing confusion in any pan of seedlings you may obtain.

Propagating media and potting composts

It is accepted that soils for growing plants in must have a correct balance between soil, water and air. It is essential that plants' roots can breathe if they are to function correctly. This rule applies not only to the soils in the open ground but also to composts, whether for propagation or potting. With composts for plants that are to be grown on it is necessary to incorporate supplies of foods, either natural organic kinds or artificial fertilisers.

There are many formulas for composts that can be used in the propagation and the growing of heaths and heathers, but the following are some that have been tried with great success. Good material must be selected for making them and the criteria of good air and water relationship observed.

PROPAGATING COMPOSTS

1. Equal parts peat and sand. The peat can be either sedge or sphagnum. The sand may be silver or even $\frac{1}{8}$in grist as recommended by the John Innes Institute for their potting composts: that is, from fine to $\frac{1}{8}$in particles, but not including dust. This really could also apply to the peat: from fine to $\frac{3}{8}$in particles but not containing dust. I often use $\frac{1}{8}$in grist elutriated sand from the china clay pits.
2. Equal parts peat and Perlite. Perlite can often be purchased as a proprietary substance called 'Loam-a-lite'.
3. Perlite can be mixed in equal proportions with peat and sand. Seed may be sown on the previously mentioned mixtures, but is often sown above a mixture of John Innes seed compost.
4. John Innes seed compost. This is two parts of loam, one part of sand ($\frac{1}{8}$in grist) and one part of peat, all by bulk. Good fibrous loam is to be preferred with a pH between 5·5 and 6·5. To one bushel of this is added $1\frac{1}{2}$oz of superphosphate of lime. The element phosphorous which is in this chemical is most essential for the germination of seed. $\frac{3}{4}$oz of flowers of sulphur may be added to assist the acidity of the compost.

POTTING COMPOSTS

1. The acid mixture of John Innes potting compost is made from seven

parts sterilised fibrous loam, three parts peat, and two parts sand, all by bulk, and to each bushel is added 4oz of John Innes base fertiliser and, if required, ¾oz flowers of sulphur. It is important to stress here that it is not all that easy to obtain the acid mixture from general horticultural sundriesmen and most of the compost sold is JI potting compost No 1. This, as well as containing the JI base, contains ¾oz of carbonate of lime per bushel, which would be detrimental to the majority of heaths and heathers. JI base fertiliser is made up by weight: two parts hoof and horn, which supplies the nitrogen, two parts superphosphate of lime, phosphorous is supplied here, and one part sulphate of potash, potassium being the element supplied in this case. If one does not wish to purchase a JI base already mixed, it is possible to mix one's own and to each bushel of compost one would add 1½oz hoof and horn, 1½oz superphosphate of lime and ¾oz sulphate of potash.

2. Sometimes a potting compost is made up of three parts loam, three parts peat and two parts sand, parts by bulk, and adding to each bushel 4oz of JI base, thus giving a far more peaty mixture.

3. Good results can be had with equal parts peat and sand and 4oz of JI base per bushel, provided the peat is not too acid.

Whenever these composts are made they should be turned sufficiently to mix them thoroughly. They should be as moist as they can be without any of the particles sticking together when squeezed. In a compost where peat is used, it is important that the peat is not allowed to dry; very dry peat is difficult to moisten.

Either John Innes potting compost No 1 acid mixture or John Innes seed compost, also acid mixture (with or without an addition of up to 50 per cent of extra peat), provides an ideal mixture in which the seeds can be sown. It is advisable that all the media should be able to pass through a ¼in sieve. This compost, after being placed in the container, is lightly firmed using the tips of the fingers. After roughly levelling the surface it is finished off with a leveller such as the bottom of a flower pot or a specially constructed presser consisting of a flat, round piece of wood that just fits the diameter of the pot.

The seed can be sprinkled carefully on to this surface, but not too thickly as, apart from the danger of damping off, it is usual to leave the seedlings undisturbed for nearly a year, and overcrowding can be fatal.

However I prefer to treat this seed as if it was the seed of one of the common Alpines. I cover the prepared surface of the compost lightly with ⅛in stone chippings and the seed is then sprinkled lightly on to these. Once it has been sown, whether directly on the compost or on chippings, it is watered in with a fine-rosed watering can. This will gently wash the seed down. Always include a well-marked label with the name, date of sowing, origin of the seed, or any reference number. Once the seed has been sown, the containers, unless they contain seed of a tender species, are placed outside and sunk to their rims in sand, gravel, well-weathered ash, peat or similar material in a cool position, preferably on the north side of a wall. The coarse gravel discourages the entry of worms into the containers.

These containers can be left to get a gentle freezing during the winter. Always have some frame lights at hand to protect them from extremes of temperature or rain. In the spring they can be brought into a warm glasshouse in a temperature of 45° F (8·1° C) to 60° F (17·1° C). Germination under these conditions is rapid. It is always possible to leave the containers outside to germinate, but this will mean a greater delay in obtaining plants of flowering size from seed. I have obtained good results by freezing seed in a domestic refrigerator.

By studying the positions where *Callunas* and *Ericas* germinate in the wild it is known that they must have a certain amount of shade and therefore a light shading, whether the plants are outside or under glass, is most beneficial. This can be a flour-and-water paste or one of the proprietary brands of shading painted on to the glass; a better method is to use hessian sheets on wire or laths, the last being easily removed if inclement weather prevails.

Moss and allied low forms of plant life which could give undue competition to the little seedlings are discouraged when the containers are covered in grit. To keep the soil surface clean and also to reduce rotting or damping off of the seedlings, which so easily occurs under the artificial conditions in pots, the water that the containers are given should have a small amount of potassium permanganate added. The recommended strength is one level teaspoonful to 1gal of water.

A point that can be noticed in the wild is that the seeds are not usually eaten by birds, or dispersed by the wind, as although fine they are relatively heavy for their size. They seem to drop to the ground, being dispersed by the sway of the inflorescence in the breeze or by browsing animals. This accounts for the fact that heaths are mostly found in colonies (plate, p 72).

The seedlings, whether they are left until they are 2in high in the containers, or pricked out as soon as they can be handled, should be treated gently as their roots and shoots are very delicate. The seedlings can be pricked out singly into pots containing one of many composts as described earlier in this chapter. This is practised by amateurs who do not have to weigh up the cost of their operations. The professional horticulturist does use this method when trying to raise special forms, or when growing the Cape Heaths from seed, usually pricking them out into boxes, pans or into frames 2–3in apart each way. It will assist the establishment of the seedlings if they are given a light spraying with a fine-rosed can at least twice a day and more often on a sunny day. Syringing is better than using a can, and a mist nozzle giving a very fine spray is probably the best. Suitable equipment, with all the technical data on nozzle size and water pressure, can be obtained from most large horticultural sundriesmen.

DIVISION

Division must be one of the worst methods of propagation of heaths and heathers, although it is practised by so many people. There have been no experiments carried out to prove or disprove the point categorically, but the evidence of numerous people who grow heaths and heathers seems to suggest that those plants grown from division suffer to a greater degree from dieback that those grown by other methods of propagation. The usual time for carrying out division is in the spring. Here the whole plant, preferably a bushy one having numerous young growths, is lifted and planted deeper (plate, p 89), in such a way that only the tips show above soil level. It is advisable to add considerable quantities of peat and sand to the soil that is to be worked in among these shoots. Provided drying out does not occur, by the following spring, and sometimes as early as autumn, rooting will have taken place. The whole plant can then be lifted and the young rooted plants (plate, p 90) severed from the parent, which is discarded. The portions are then lined out 4–6in apart in a moist, shady nursery bed.

A variation of this method is to place a 3–6in deep box around the plant and fill this with rooting media until only the young tips appear above the surface (plate, p 89). This practice is apt to lead to drying out, and is better suited to areas of high rainfall where burying the root ball of the parent plant well below the existing soil level is likely to kill it.

LAYERING

Layering is probably the easiest method for the amateur, although it may produce an unshapely plant which can suffer from dieback, like rooted pieces from division. Many heaths and heathers will layer naturally when they are established. No one need go to the trouble of artificially layering some plants, such as *Erica carnea* (syn *E. herbacea*) 'Springwood White'. On the other hand some upright-growing heaths are too brittle to bend down and layer. The shoots for rooting can be sizeable and can save a year of growing on. The method is certainly better than normal division, and a great advantage is that only a part of the plant need be used.

Layering can be done at any time of the year, although the best time is in spring or autumn. Shoots are pinned down on to the surface of the ground around the plant. They are held down by bent pieces of wire (loops made out of 6in lengths of 12 SWG wire are ideal) or a small stone, and then covered with a 1–2in layer of peat and sand in equal parts (plate, p 89). The tips of the shoots are bent up to show through the media. A better method is to scrape some soil away from the plant, thereby creating a shallow trench. The shoots are pinned down into this trench and then bent sharply upwards. The trench is filled up with equal parts of peat and sand, although many people use normal garden soil. Better results are obtained by the trench method, provided all other factors are equal. It is generally realised that a sharp bend in the stem constricts the flow of sap and hormones and encourages rooting. Sometimes the foliage that would be buried is carefully removed. This is more of a fad than a necessity. It is essential that the compost used is moist and never allowed to dry out. The system of pegging down must be such that the layered material does not move about and thereby hinder rooting.

Rooted layers are severed from the plant up to one month before removal, which is usually about a year after being layered, but can be after six months. Many growers, both amateur and professional, have layered plants at the end of April and removed them, well rooted, in early September. After removal, layers can be lined out 6in apart in rows 12in apart and grown on before planting in their permanent position.

CUTTINGS

The way to build up a good quantity of a particular cultivar quickly is by taking cuttings. It is a simple method that is still regarded by some amateurs as only of use to the professional horticulturist. There is a great deal of 'bally-hoo' as to the correct size, treatment and time of taking cuttings: I well remember reading a book by a well-known horticulturist who was adamant that all cuttings should be taken with a

Page 71 (above left) Erica glandulosa; (above right) Erica pageana; (below left) Daboecia
cantabrica 'Atropurpurea'; (below right) one-sided raceme of Erica carnea (herbacea)

Page 72 (*above*) Colonies of *Calluna vulgaris* on the Long Mynd, Shropshire; (*below*) *Calluna vulgaris* 'Foxii Nana' and *Erica cinerea* 'Golden Drop' in the Royal Horticultural Society's gardens, Wisley

heel of old wood trimmed with a sharp knife; then the lower third of
the cutting was to have all its leaves removed, not by just pulling them
off, but by cutting them off with a knife or scissors so as not to damage
the bark. However I have seen and actually rooted thousands of nodal
cuttings that did not even have the lower leaves removed. It certainly
cannot be denied that some cuttings are harder to root than others.
Many a person will have found out by bitter experience that a great
percentage of cuttings of Erica australis 'Mr Robert', the fine white-
flowered tree heath, will rot, and what a very small percentage eventually make decent plants.

The obvious questions that anyone is going to ask are, 'When do I
take my cuttings?' and, 'How do I treat them, in what compost and
where do I put them? And having put them somewhere, what do I do
with them and how long will they take to root?' There are so many
different ways of rooting the cuttings, from a mist unit to cold frames,
bell jars to compost rolled up between strips of polythene, that obviously one cannot give dogmatic answers.

With the exclusion of Cape Heaths I can say that the time for taking
the general batch of Ericas and Callunas is July and August. One can
start as early as June and this is advised for Erica carnea (syn E. herbacea).
August is often regarded as too late by many people because the plants
will have started flower-bud formation and this tends to reduce not
only the amount of available material but also the percentage of cuttings that will root. Where, for one reason or another, material is still
soft and sappy and wilts when inserted in the propagating medium, it
is usual to take the cuttings a little later—this probably explains why so
many people root them in August. Some people take cuttings as late as
October and November, but then these are only a small group who
like to use very hard side shoots and place them under bell jars or
small hand lights in prepared spots in the open ground. Here the cuttings stay over winter and root sometime in the spring. Material for
vegetative propagation should always be true to type and free from
pests, diseases and abnormalities, so always check that good material is
being used for propagation.

I have mentioned that material can be of firm side shoots if propagation is being carried out during October or November, but it is usual
to use half-ripe, unflowered material (plates, p 90), not hard and woody,
not soft and liable to wilting, but somewhere between these two extremes. Sometimes, because of shortage of material, every shoot on the
plant must be used, so instead of using only tip cuttings one also has to

E

use the lower and flowering shoots, except the really woody material which must regretfully be discarded. The flower buds or flowers are picked off and it is surprising just how many of these poor cuttings will root. Although the usual length for cuttings is about 1in, mine vary from ¼in upwards and I get excellent results. Best results with *Callunas* result from cuttings of a maximum ½in in length. Many people advocate larger cuttings of about 3in, particularly for the tree heaths with a heel of older wood. I feel this is not in any way essential; it is just that it is possible to root them from larger material.

Some propagators have rooted pieces of heaths and heathers up to 2ft long; American growers often root some of the tree heaths from 12in long pieces. The usual length is only 1in except for the tree heaths, which will often root more easily from 3–4in cuttings.

Young material has been known by propagators to root generally more quickly than older material. This is almost certainly due to the younger tissue being capable of meristematic activity and therefore quickly forming new tissue to produce the roots. Good examples of this are the taking of *Cupressocyparis* × *leylandii* cuttings from young material, often only two to four-year-old plants, or the taking of hardwood cuttings for fruit-tree rootstocks from vigorously growing, well-fed hedges of the desired rootstock.

It is my strong opinion that it is unnecessary to remove any leaves from cuttings prior to insertion and it probably does more harm than good by damaging the tissue.

Given the right conditions these little cuttings will root so rapidly and so easily that the use of hormone rooting compounds is a complete waste of time and materials. Cuttings may be inserted up to one-third of their length in the rooting medium. For anyone with a mist unit, or a good sun frame, I would recommend that cuttings be inserted as shallowly as possible, just deep enough into the media not to fall over. If you are a little clumsy, however, the combination of very small cuttings and shallow insertion in the medium can be a risky operation: on innumerable occasions I have seen some of my horticultural students painstakingly dibble in these cuttings, 21 rows by 11 rows to one standard seed tray, and then on their way to the mist unit jar their arm against a door post or bump into a fellow student, thereby undoing in a split second a considerable amount of effort.

It is possible to have the cuttings very close together and up to 250 cuttings can be inserted in a 6in pot. The closeness will often depend on just how long the cuttings will have to stay in the media once they have rooted, as once the roots intertwine a considerable amount of root damage will occur, and therefore there will be a check in growth, when they are removed from the propagating media.

Many people will be rather surprised to learn that the operation of firming in the cuttings can be dispensed with and that the degree of firming required can be given by simply watering with a very-fine-rosed can. Because of the possibility of rotting taking place in many of the amateur's propagating frames or pits, due to incorrect temperature and humidity, it is a good idea to make a weak solution of potassium permanganate and water the cuttings in with this. I must admit that I have not carried out any large-scale experiments on the effect of potassium permanganate on rooting, but I do know that the use of captan fungicide in the mist-unit water at Liverpool University Botanic Gardens did in fact slow down the rooting. Recently some of the Dutch nurserymen have claimed that captan encouraged rooting and obviously a great deal has yet to be done on this subject.

I prefer to use some form of bottom heat for rooting heaths and heathers, but it is not essential. The bottom heat should be about 10° F higher than the air temperature surrounding the cuttings.

It is essential that a high humidity should accompany a moderately high temperature and not a low temperature, as under these muggy conditions rot will quickly set in. It is where the cutting has a cool top due to the evaporation of moisture from the top of the propagating material, a misty middle due to the humid conditions of the frame or mist unit, and a warm base from the propagating media often warmed by heating cables, that rooting is quickest. The usual temperature is 60° to 65° F air temperature, 70° to 75° F compost and bottom temperature.

There are many suggestions and formulas for rooting media, but the essential feature is that it should be well drained but retentive of moisture. A well-mixed compost of equal parts peat and ⅛in grist sand makes an ideal medium. Some people suggest charcoal and leafmould; I certainly would not recommend these, particularly the latter which is likely to encourage various rots rather than good rooting. The medium can be placed in frames, on glasshouse staging, in boxes, pans (clay or plastic), or even in the folds of a sheet of polythene. The compost should not be firmed but just levelled prior to insertion of the cuttings. Mist units certainly provide the easiest way of rooting heaths and heather cuttings.

There are a number of makes of mist units on the market at present, all of which are satisfactory. There is a very useful portable unit, at least portable as regards power supply—it runs from a small 12 volt television battery or an accumalator battery. Like all other units it must be connected to a water supply of a minimum 20lb pressure. It is possible to have cuttings ready for potting up within fourteen days of insertion, although three to four weeks is more usual.

Erica cinerea can take from six to ten weeks to root from cuttings; *E. carnea* (syn *E. herbacea*) from four to eight weeks; the cultivar 'Eileen Porter' can often take as long as three months. Obviously the length of time taken to root cuttings will be increased considerably beyond these times if cold frames are used for autumn cuttings, when rooting often does not take place properly until the early spring.

Similar results can be had with a good sun frame, which is really a laborious mist unit, all the spraying and the humidity control being carried out by a skilled gardener and not by the little electronic leaf and spray nozzles as in the mist unit.

Bell jars are similar to sun frames when used in the height of the summer and there are a number of nurseries today still using this method. The bell jars are placed out at 2–3ft intervals in a little sunny border of the nursery area. The area where they are standing is then prepared by working in large amounts of peat and sand. The cuttings are inserted, well watered, and then covered with a bell jar, which is usually whitewashed all over to protect the cuttings from being burnt up by the sun; or pots of cuttings are half sunk in the ground (plate, p 89). Cold frames and bell jars can also be used for the late-autumn cuttings, which I mentioned were of hardened side shoots and were not expected to start rooting until the spring. Once the cuttings have obviously rooted in the bell jar then more air is gradually admitted. This is done just by propping up the rim of the bell jar with a wedge-shaped piece of wood. Drying out around the edges of bell jars can occur, so it is usual to have some form of irrigation near at hand. I consider there is a lot to be said for the volumatic type of watering. In this system fine hair-thin tubes (like spaghetti) run off at regular intervals from an alkathene water pipe. One or more of these thin tubes can be put into each batch of cuttings.

The cuttings can be placed directly into the media, whether it be in a mist unit, frame, bell jar, glasshouse staging, etc, or they can be put in containers. I prefer the plastic seed trays; they are much easier to clean, stack fairly well and although many do tend to crack when mis-handled, they still work out considerably cheaper in the long run than wooden boxes. My experience has been that clean boxes or other containers induce slightly quicker rooting. Cuttings can be inserted in pots or pans (plate, p 89), but this depends on the number to be propagated.

The roots of heaths and heathers are very fine and they do not penetrate all that deeply (plate, p 90), so the use of boxes or other containers over 2½in deep is a waste.

Cuttings may be placed on a bed of sphagnum moss, which is laid in a strip on a piece of polythene. The polythene is then rolled up leaving the cuttings just appearing from the open ends of the polythene, while their base is inserted in the moist sphagnum moss. When placed in a cool, well-lit position (not in direct sunlight), a reasonable percentage will root. A more sophisticated method is the use of glass instead of polythene. A sheet of glass measuring 18in long by 9in wide has the bottom 4½in covered with sphagnum moss. The cuttings are laid on this with their tips just showing. The sphagnum and cuttings are then sandwiched with another piece of glass, and the two sheets are bound together with string or tape. Fine sand is often sprinkled into the top between the cuttings. The base of the sandwich is stood in water away from the direct sunlight until rooting has taken place.

Excellent results have been achieved during late summer with cuttings in a frame which was prone to drying out. The clay pan that contained the cuttings was put inside a slightly larger pan, the space between the two being filled with fine sand. The base of the larger pan was stood in a saucer of water and the capillary action of the water in the sand kept the cuttings perfectly moist, but not too wet to cause harm to the propagating material.

Cuttings may be placed in pans at an acute angle, the media in which the cuttings are placed being level with the top of the pan; a piece of glass is then carefully placed on top of the pot, gently pressing the cuttings on to the moist compost. A good percentage of rooting has taken place under these conditions. Professor Broadbent of Bath University of Technology tells me that cuttings placed in a suitable medium in the open ground at an acute angle and covered with a piece of glass as in the pot method have rooted very well, with a very high percentage take.

It is imperative that propagating material is labelled, whether it be with just an index number, further details of which would be on an index card system or in a notebook, or with the name, date on which the material was taken and where it came from, etc, on a good label. It is surprising how quickly one can forget what propagating material it is and where it came from, when it stands for a few weeks in a propagating frame or unit.

There are many types of labels and it does not matter which is used, provided the information recorded on them is not quickly erased. Some people use wooden ice-lollipop sticks but in a couple of weeks these lose all their data. The Hartley metal labels, the McPenny plastic labels or lengths of xylonite, used with a hard pencil, are preferable.

Once cuttings are well rooted we are really left with a dilemma; should we pot up at once, or leave them until the following growing season? This will largely depend on the media that the cuttings were put in; if it is reasonably rich in foods then obviously it is not so imperative to move on the rooted cuttings. If, on the other hand, they were rooted in an inert media such as sand, then urgent treatment is required. Once the cuttings are known to have rooted air is admitted more and more freely to harden them off.

When the cuttings are well rooted, a week or so before either potting up, then when established, planting in a nursery bed (plate, p 36), or pricking out direct into nursery beds, etc, it is advisable to nip out the top of the cuttings to encourage them to bush.

Excellent results have been obtained by planting rooted cuttings directly into their final positions. The ground should be moderately rich organically and a careful check kept on weeds, which would so quickly compete with the little cuttings for light and moisture. If they are to be potted up then a good soil mixture should be used, such as acid John Innes potting compost or general garden soil mixed well with a liberal amount of peat.

Peat pots, particularly $2\frac{1}{2}$in square types (plate, p 90), make ideal containers if small plants are required. These are being superseded by the Jiffy 7 (plate, p 90), a new type of pot purchased as a flat disc $1\frac{3}{4}$in across and $\frac{1}{4}$in thick. When soaked in water it expands to a height of 2in and looks like a cylinder of peat in a nylon net bag. The rooted cutting can be inserted in the top. Some nurseries still put rooted cuttings individually into 3 or $3\frac{1}{2}$in clay pots.

If clay pots are used they must be perfectly clean, as problems arise when knocking them out of the pots at the planting stage. The root ball sticks very badly to the sides of dirty pots and does not come out very easily; thus many roots get damaged.

The practice of potting heaths and heathers varies from nursery to nursery. Some establishments will pot up the rooted cuttings and then place them in a cold frame, the pots often not even being plunged. If the frame is not facing north then this freshly potted material will need to be shaded. I prefer to leave the freshly potted plants in a warm environment, either a heated frame or on a glasshouse bench, until the following April or May (eight to nine months after taking the cuttings), when they could go out into a sheltered frame.

Potting as soon as rooted and following the last mentioned procedure can produce a good-sized plant in a very short period of time. This is putting into practice the principle that to get the best from a plant it should not suffer a check in its growing cycle. This is, I know, rather a sweeping statement as there are many species of plants that must have a check before they will break into growth and flower, but it is certainly a recognised principle that a slight check can considerably slow down and reduce growth. For propagation of Cape Heaths for pot work see Chapter Three.

Many of the methods described under propagation are obviously those carried out commercially when large quantities of heaths and heather are required. There is no reason why the amateur should not adopt, or adapt, these methods to fit the smaller quantities he wishes to produce.

A sun frame could well be dispensed with and replaced with a pot covered with a simple wire frame supporting a polythene bag, the cuttings being put in the pot, the pot well watered and stood a bright window-ledge in the kitchen. Or a pot or small box could be sunk in the open ground and covered with glass.

Where small numbers of plants are grown and therefore several species, varieties or cultivars are grown in one pot, great care must be taken with labelling. It is so very easy to get the plants mixed. Even the only slightly 'green-fingered' gardener should have no difficulty in propagating heaths and heathers and getting a high percentage to root.

Looking after a frame

If young plants are to be over-wintered and a warm glasshouse bench cannot be spared, then the next best treatment is to place them in a cold frame. Here the pots are usually stood close together, so as to reduce drying out and to get the maximum number of plants under protection. Great care should be taken in watering, as it is so easy to give more water than is required to some plants and not enough to others when they are packed tightly together; also, when packed tightly the pots cannot easily lose their moisture and dry out if they have been accidentally over-watered.

During the winter months of low-light intensity the protection of a frame is all that is required, provided as much good ventilation is given as possible. When the spring arrives with its stronger sunlight the frames, particularly if they are facing south, will need shading.

Sometimes the pots are plunged in sand or just stood on sand or weathered ashes. If sand is purchased for a frame make certain it is lime-free. Likewise, in the early stages of establishment in a frame when one is syringing daily or watering the plants, the water must be lime-free if lime-intolerant plants are being grown.

Five

Characteristics and variations of heaths and heathers

The three genera dealt with in this book, *Calluna, Erica* and *Daboecia*, are botanically described and identified as follows:

Calluna: The leaves are small, scale-like and persistent, opposite and decussate with two backwardly projecting tails. The corolla is persistent and encloses the capsule. The calyx, which is larger than the corolla, is deeply four-parted and is brightly coloured. It has eight stamens. The name is Greek—*Kalluno* means to cleanse or adorn—and derives either from the use of the twigs in brooms or from the effect of the flowers.

Erica: This genus has needle-like leaves, usually in whorls of from three to six and strongly revolute. The corolla lobes are united into a tube, the calyx is shorter than the corolla. The inflorescence is usually made up of flowers in axils or in terminal clusters or racemes. The stamens are inserted at the base of the ovary. The flower is usually bell-shaped and most are pendulous. Many are fertilised by bees: the honey is secreted by the disc and an insect flies on to the flower and while probing shakes the bloom and covers itself with pollen. On many, a horn-like projection (awn) on the anthers ensures contact with the insect's proboscis. *Erica* is from the *Ereike* of Theophrastus, the Greek name of a heath, meaning to break, perhaps derived from the medieval theory that it could dissolve gallstones. It may be a reference to the fact that some have easily broken branches.

Daboecia: The leaves of this genus are alternate and entire; the corolla is deciduous, glabrous, campanulate or urceolate, and is four-lobed.

The flowers are held in a terminal elongated raceme and have eight stamens. The fruit is a four-celled septicidal capsule. *Daboecia* is derived from the plant's Irish name, St Dabeoc's Heath.

Forms and variations

There are many reasons for selecting a certain piece of plant material for propagation and eventually distributing it as a new form or variant for the garden. There are also different ways in which these sports or variations occur.

VARIATION IN FLOWER COLOUR

The flower may be a single colour throughout, or a bicolour, or change with age from one colour to another. The calyx may be the same colour as the flower, a slightly different shade or completely different.

FLOWER FORM

The flower may be single, or double as occurs in *Erica mackaiana* 'Plena' and in many *Callunas*. The corolla may fail to open as in *Calluna vulgaris* 'Underwoodii' and *C. vulgaris* 'David Eason'. The corolla may be larger than the type as in *Erica ciliaris* 'Stoborough', or smaller than the type as in *Daboecia cantabrica* 'Porter's Variety'. Corolla shapes—as well as being larger or smaller than type the corolla lobe may be a different shape, rounder, more constricted in the mouth or more tubular. There may be no corolla at all. The calyx may be split as in *Erica cinerea* 'Schizopetala' or *E. tetralix* 'Mary Grace'.

INFLORESCENCE

Some are larger—with more flowers in each cluster, as in *Erica tetralix* cultivars. Some are longer—as in many of the cultivars of *Erica cinerea*, such as 'P. S. Patrick', 'Rosea', or 'Domino'. *Callunas* such as 'H. E. Beale', 'Elsie Purnell' and 'White Gown' all have longer inflorescences and therefore more flowers than the type plant.

FOLIAGE

Some plants have hairy foliage, such as *Calluna vulgaris* 'Hirsuta Typica', while others are devoid of hairs. Some may be glandular and others eglandular. The foliage may be of a different colour from the normal all the year round, as with *Calluna vulgaris* 'Ruth Sparkes', or

Erica tetralix 'Alba Mollis'. The colour may intensify in the winter as in *Calluna vulgaris* 'Cuprea', or take on winter tints as in *C. vulgaris* 'Robert Chapman', *C. vulgaris* 'Golden Feather', or *Erica cinerea* 'Golden Drop'.

GROWTH FORMS

Creeping—some forms are prostrate and only grow to 1–2in high, such as *Calluna vulgaris* 'Mrs Ronald Gray'. Drooping—instead of the normal twiggy nature some cultivars, for example *Calluna vulgaris* 'Joan Sparkes', seem to have softer growth and gently flop. Erect—the upright growths of *Calluna vulgaris* 'C. W. Nix', 'Alportii' or 'Darkness' have a characteristic erect growth showing very little tendency to spread. Dumpy and rounded—some forms are dense and prominently dumpy and rounded like a giant pin cushion, such as *Calluna vulgaris* 'Foxii Nana'. Tenderness—*Calluna vulgaris* 'Elegantissima Walter Ingwersen' is a more tender form of the common heather and therefore is more susceptible to winter damage during a cold spell. Also, *Erica australis* 'Aragonensis' is a more tender cultivar than *E. australis*.

TIME OF FLOWERING

Often in the wild a plant is noted for its floriferousness or for flowering before or after the other plants; these give us both the early and the late cultivars of the many species that we grow.

These variations can be major or minor, perhaps due to environmental factors or constant natural hybridising. They may be due to 'sporting', as is the case with *Calluna vulgaris* 'Joan Sparkes' which arose as a different shoot growing on *Calluna vulgaris* 'Alba Plena', or *Erica mediterranea* (syn *E. erigena*) 'Golden Dome' which arose from *E. mediterranea* 'W. T. Rackliff'. *Calluna vulgaris* 'Ruth Sparkes' is unstable, and one form has a tendency to revert from the yellow-foliaged and double white-flowered form to its original parent stock which has green foliage and single white flowers.

Some variations can be induced when the growing point is damaged or when hybridising takes place and a new form arises, as is believed to be the case with *Erica mediterranea* 'Rosea' which arose as a seedling from 'Brightness'. When the growing point is damaged it is possible (but very rare) for a cell to grow in a different manner from before and produce a new type of growth such as a 'Witches Broom'.

Dichotomous key of some hardy Erica species

(a) Leaves ciliate or glandular ciliate
  (b) Cilia terminate in glands (glandular)
    (c) Leaves in threes, corolla urn-shaped ....*ciliaris*
    (cc) Leaves in fours
      (d) Corolla cylindrical ....*australis*
      (dd) Corolla urn-shaped ....*tetralix*
  (bb) Cilia plain
    (c) Leaves in fours
      (d) Flower pink
        (e) Calyx glabrous ....*mackaiana*
        (ee) Calyx pubescent ....*tetralix*
      (dd) Flower yellow ....*pageana*
    (cc) Leaves in threes
      (d) Anthers awned, calyx without cilia ....*cinerea*
      (dd) Anthers awnless, calyx with cilia ....*ciliaris*

(aa) Leaves not ciliate
  (b) Anthers included
    (c) Young wood smooth ....*scoparia*
    (cc) Young wood downy or hairy
      (d) Flower pink ....*terminalis*
      (dd) Flower white
        (e) Stigma white...................................*arborea*
        (ee) Stigma pink ....*lusitanica*

  (bb) Anthers exserted
    (c) Shrubs 4ft and over
      (d) Leaves in threes, flower open campanulate ...*canaliculata*
      (dd) Leaves in fours, flower ovoid urceolate ......*mediterranea*
                                       (*erigena*)
    (cc) Shrubs under 4ft
      (d) Flowers in terminal umbels.......................*umbellata*
      (dd) Flowers in raceme
        (e) Raceme one-sided.............................*carnea*
                                        (*herbacea*)
        (ee) Raceme columnar
          (f) Young wood smooth
            (g) Anther lobes united almost to
               apex ....*multiflora*
            (gg) Anther lobes separated to base ...*vagans*
          (ff) Young wood minutely puberulous ...*manipuliflora*

Six

Calluna vulgaris cultivars

KEY TO ABBREVIATIONS

F = Good foliage colour
* = Outstanding variety or cultivar
D = Double flowers
FCC = First Class Certificate from the Royal Horticultural Society
AM = Award of Merit from the Royal Horticultural Society
AGM = Award of Garden Merit, which means that it is ideally suited to garden cultivation, awarded by the Royal Horticultural Society
HC = Highly Commended by the Royal Horticultural Society
PC = Preliminary Commendation by the Royal Horticultural Society

Name and authority	*Calluna vulgaris* (L) Hull
Syn names and authorities	*Erica vulgaris* Linnaeus
Common names	Heather, Ling, Hadder, He Heath, Red Heath, Grig, Hull, Basam Bend, Breon, Gawlins, Griglors Heather, Dog Ling, Heth, Black Ling
Shrub, etc, height	Shrub up to 3ft, often only 9in to 2ft high
Habit	Low, evergreen, straggly, strongly branched, prostrate to erect
Stems	Young shoots leafy
Leaf arrangement	Opposite, decussate
Leaves—shape, size, description	Linear, 1/20 to 1/10in long, scale-like, sessile, somewhat ciliate
Inflorescence	One-sided, dense raceme, 1 to 12in long
Fragrant	—
Corolla—shape lobes, colour	Polypetalous, persistent, campanulate, half as long as calyx, purple/pink, $\frac{1}{8}$in
Calyx—shape, colour, etc	Twice the size of corolla, lobes ovate to oblong, same colour as corolla, $\frac{3}{10}$ to $\frac{1}{4}$in, four tiny bracts at base of large calyx

Stamens—shape, colour	Eight anthers, spurred, with eight black honey glands at the base between each filament, which is shorter than the corolla
Stigma—shape, colour, exserted or included	Four-fid, exserted and projects before anthers for cross-pollination by wind and insects
Pedicel	—
Flowering time	July to October
Introduction (Great Britain)	Natural habitat

General

The only species of a distinct genus. It became naturalised in Nova Scotia, Canada, where it is believed to have grown from seeds dropped out of the heather beds or from packing around belongings taken by the settlers from

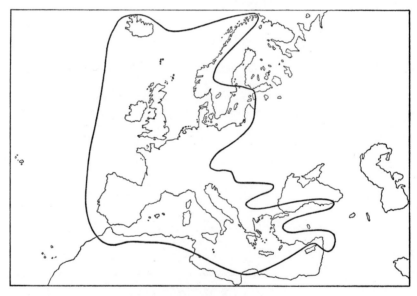

Distribution of *Calluna vulgaris*

Scotland. It is very hardy, dislikes lime, but grows very well in a good soil. However if the soil is too rich the plants will grow fast and become straggly and suffer in a bad winter. Some cultivars grow well on clay soils, particularly 'H. E. Beale'. The species is very tolerant of salt spray. In a sandy soil it will usually grow without a main stem. It stands exceptionally hard wear; being burnt, walked upon, eaten by game, sheep, cattle, deer, etc. It is a very useful plant for honey and many beekeepers will go to great lengths to get their hives taken up to heather moors for the autumn. The nectar is more accessible than in *Ericas* and the flower is visited by a large number of insects.

Cultivars

alba — — 18in white August to September
The lucky white heather that is found growing wild. This name covers a multitude of white heathers which are very variable in height and habit.

'Alba Aurea' F — 4in white September to October
Maximum height of 4in and with bright green foliage that produces yellowish tips in the spring. It bears pure white flowers, sometimes as early as August.

'Alba Carlton' — — 18–24in white August to September
Syn 'Carlton'
Found by Mr S. H. Ward of Malton. Introduced by Maxwell and Beale. Has a spreading habit. It is very floriferous, flowering on the laterals as well as the main spikes. The foliage is dark green.

'Alba Compacta' — — 12in white August to September
Has a close compact habit.

'Alba Cunneryensis' See 'Cunneryensis'.
'Alba Dumosa' See 'Dumosa'.
'Alba Elata' — — 24in white September to October
Syn 'Elata' and 'Elata Alba'
An improved Scottish white heather of bushy habit, free flowering.

'Alba Elegans' — — 18in white August to September
Syn 'Elegans'
HC 1962
An old cultivar with a straggly habit, but good white single flowers. The cultivar 'Alba Plena' originated as a sport from this.

'Alba Erecta' — — 18in white July to August
Syn 'Erecta'
Flowering a little earlier than most white cultivars, it has an attractive upright habit.

'Alba Florepleno' See 'Alba Plena'.
'Alba Gracilis' See 'Tenella'.
'Alba Hammondii' See 'Hammondii'.
'Alba Hayesensis' See 'Hayesensis'.
'Alba Jae' — * — 9–12in white August
AM in 1960

It was raised and introduced by Fred J. Chapple. It grows to a height of between 9 and 12in with a similar spread, being very compact and erect in habit, as well as vigorous. The single, pure white flowers are held in clusters of generally about fifteen, making an inflorescence of some 3in long on flowering stems of 7 to 9in. The foliage is a bright medium green with paler tips. It is generally regarded as an August-flowering cultivar.

'Alba Mair's White'   See 'Mair's Variety'.

'Alba Minima'   – – 3in white   August to September
Bears a few flowers, not outstanding.

'Alba Minor'   – – 6–9in white   July to August
Syn 'Minor'
A dwarf form with small sprays of single blossoms above bright green foliage.

'Alba Multiflora'   – – 24in white   September to October
Upright habit with medium green foliage.

'Alba Pilosa'   – – 12in white   August to October
'Syn 'Pilosa'
Its fresh green downy foliage is very attractive at times. A useful long-flowerer, sometimes commencing in July.

'Alba Plena'   – * D 12–18in white   September to October
Syn 'Plena', 'Alba Florepleno'
AM 1960
A popular cultivar of German origin which was introduced to this country by an English climber in the Schwazwald in 1938, and introduced to the trade by Maxwell and Beale. It is very quick growing and therefore useful for smothering weeds. It will reach a height of 12 to 18in, although sometimes it can have a straggly and floppy habit. The foliage is medium green. From mid-August to October very double white flowers are produced on 8 to 10in spikes. It is very good for cut flowers. It is not unusual for the first few flowers to open to be single and likewise, when the plant gets old, parts of it will revert to the single form. It is believed to be a sport of 'Alba Elegans'. It stands wet conditions well and is almost identical to 'Else Frye'.

'Alba Praecox'   – – 9in white   July to August
It was introduced by Messrs G. Arends of Wuppertal, Germany, in 1938. It has a dwarf erect habit.

Page 89 (*above left*) *Erica carnea* (*herbacea*) showing a stage in the preparation to promote rooting for division; (*above right*) box system of promoting rooting prior to division; (*below left*) layering with the use of a stone; (*below right*) well-labelled pots of *Daboecia*, *Calluna*, and *Erica* cuttings under a bell jar

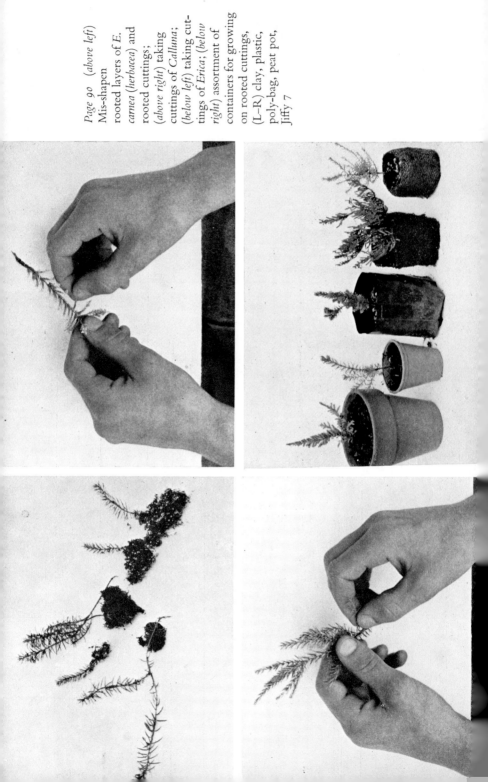

Page 90 (above left) Mis-shapen rooted layers of *E. carnea* (*herbacea*) and rooted cuttings; (above right) taking cuttings of *Calluna*; (below left) taking cuttings of *Erica*; (below right) assortment of containers for growing on rooted cuttings, (L–R) clay, plastic, poly-bag, peat pot, Jiffy 7

'Alba Pumila' – – 9in white July to September
Syn 'Pumila'
Often only 4in high. Has small light green leaves on a
compact tufted plant.

'Alba Pyramidalis' See 'Pyramidalis'.
'Alba Rigida' See 'Rigida'.
'Alba Searlei' See 'Serlei'.
'Alba Serlei' See 'Serlei'.
'Alba Spicata' See 'Spicata'.
'Alba Tenella' See 'Tenella'.
'Alba Torulosa' See 'Torulosa'.
'Alboviolacea' – – 18in white, flushed lavender August to September
The white flowers are flushed with the palest lavender,
often described as a palest mauve.

'Alportii' – – 24–36in purple August to September
Syn 'Atrorubens'
AGM in 1947
Its ultimate height is somewhere between 24 and 36in.
It has dark foliage, that goes somewhat darker in the
winter, held on upright growths. It is a very free
bloomer, having dense spikes of vivid rose-purple,
usually from August to September, but sometimes in
July. It is very similar to 'Darkness'.

'Alportii Late' See 'Goldsworth Crimson'.
'Alportii Praecox' – – 18–24in purple July to August
Raised and introduced by Messrs Arends, Wuppertal,
Germany, in 1938. Starts flowering about three weeks
earlier than 'Alportii' and often is a little dwarfer when
mature.

'Alportii Rigida' See 'Rigida'.
'Argentea' F – 12in pale mauve August to September
It has a silvery foliage throughout the year, a somewhat
straggly habit and has a few pale mauve flowers. In
some conditions the tips of the foliage turn to an
anaemic lemon-yellow.

'Atrorubens' See 'Alportii'.
'August Beauty' – * – 12in white August to September
AM in 1960
The award was not just for its freeness in producing
4½in long inflorescences, but also for its habit which is
very compact, but vigorous, with slightly spreading
stems bearing dark green foliage. This spreading habit
encourages the flower stems to curl downwards to-

F

Calluna vulgaris (single flowers)

wards ground level. Flowering commences in the last
few days of July and continues into early September.

'Auraefolia'   See 'Hammondii Aureifolia'.

'Aurea'   F - 12in purple August to September
AM in 1961
It reaches a height of 12in, although sometimes it will
grow taller. The foliage is a good golden colour and the
upper surfaces of the leaves turn a reddish-bronze in
winter. The stems are slender, somewhat feathered and
give the plant a spreading but overall erect habit. In
August and September it bears a limited number of
purple blooms. Like most other winter-colouring heaths,
the tinges are on the southern side. Because of its
tendency to die out in parts, its appearance must be
preserved by regular removal of dead tissue.

'Aureifolia'   See 'Hammondii Aureifolia'.

'Barnett Anley'   - * - 12-24in purple August to September
AM 1960, FCC in 1962
Raised by Mrs B. L. Anley of Woking. Its maximum
height is usually between 18 and 24in, although in some
situations it only reaches 12in. It is compact and erect in
habit and the foliage is bright green, darkening to
purple tints on the southern side. Its flowering stems are
some 10 to 12in long often covered for about half their
length with single petunia-purple flowers in August and
September.

'Beechwood   - - 18in deep crimson August to September
Crimson'   Raised by J. W. Sparkes, it is an improvement on
'C. W. Nix' and has an upright habit. The deep
crimson flowers are displayed on dark green foliage.

'Beoley Elegance'   - * - 24in white August to September
Syn 'Beoley Elegans'
Raised by J. W. Sparkes. A good white-flowering
plant, very similar to 'Elegantissima Walter Ingwersen'
which has soft lilac flowers.

'Beoley Elegans'   See 'Beoley Elegance'.

'Beoley Gold'   F * - 18in white August to September
AM 1968
Raised by J. W. Sparkes. This cultivar did not for a
time show up well in the trials at the RHS Garden at
Wisley. There the foliage looked somewhat pale and
the flowers made the plant look rather dirty, but in a
number of places, and none more so than at Sparkes'

Calluna vulgaris (double flowers)

Nursery, its foliage does well, being very bright yellow with golden tints on the exposed southern side. It does have a number of white flowers in August and September but not as many as 'Gold Haze'. The maximum height is 18in.

'Betty Baum' – – 18in pink-purple September to October
Of spreading habit and free flowering but a little straggly.

'Blazeaway' F – 18–24in light mauve August to September
Raised by J. W. Sparkes. Similar to 'Robert Chapman' but flowers two weeks earlier. Its main attraction is its orange and red foliage tints that are intensified in the very cold weather on the southern side of the growths.

'Bognie' F – 12in purple August to September
Its foliage is not as strong as 'Cuprea', but has bronze to golden tints. Named after a farm on Forestry Commission land in the north of Scotland, near where it was found growing.

'Brachysepala Densa' – – 16in reddish-purple August to September
Bushy habit with dark green foliage. The name is a taxonomic sub-form of which Beijerinck says 'Darleyensis' is an example. The Dutch and the Americans are growing a form under the name 'Brachysepala Densa'.

'Bransdale White' – – 12in white July to August
Not an outstanding cultivar, it has light green foliage. Found by the late Earl of Feversham's gamekeeper while on a shooting party on the moors.

'Caerketton White' – * – 18in white June to July
The heathers are usually associated with the autumn, but this 18in high cultivar is one of the earliest to bloom, having pure white flowers in profusion from June or July. It has a further asset in that in the spring its basically dark green foliage is enhanced by light green tips.

'Californian Midge' – – 3in pink-purple August to September
Syn 'Midge'.
A curiosity sent to Mr F. J. Chapple from California. At a maximum height of 3in it bears minute leaves and tiny pink-purple bells during August and September.

'Camla Variety' – * D 9in pink August to September
Syn 'County Wicklow'?
Named after the house where Mr F. W. Millard, who

introduced it, lived. Some authorities say it is the same as 'County Wicklow', but its double pink flowers are slightly larger and are in longer spikes. It is thought that the same plant was given to two nurseries, who both named it without either knowing the other had it. Perhaps it is the better collection of propagating material from 'Camla' over the years that would account for the slight difference. I believe that one of the clones has at some time altered slightly its characteristics, accounting for the difference.

'Carlton'   See 'Alba Carlton'.

'Carole Chapman'   F * – 12in September
Raised by J. W. Sparkes. This appears to be a golden form of 'Foxii Nana' and makes a tight pincushion in its early years of 4in, then grows suddenly to 12in.

'Coccinea'   – – 9in deep crimson August to September
Very similar but slightly inferior to 'Coccinea Smith's Variety'.

'Coccinea Smith's Variety'   – * – 9in deep crimson August to September
The best form to have. It grows to a height of 9in with grey downy young foliage. The greyness persists to a lesser degree throughout the year and in August and September it has deep crimson flowers slightly darker than 'Coccinea'.

'County Wicklow'   – * D 9in pink August to September
See 'Camla Variety'
AM 1960, FCC 1961
It would appear that the same plant material was given to two different nurseries, hence the confusion over the naming. 'County Wicklow' is the name it is generally known by, but it was given first to the Camla Nurseries, East Grinstead.

'Cramond'   – D 18–24in deep pink September to November
Medium green foliaged heather similar to 'Peter Sparkes'.

'Crispa'   – – 12in white August to September
An American cultivar that is horticulturally useless.

'Cronix'   See 'C. W. Nix'.
This name has probably arisen through bad spelling.

'Cunneryensis'   – – 24in white August to October
Syn 'Alba Cunneryensis'
Introduced by W. Goodwin, Tansley, Derbyshire. Long sprays of single white blooms are borne on this plant of tall loose habit.

'Cupraea'   See 'Cuprea'.
'Cuprea'   F * - 12in purple August to September
                Syn 'Cupraea'
                An old cultivar getting an FCC as long ago as 1873.
                A good copper-foliaged *Calluna* that turns deeper in
                colour in the winter. It will bear a limited number of
                purple flowers in August and September, but it is for its
                coloured foliage, which reaches a height of 12in, that it
                is grown. It has a somewhat loose habit and is straggly
                by nature, but careful pruning can alleviate this problem.
'C. W. Nix'   - - 24in purple-crimson August to September
                Syn 'Cronix'
                AM 1961
                Introduced by Maxwell and Beale. Similar to 'Alportii'
                with upright stems of purple-crimson flowers above
                dark foliage. The flower spikes are larger than 'Alportii'.
                In some districts it does not bloom freely.
'Dainty Bess'   - - 4in pink August to September
                Similar to 'Sister Anne', but is slightly smaller and
                slower growing. It is an American cultivar.
'Darkness'   - * - 12in crimson-purple August to September
                A reasonably new cultivar raised by a keen gardener,
                Mr Pratt, living in the Wirral, Cheshire. Propagating
                material was presented to Liverpool University Botanic
                Gardens (known locally as Ness Gardens), a short dis-
                tance from his home, and it is from there that the plant
                has been distributed. It has a somewhat erect compact
                habit to a height of 12in, and has a very dense spike of
                flowers of a bright crimson-purple. It is a very free
                bloomer and the old flowers, although fading some-
                what, are still attractive throughout the winter. From a
                distance the flowers appear to be slightly more vivid
                than 'Alportii', which is also a taller, less compact and
                more sprawling plant.
'Darleyensis'   - - 18-24in pink-red August to September
                Introduced by James Smith & Sons, Darleydale, Derby-
                shire. This has unusual curled foliage, with deep bronze
                tints in the winter. Its general habit is to form tussocks
                from 18 to 24in in height. In August and September
                deep pink-red bells are produced on curly shoots.
'David Eason'   - - 12-18in purple-red October to November
                Raised and introduced by Maxwell and Beale. It is of a
                spreading habit, grows from 12 to 18in high and has

light green foliage. It is most unusual, as its flower buds of deep purple and red, borne between October and November, do not open properly.

'Decumbens Alba'   – – 9in white August to September
Spreading habit with light green foliage. A Dutch cultivar which is similar to 'Rigida'.

'Drum-Ra'   – – 12–18in white August to September
AM in 1961
Introduced by Jack Drake, Inshriach Nursery, Aviemore. Of compact and erect habit and foliage of medium to apple green. The single flowers are held on erect spikes of varying heights, each inflorescence being approximately 3½in long.

'Dumosa'   – – 18in white July to September
Syn 'Alba Dumosa'.

'Durfordii'   – – 18in pink-purple October to December
Syn 'Hyemalis Southcote'
A very late flowerer with spiky habit. Its foliage, which is very dark, makes a good foil for the flowers.

'E. F. Brown'   – – 18in mauve September to October
Found by an American friend of Mr and Mrs Letts. The foliage is light green and it is not of a dense growth.

'E. Hoare'   – – 18in crimson-purple August to September
HC in 1960
Introduced by Maxwell and Beale. Usually of bushy habit, but in some soils becomes loose and floppy. The dark green foliage shows purple tints at its tips in winter and 4 to 5in long inflorescences of crimson-purple flowers, deeper than 'Alportii', are borne from early August. The dead flowers take on a russet effect.

'Elata'   See 'Alba Elata'.
'Elata Alba'   See 'Alba Elata'.
'Elegans'   See 'Alba Elegans'.
'Elegantissima'   – – 24in white September to October
'Elegantissima   – * – 24in soft-lilac September to December
   Walter   The plant being described is the British 'Elegantissima'
   Ingwersen'   and not the pure-white-flowered one of Dutch origin. The one in circulation in Britain is really Portuguese, being introduced by Ingwersens. It is for this reason that it thrives best in a sheltered position, where it grows to a height of 24in. Given a sheltered spot, or the protection of a cold greenhouse, it will produce, on its 14in long graceful, tapering spikes, soft lilac flowers in profusion

from as early as August into January. Found just below 1,000ft near Coimbra, Portugal in 1928.

'Elkstone White' – – 5–6in white July to August
Introduced by John Ravenscroft, Bridgemere Nurseries, Nantwich. This plant was collected in the early 1950s, being the only plant in flower on Morridge Moor at the time when spotted. It grows to just over 6in high and has a spreading habit. Its white flowers appear from July to August above bright green foliage.

'Elongata' See 'Mair's Variety'.
'Else Foye' See 'Else Frye'.
'Else Frye' – D 9in white August to September
Syn 'Else Foye'
Of American origin, arising in Mrs Frye's garden in Seattle in 1940 and introduced by Fred J. Chapple. It is similar to 'Alba Elegans' but the foliage is darker and slightly smaller. The first few flowers are often single. A sport from a pink-flowered plant.

'Elsie Purnell' – D 30in rose-pink September to October
AM in 1963
It was introduced by J. W. Sparkes as a sport from 'H. E. Beale'. It reaches a height of 30in and has greyish-green foliage and a rather open habit. It is very similar to 'Peter Sparkes' and 'H. E. Beale', but is slightly paler and a little later. The flowers, produced in September and October, are rose-pink.

'Erecta' See 'Alba Erecta'.
'Fabiana' Similar to 'Sister Anne'; the grey-green foliage turns bronze in the winter. Sometimes this name is given to the False Heath, 'Fabiana imbricata', a member of the family Solonaceae.

'Fairy' F – 12in pink August to September
Raised by J. W. Sparkes. Various shades of orange and gold in the autumn and winter.

'Flore Pleno' – D lilac-pink August to September
Syn 'Flora Pleno', 'Flora Plena', 'Plena'
AM in 1929 (London)
This is reputed to be the first double Calluna cultivated, but has now been superseded by other cultivars. Its spikes are not as long as in 'H. E. Beale', but are slightly deeper, being a soft lilac-pink. It is still an attractive and useful cultivar. 'Multiplex' is identical to 'Flore Pleno'.

'Foxhollow   – – 6in purple August to October
  Wanderer'   A new cultivar found and introduced by Mr and Mrs Letts. It was found on an old copper mine in Cornwall. It is a vigorous prostrate plant just over 6in tall with long raking branches carrying pleasing rich-green dense foliage. It bears long spikes of purple flowers from August to October. Mr and Mrs Letts described it as an ideal carpeter and weed smotherer. They are so taken with this plant that they have named it after their nursery 'Foxhollow'.

'Foxii'   – – 3–6in purple August to September
Soft mid-green foliage forms a little hummock, often only 3in in height and in many seasons the plant bears no flowers. At other times one or two.

'Foxii Floribunda'   – – 4in purple August to September
At 4in it is a little taller than 'Foxii' and 'Foxii Nana' and is considerably more free flowering. The purple flowers are produced usually in August and September. It tends to be a little looser in growth right at its top than the other 'Foxii' kinds.

'Foxii Nana'   – * – 3in purple August to September
AM 1962
Usually only grows to a height of 3in, though very old specimens, 18in across, can be as much as 9in high, and roots are formed inside the mound from old wood. Usually forms minute deep green pincushions studded with single purple flowers (plate, p 72).

'Frances Grey'   – – 15in pale purple August to September
Syn 'Francis Gray', 'Francis Grey', 'French Grey'
It is of spreading habit and has pale purple flowers and bright green foliage.

'Francis Gray'   See 'Frances Grey'.

'Fred J. Chapple'   F * – 15–30in purple August to September
AM 1961
This was raised and introduced by Fred J. Chapple. Its performance for both flowers and foliage make it worthy of bearing his name. In August and September it bears prolifically single, pretty purple flowers and in the spring its foliage, which is normally a medium green, varies in shades of green, gold, medium pink and copper, the tips being a pinky red. A considerable improvement on 'Tricolorifolia Smith's Variety'. Easily identified from *C.v.* 'Tricolorifolia' and 'Hammondii

Rubrifolia' by yellow flecks in the foliage persisting into mid summer. Its overall height is between 15 and 30in, and its habit is compact and erect.

'French Grey'   See 'Frances Grey'.

'Gnome'   – * – 9in white September to October
Raised by J. W. Sparkes. It reaches a height of somewhere between 9 and 12in and is another one of the rock-garden type, making an ideal substitute for a dwarf conifer. It is similar in habit to 'Humpty Dumpty', but the growths are tighter and it has a greenish-yellow tip to the foliage. The dwarf-conifer image is spoilt only in September and October by an occasional white flower.

'Gnome   – – 9in pink September to October
(pink form)'   Has the same foliage and habit as 'Gnome', but pink instead of white flowers, which are also more numerous.

'Goblin'   – – 2–3in purple August to September
Introduced by J. W. Sparkes. Appears to be identical to 'Minima' and is probably the same plant under another name.

'Golden Carpet'   F * – 2in purple August to September
A relatively new and untried cultivar, raised by Mr and Mrs Letts from a seedling found in a group of 'Mrs Ronald Gray' in their garden. It reaches a height of only 2in and is slow growing, eventually making a strong yellowish-gold carpet, but taking on orange and red tints in the winter. It appears to like good drainage as does 'Mrs Ronald Gray'.

'Golden Feather'   F * – 18in mauve August to October
AM 1965, FCC 1967, as a summer and winter foliage plant. Raised by J. W. Sparkes. It is aptly named. Its long stems are rather feathery in habit. The foliage is golden in early summer and then takes on orange tints throughout the year. It will reach a height of 18in, although it is often shorter than this.

'Golden Haze'   See 'Gold Haze'.

'Gold Haze'   F * – 24in white August to September
Syn 'Golden Haze'
Received an AM in 1961 for its flowers and an FCC in 1963 as a foliage plant
Raised by J. W. Sparkes. Looks like an enlarged form of 'Ruth Sparkes'. Throughout the year it bears brilliant golden foliage and in the autumn has long sprays of pure white single flowers.

'Gold Pat'   F – 6in pink August to September
Raised by J. W. Sparkes. A sport of 'Mrs Pat'. It is more
dwarf than its parent. The pink tips typical of 'Mrs Pat'
are displayed against the golden foliage in the spring.
This combination of colours sounds lovely but the
plant appears to be weak in constitution and under most
conditions it does not grow well.

'Goldsworth   – – 24–30in red-crimson September to November
Crimson'   Syn 'Alportii Late'
This was the name given by W. C. Slocock of Woking,
Surrey in 1925, but then in 1933 it was renamed after
the firm's Goldsworth Nursery. A useful late-flowering
cultivar with dark green foliage and spikes of deep red-
crimson flowers. In some soils it is regarded as a shy
bloomer, having only a few flowers near the tip, and
the whole plant grows straggly.

'Goldsworth   F – 30in red-crimson September to November
Crimson   The growth and flowers are similar to 'Goldsworth
Variegata'   Crimson', except that odd pieces of growth with tints
of orange and yellow are spasmodically produced on
the plant. More of a novelty than a plant of beauty.

'Goldsworth Pink' – – 24in pink August to November
Dark green foliage with an upright habit.

'Gotteborg'   – – 6in pink August to September
'Grasmeriensis'   – – 12in pink August to September
Propagated in 1930 and introduced by Mr Robert
Hayes of Geoffrey Hayes Ltd. A little-known floriferous
heather with very long erect spikes of pink blooms.

'Gregor's Variety' – – 24in white September to October
Upright growth with mid-green foliage. The pure
white single flowers are borne in short spikes.

'Hammondii'   – – 24–30in white August to September
Syn 'Alba Hammondii', 'Hammondii Alba'
This must be included in a selection of taller-growing
heathers because of its pure simplicity. It has beautiful
dark green foliage on a strong, quick-growing plant
from 24 to 30in in height. The new growth always
tends to be a little paler and most noticeable during the
winter. In August and September long spikes of white
flowers are produced which are ideal for cutting.

'Hammondii Alba' See 'Hammondii'.
'Hammondii   See 'Hammondii Aureifolia'.
Auraefolia'

'Hammondii Aurea' See 'Hammondii Aureifolia'.

'Hammondii
Aureifolia'

F - 18–36in white August to September
Syn 'Hammondii Auraefolia', 'Hammondii Aurea',
'Hammondii Aurifolia', 'Aureifolia', 'Auraefolia'
Some nurserymen classify 'Hammondii Aurea' as a
separate cultivar saying that its young growth stems are
more golden than 'Hammondii Aureifolia'. It is an exceptionally good heather growing to a height of between 18 and 36in and is of rather dense habit. In spring
all its new growths are of a bright golden colour, con-
trasting well with the normal older green foliage. In
August to September it bears a moderate number of
white flowers.

'Hammondii
Rubrifolia'

F - 18in purple August to September
Syn 'Rubrifolia', 'Rubraefolia'
A variable seedling from 'Hammondii'. This foliage is
green but has markings, particularly on the new spring
growths, of yellow, gold and red. It produces a
moderate number of purple flowers.

'Hayesensis'

- - 18–24in white August to September
Syn 'Alba Hayesensis'
Raised and introduced by Geoffrey Hayes Ltd of Grasmere. A very vigorous grower, having very long, finely
tapered spikes of white flowers.

'H. E. Beale'

- * D 24in soft pink September to November
AGM 1942, FCC 1943
There must be very few gardeners who do not know
this cultivar. It reaches an average height of 24in. Its
foliage is a greyish colour and takes on mauvish tints in
the winter. From September to November, 10 to 14in
sprays of double, soft pink blooms are produced, the
petals being imbricate. At the base of each flower spike
are short lateral spikes that enhance its beauty. The
major disadvantage of this cultivar is that older plants,
unless fed regularly and pruned strongly, will eventually
produce flower spikes of only a couple of inches in
length. The best spikes are produced on three- to five-
year-old plants. This cultivar was found in the New
Forest in 1925 and two out of three cuttings were rooted
by the nursery of Maxwell and Beale (plate, p 53).

'Hibernica'

- - 6in bright pink October to November
A very useful late-flowering cultivar with a reputation
of nearly flowering itself to death. Although nearly 6in

in height its growths are somewhat prostrate and are covered with numerous bright pink flowers in October and November. These blooms later fade to an off-white.

'Hiemalis'   – * – 15in pink-lilac October to November
Syn 'Hyemalis', 'Johnson's Variety'
Collected in 1927 near Hyères, Southern France, by the late A. T. Johnson. It is very upright, growing up to 15in high. It has delightful pink-lilac blossoms in profusion from October to December, but its inherent failure of being damaged in severe cold weather is due to its origin. It is well suited to the milder climates or the sheltered garden.

'Hirsuta Albiflora'   – – 18–30in white August to September
Of bushy habit with growths of various lengths. The foliage is not as grey as the name might suggest. From August to September it has very long white tapering spikes.

'Hirsuta Compacta'   See 'Sister Anne'.

'Hirsuta Typica'   F – 24in pale mauve August to September
Syn 'Incana'
AM 1962, FCC in 1964 as a grey-foliaged plant.
It is very vigorous and grows to a height of 24in or more. Its foliage is very dense and is a fluffy grey. It produces harmonising light mauve flowers in August and September.

'Hookstone'   – – 18–24in pink-rosy purple August to September
Collected in 1935 by Mrs C. E. Underwood at Hangmore Hill on the Cobham Ridges in Surrey and introduced by G. Underwood and Son. It is an erect, sturdy plant with greyish-green foliage and is very floriferous.

'Hugh Nicholson'   F – 12in – –
Raised by J. W. Sparkes. Similar to 'Hammondii Aureifolia', but its mottled green and cream foliage is held throughout most of the summer.

'Humilis'   See 'Mrs Ronald Gray'.

'Humilis Compacta'   See 'Mrs Ronald Gray'

'Humpty Dumpty'   – * – 6–9in white August to September
HC 1965 as a foliage plant
This produces very dumpy hummocks of parsley-green foliage that shows a great similarity to a dwarf conifer from a distance. Although it only reaches a height of between 6 and 9in, there is a tendency for the branches

to splay out, spoiling the overall shape. It is usually a shy bloomer (only one or two white flowers in August and September) but J. W. Sparkes, its raisers, reported it as being very floriferous, having been almost covered in 1964.

'Hyemalis' See 'Hiemalis'.

'Hyemalis Southcote' See 'Durfordii'. Introduced by the late Dr Ronald Gray, Hindhead, Surrey.

'Hypnoides' – – 12in purple August to September
An old cultivar.

'Incana' See 'Hirsuta Typica'.

'Janice Chapman' – – 12in white August to September
Raised and introduced by J. W. Sparkes. Similar to 'Alboviolacea'. It has rich green foliage and white flowers that with age become lavender tinted.

'J. H. Hamilton' – * D 6–9in bright pink August to September
Syn 'Mrs J. H. Hamilton'
AM (London) 1935, AM 1960, FCC 1961
This 6in high heath was found in Yorkshire and was connected with the name 'J. H. Hamilton' who, in 1935, was director of Maxwell and Beale. It has spreading stems bearing dark green foliage. It is a vigorous plant which, in August and September, bears numerous upright spikes, some 5 to 7in long, with the top 3 to 3½in densely covered with fuchsia-pink double flowers without the slightest trace of purple. It is a very popular cultivar, particularly for small posies or arrangements.

'Joan Sparkes' – * D 9in pink August to September
AM (London) 1957
It was raised by J. W. Sparkes and reported to be a sport from 'Alba Plena' which occurred in 1950. It grows to a height of 9in and has dark green foliage. During August and September its feathery spikes are clothed prolifically with double pink flowers. Unfortunately in some areas, particularly in very sandy soils, this plant becomes straggly and loses a lot of its charm, but nevertheless always seems to flower well (plate, p 107).

'John F. Letts' F * 4–6in soft mauve August to September
Raised and introduced by Mr and Mrs Letts. A compact plant similar in habit to 'Sister Anne' which arose from a seedling found near 'Mrs Ronald Gray'. Its foliage is soft gold in summer, becoming flushed with shades of orange and red in the late autumn and winter.

'Johnson's Variety'   See 'Hiemalis'.

'Joy Vanstone'   F – 18in   rose-purple   August to September
HC 1965
Raised and introduced by J. W. Sparkes. It looks
somewhat like 'Beoley Gold' until the winter, when the
colour deepens through stages of orange to red. During
August and September it produces 4in spikes of rose-
purple flowers, but regrettably as they fade the plant
does take on a somewhat dirty appearance, although
only for a short time.

'Kirby White'   F – 18in   white   August to September
Similar to 'Hammondii Aureifolia' with bright yellow
tips on green foliage all year round.

'Kit Hill'   – – 9in   white   August to October
A dark green foliaged cultivar found by J. A. Mitchell at
Kit Hill in Cornwall and introduced by Maxwell and
Beale. It has white flowers which are produced on both
terminal and lateral spikes, the tapering branches
drooping in a delicate curve.

'Kuphaldtii'   – – 6in   rose-purple   August to September
Syn 'Prostrata Kuphaldtii', 'Prostrata Kuis'
Collected by Herr Kuphaldt and introduced by Messrs
Hesse of Weene, Germany in 1932. Its very open foliage
is held on almost prostrate twisting growths, forming a
loose mound with rosy-purple flowers on curling spikes.

'Kynance'   – – 12in   bright pink   August to September
It was found in the Lizard district of Cornwall in 1923
by Maxwell and introduced by Maxwell and Beale. A
useful 12in high cultivar that has masses of close-
feathered spikes of bright pink flowers in August and
September.

'Lambs Tails'   F – 4in   pink   August to September
It was raised by J. W. Sparkes. It has a very spreading
habit, with the young growths giving the appearance of
lambs' tails. The golden foliage reaches a height of 4in
and has a slight touch of orange, which is accentuated
during winter months, particularly on the southern side.

'Late Crimson Gold'   F – 12in   crimson   September
Raised by J. W. Sparkes. A golden-foliaged heather
bearing crimson flowers during September and occasionally into October.

'Loch-Na-Seil'   – – 6in   purple   August to September
A slow growing, semi-prostrate heather.

Page 107　(above) Calluna vulgaris 'Joan Sparkes'; (below) Calluna vulgaris 'Rigida'

Page 108 (above) Erica
australis 'Mr Robert';
(below) Erica carnea (herbacea)
'Springwood Pink' planted
in a pocket in a rock garden

'Long White' – – 18in white September to October
An upright grower with an open habit. The foliage is bright green and has long spikes of pure white flowers. A good grower.

'Lyle's Surprise' – – 12in white August to September
It was found by Ronald E. Lyle of Alloa in Morayshire, while out walking. Its highly branched foliage when combined with the small spikes of white flowers in August and September gives a laced effect.

'Mair's Variety' – * – 36in white August to September
Syn 'Elongata', 'Alba Mair's White'
AM 1961, FCC 1963
A strong grower with good green foliage, the tips of which go yellowish-green in the early parts of the year. In some positions and soils it does not flower well and its habit becomes straggly. When flourishing, its single white flower spikes are often from 9 to 12in long and are very good as cut flowers.

'Midge' See 'Californian Midge'.

'Minima' – – 2in purple August to September
A good ground-cover plant forming close mats of foliage, the leaflets being held at right angles to each other. The purple flowers are produced sparsely through August and September. This cultivar is now being superseded.

'Minima Smith's – – 2-4in purple August to September
   Variety' The late Mr Thomas Smith found this 'Witch's Broom' at Newry, Northern Ireland, and it was introduced by his Daisy Hill Nursery at Newry. The 2 to 4in high close-growing mats are this plant's characteristic, the close cushions of growth turning dark red in winter, although some people would regard it as a dirty bronze. The individual shoots look like little pear trees. 'Minima' does not flower very well, but the 'Smith's Variety' of it has a considerable number of purple flowers in August and September.

'Minor' See 'Alba Minor'.
'Miss Appleby' See 'Radnor'.
'Molecule' – – 6in pink August to September
The pink flowers are held on short spikes of minute dark green foliage.

'Mousehole' – – 6in pink August to September
Found and introduced by Mr and Mrs J. F. Letts.

G

'Mrs Alf'

Originated in the Penzance district of Cornwall. A compact spiky plant with dark green, somewhat hairy foliage, and tiny pink flowers in August and September.
– – 6–12in pink August to November

'Mrs Dunlop'

Collected in Glenisla. A weak grower with sparsely produced single pink blooms. Of little horticultural value.
– – 18in white August to September

'Mrs J. H. Hamilton'

Not an outstanding cultivar. The flowers fading rapidly to a dirty white.
See 'J. H. Hamilton'.

'Mrs Pat'

F – 6in light purple August to September
It was collected by Mrs P. S. Patrick on the Broadstone Moors, Dorset, and introduced by Maxwell and Beale. It will just reach 6in when growing well. It is a delicate heath with bright green foliage, but in the spring the tips, which are pink, turn particularly bright. A moderate number of light purple flowers open from the mauve-pink buds in August and September. In many soils it does not grow well, but if a suitable home can be found it is a very good plant. There is a golden form in cultivation—'Gold Pat'.

'Mrs Pat (Golden Form)'

See 'Gold Pat'.

'Mrs Ronald Gray'

– * – 2in purple August to September
Syn 'Humilis Compacta', 'Mrs R. Gray', 'Humilis'
Found in the wild on a North Devon cliff by the late Dr Ronald Gray when out rambling, and introduced by Maxwell and Beale. It is most unusual, growing absolutely prostrate at a maximum height of 2 in and can be walked upon, although it would not stand heavy wear. Its carpet of foliage hugs the ground and, to avoid deterioration in winter, the soil beneath it should have sharp drainage. During August and September it bears spikes of purple flowers.

'Mullion'

– – 5–9in orchid purple August to September
AM in 1963
Found near Mullion Cove by Mr and Mrs Maxwell when on their honeymoon and introduced by Maxwell and Beale. Its ultimate height is somewhere between 5 and 9in, usually the latter; it is semi-prostrate and much branched, making a good ground-cover plant. It is not as hardy as some cultivars, the foliage often being

damaged in winter, but it will quickly recover in the spring. In August and September it will cover two-thirds or more of the 4in flower stems densely with single orchid-purple flowers.

'Multicolor'   F * – 12–15in   pale purple   August to September
Syn 'Prairie Fire' from the USA
It received an AM in 1961, and again in 1962 as a winter-foliage plant.
Its height is somewhere between 12 to 15in. The normal foliage colour is a yellowish-green, the tips of which become red in winter, often all the way around and not just on the southern side, as occurs in most winter-colouring *Callunas*. The young growths in spring are a reddish bronze, looking attractive over the older foliage.

'Multiplex'   – D   12in   mauve   August to September
Syn 'Plena' (it is a very old name)
An American cultivar, identical to 'Flore Pleno'.

'Nana'   – –   8–9in   purple   August to September
'Nana Compacta'   – –   3–6in   pink   August to September
It generally reaches only 3in high and a height of 6in under certain conditions. The plant, with its good green leaves, resembles a small pin cushion. It is the most floriferous of the carpet cultivars, producing tiny pink flowers in August and September. Although taking its time a good clump can be 12in or more square.

'October Crimson'   – –   18in   crimson   October
Raised and introduced by J. W. Sparkes. The good strong green foliage makes a good foil for medium length spikes of crimson flowers.

'October White'   – –   24in   white   October to November
A cultivar used mainly for cut-flower work, having long erect spikes of pure white flowers very late in the season.

'Orange Queen'   F –   12in   rose-purple   August to September
HC 1965
Raised and introduced by J. W. Sparkes. Its pale green foliage turns to yellow with orange tints during the winter months. The tips of the young shoots have red tints. In August and September it bears 4in long spikes of single rose-purple flowers.

'Oxshott Common'   – *   24in   pale mauve   August to September
AM 1968
Its long spikes of pale mauve flowers are exceptionally

attractive when borne in profusion above its greyish
tinted foliage.

'Pallida'   – – 12in soft purple August to September
A little grown but vigorous cultivar.

'Penhale'   – – 12in rosy-purple August to November
It is not a well-known cultivar. It grows to a height of
12in and its stems are very branched. The foliage is a
dark green and turns to bronze in winter. Between
August and November it is usual to find its bright rosy-
purple flowers.

'Peter Sparkes'   – * D 18in lilac August to October
AM 1958, FCC 1962
Found as a sport on 'H. E. Beale' by J. W. Sparkes,
who introduced it. It reaches a height of 18in and is
vigorous. Its dense spikes of flowers are slightly deeper
than 'H. E. Beale', the blooms being double and of a
lilac-pink.

'Pilosa   See 'Alba Pilosa'.

'Plena'   See 'Alba Plena', or 'Multiplex', or 'Flore Pleno'

'Prairie Fire'   See 'Multicolor'

'Prostrata Kuis' See 'Kuphaldtii'.

'Prostrata Kuphaldtii' See 'Kuphaldtii'.

'Prostrate Orange' F * – 9in pink August to September
Raised and introduced by J. W. Sparkes. As a foliage
plant at a height of between 6 and 9in, this is most outstanding. The foliage is a pale yellow-green, but the
reddish tints in winter give an orange effect deeper than
'Orange Queen'. It is not very good as a flowering
plant, as the pink flowers, produced in August and
September, give the plant a somewhat dirty effect when
ageing.

'Pubescens'   – – 9-15in pink August to September
Leaves and branches densely villous-pubescent.

'Pumila'   See 'Alba Pumila'.

'Purpurea'   See 'Serlei Purpurea'.

'Pygmaea'   – – 3in pink-mauve August to September
AM 1962
A dwarf, closely growing plant, somewhat similar to
'Foxii', with dark green foliage, making it a useful ever-
green for rock-garden work. It is dumpy in habit, and
in August to September it does bear a few single pink-
mauve flowers.

'Pyramidalis'   – – 24in white August to September

Syn 'Alba Pyramidalis'.
A taller and more robust plant than the wild white forms.

'Pyrenaica'   – – 6in pink-mauve   August to September
A dense mat of dark green foliage, produces only a few spikes of pink-mauve flowers. It is not a free-flowering cultivar.

'Radnor'   – * D 9in soft pink   August to September
Syn 'Miss Appleby'
Its flowers are so similar to 'H. E. Beale', being of a double soft pink, that it may, in many people's gardens, oust the old-established cultivar. The inflorescence is somewhat short and is characteristically curved.

'Ralph Purnell'   – – 18in red-purple July to September
Raised and introduced by J. W. Sparkes. A strong upright grower with good length spikes of reddish-purple flowers.

'Rigida'   – – 4in white July to September
Syn 'Alba Rigida', 'Alportii Rigida'
AM 1962
It is very compact and usually grows to only 4in, although occasionally it will reach 9in. The flowers are single and a clear white. It is not unusual for the flowers to be over by mid-September, the first blooms appearing in mid-July (plate, p 107).

'Robert Chapman'   F * – 18in purple-pink August to September
Two AMs in 1962, one as a winter-foliage plant
It is a very popular cultivar and grows to a height of 18in. It is of a dense habit and the growths are rather variable in height on each plant, giving a very pleasing effect, particularly as the golden-bronze foliage takes on tints of red during the winter months on the southern side. It bears a very good number of purple-pink flowers in August and September.

'Roma'   – – 9in deep pink August to September
Raised and introduced by Maxwell and Beale. Similar in habit to 'Mullion', but has more longer, feathery spikes of deeper pink flowers.

'Rosalind (Crastock   F – 18in mallow purple August to September
Heath Variety)'   AM 1961
Has golden, upright foliage. Surprisingly not as golden as 'Underwood's Variety'. When ageing the plant starts to look untidy, having a lot of dead material in the

centre of it, a looser habit and a number of greenish shoots at the base of the plant. Produces occasionally a red-foliaged shoot.

'Rosalind (Under-   F – 18in mallow purple   August to September
wood's Variety)'   Brilliant golden foliage, particularly in some soils, and an upright habit. When ageing the plant gets untidy and has a number of greenish shoots lower down. Spasmodically produces a red-foliaged shoot.

'Rosea'   – – 15in red-purple   August to September
An American cultivar with light green foliage.

'Rubra'   See 'Serlei Rubra'.

'Rubraefolia'   See 'Hammondii Rubrifolia'

'Rubrifolia'   See 'Hammondii Rubrifolia'

'Ruby Slinger'   F – 12in white   August to September
A new cultivar similar to 'Kirby White' introduced by Slieve Donard, Northern Ireland. New growth is a soft sulphur-yellow changing to green as the summer progresses.

'Ruth Sparkes'   F D 9in white   August to September
HC 1962 as a summer foliaged plant
It arose as a sport from 'Alba Plena' in the late 1950s on the nursery of J. W. Sparkes at Beoley, near Redditch, Worcestershire, who introduced it. This is a lovely golden-foliaged heather with a very compact habit. It has double white flowers in August and September. It does have a habit of reverting to the green form which bears single flowers, but it is reported that there are plants in cultivation of 'Ruth Sparkes' that do not revert, available as 'Ruth Sparkes (Improved Form)'.

'Ruth Sparkes   F * D 9in white   August to September
(Improved Form)'   The form of 'Ruth Sparkes' which does not readily revert to the green and single form.

'Sally Anne   F – 12in pale pink   August to September
Proudley'   Attractive golden foliage in spring and summer.

'Salmonoides'   – – 12in salmon-pink   August to September
Introduced by James Smith & Sons of Darleydale, Derbyshire. A sturdy erect heather, but the plant has a washed-out and anaemic appearance.

'Searlei'   See 'Serlei'.

'Searlii'   See 'Serlei'.

'Searly'   See 'Serlei'.

'September Pink'   – – 12–18in pink September to October
'Sericea'   I do not know this cultivar but suspect it arose by the
                        bad spelling of 'Serlei'.
'Serlei'   – – 24in white August to November
                        AM 1961, FCC 1962
                        Syn 'Alba Searlei', 'Searlei', 'Searlii', 'Searly', 'Serlii'
                        'Sericea', 'Shirley'
                        A tall and upright cultivar with emerald-green foliage,
                        but more compact and robust than 'Mair's Variety'. It
                        bears long sprays of white flowers from September to
                        November and is a good cut-flower plant.
'Serlei Aurea'   F * – 18in white August to September
                        AM 1961
                        All the year round its bright golden foliage remains the
                        same, and in August and September it bears a moderate
                        number of single white flowers. A sport from 'Serlei'.
'Serlei Grandiflora'   See 'Serlei Rubra'.
'Serlei Purpurea'   – – 24in lavender-purple September to October
                        Syn 'Purpurea'
                        Of bushy habit and bears erect spikes of lavender-purple
                        flowers.
'Serlei Rubra'   – – 24–36in purple August to November
                        Syn 'Serlei Grandiflora', 'Rubra'.
'Serlei White Gown'   See 'White Gown'.
'Serlii'   See 'Serlei'.
'Serotina'   I do not know this cultivar but its name indicates late
                        flowering.
'Shirley'   See 'Serlei'
'Silver Knight'   F – 12in pink August to September
                        Raised and introduced by J. W. Sparkes. A new cultivar
                        very similar to 'Silver Queen', having woolly silver
                        foliage and pink-mauve flowers from August to
                        September. Although both reach a height of 12in,
                        'Silver Knight' is reputed to be a little more compact.
'Silver Queen'   F * – 12–18in mauve August to September
                        It is a shy bloomer normally, although there are years in
                        which its mauve flowers can be seen in August and
                        September. Its beauty lies in its woolly, silvery foliage
                        which is best in a clean atmosphere. Like a number of
                        the other hairy-leafed heaths and heathers it is not
                        among the easiest to propagate.
'Silver Spire'   – – 24in white September to October
                        Introduced by Robert Hayes of Grasmere, Westmor-

land. The foliage is an attractive light green and the good white flowers are produced on laterals, as well as the terminal spike, and can be from 3 to 6in long.

'Sir John Charrington'   F – 18in deep crimson August to September
Raised and introduced by J. W. Sparkes and named in honour of the chairman of the Heather Society. Its foliage of orange and red is very similar to that of 'Robert Chapman', but its flowers are deep crimson as opposed to a purplish-pink.

'Sister Anne'   – * 4in pink August to September
Syn 'Hirsuta Compacta'.
Introduced by W. E. Th. Ingwersen Ltd, East Grinstead, Surrey. Found by Miss Anne Mosely about 1929 above the Serpentine Rocks in the Lizard, Cornwall. Some nurserymen regard 'Hirsuta Compacta' and 'Sister Anne' as different plants. The usual height is about 4in and the foliage is somewhat silvery and downy. During the winter reddish tints are shown, but the foliage is generally dirty. In August and September pink flowers are produced right at the end of the shoots and laterals. The plant is very floriferous and the dead flowers take on silvery-lavender colours to make this a very popular cultivar.

'Spicata'   – – 12in white August to September
Syn 'Alba Spicata'
Very free flowering.

'Spicata Nana'   – – 9–12in white August to September
Medium green foliaged cultivar with little or no flowers. Slightly dwarfer than 'Spicata'. Not worth growing.

'Spitfire'   F * – 12in pink August to September
Raised and introduced by R. E. Hardwick of Newick in Sussex. Similar to 'Aurea', being a good golden heather. Its foliage turns bright red in the winter, described by some people as a fiery red, particularly on the southern side. Its pink flowers are moderately produced in August and September.

'Spring Cream'   F – 18in August to September
Raised and introduced by J. W. Sparkes. Its bright green foliage in the spring has attractive cream tips.

'Spring Torch'   F – 12in pink August to September
Raised and introduced by J. W. Sparkes. The green foliage has vermilion-coloured tips in the spring.

'Stricta Nana'   – – 12in August to September
An American cultivar not worth growing.

'Summer Elegance'   – – 18in silver-lilac August to September
The flower spikes are long and tapering.

'Summer Orange'   F – 18in pink August to September
Raised and introduced by J. W. Sparkes. A very good orange-foliaged cultivar, the tints of which turn darker in the winter.

'Sunset'   F * – 6–12in pink August to September
AM 1967 as a winter foliage plant, FCC 1968
The foliage is yellow-orange with deeper-coloured tips. During the winter it takes on strong red tints deeper than in 'Robert Chapman'. Its habit is rather loose and it produces only a few pink flowers in August and September.

'Tenella'   – – 12in white August to September
Syn 'Alba Gracilis', 'Alba Tenella'
Its habit is very distinctive, being in a tangled criss-cross manner and the stems and flowering spikes are slender.

'Tenuis'   – – 6in scarlet-purple July to September
It is a very early and continuous flowerer, the first blooms coming in July and continuing on to September. The flowers are scarlet-purple, fading to red, and are produced on spikes growing in a criss-cross manner. It is often called the 'scarlet heath'.

'The Pygmy'   – – 2in rosy-purple August to September
Collected by Maxwell at Arne, near Wareham, Dorset, and introduced by Maxwell and Beale. A true dwarf carpeter that will endure a reasonable amount of traffic. Although shy blooming on some soils, it can bear a profusion of rosy-purple flowers.

'Tib'   – * D 10in cyclamen-purple July to October
AM 1960, FCC 1962
It was found in the Pentland Hills near Edinburgh, Scotland, in 1934 by Miss Isabel Young of Currie, and it was put on the market in 1938. It was named 'Tib' after her, as Tib is a nickname for Isabel. It is very compact and vigorous and the growth is erect; the foliage is a dark green. It is not unusual to find the odd flowers still opening in January on this very floriferous plant, but by late autumn, when three-quarters or more of the flowers are over, the plant tends to have a somewhat scruffy appearance.

'Tomentosa'   – – 18in white September to October
It has greyish-green foliage and long sprays of white
flowers, which are also produced on the laterals.

'Tom Thumb'   – – 6in pink August to September
Introduced by Maxwell and Beale. It is another member
of the group of heathers that resemble miniature
conifers. Its foliage is upright, very close and of a fresh
green. This is somewhat spoilt however in August and
September by being dotted with pink flowers.

'Torulosa'   – – 12–18in white August to September
Syn 'Alba Torulosa'
A very characteristic heather with light green foliage. It
is very floriferous and has long whippy spikes tapering
to a point of single white flowers in August and
September, that slowly fade as the winter progresses.
Each bloom is enhanced by the visible brown stamens.

'Tricolorifolia   F – 24in pink August to September
  (Smith's Variety)' Discovered and introduced by James Smith & Sons of
Darleydale. The dark green foliage has bronze tints in
the winter, while the terminal points are a paler green.
There are three distinctive colours in its summer foliage:
bronze, red and grey. These are at their best in April
and May. It is not very floriferous.

'Underwoodii'   – – 15in silvery-pink September to November
AM 1960
This was found in 1936 by George E. Underwood of
Woking on Cobham Ridges, Surrey, and introduced by
Messrs G. Underwood and Sons. It is most unusual in
that the buds do not open into flowers, but turn from an
ivory-pink to a silver-pink and purple. It reaches a
height of 15in and has inflorescences some 6½in long.
The flowers are single, although, as mentioned, they
never open, and are at their peak from September to
November, but often still look effective in January. The
base of each bud is white. The foliage of this slightly
spreading plant is dark green, although in the winter it
takes on blue-mauve tints.

'Variegata'   An old cultivar.

'White Bouquet'   – – 9in white July to August
A useful early dwarf white.

'White Gown'   – – 30in white September to October
Syn 'Serlei White Gown'
It has greyish-green foliage and tall feathery spikes. It

does not do very well in cities because it is affected by atmospheric pollution.

'White Mite' – * – 9in white July to August
A very free-flowering cultivar found in the Cairngorms above 3,000ft. It has light green foliage and is very floriferous. One of the first white heathers to flower.

'White Queen' – – 24in white August to October
An old cultivar with greyish-green foliage.

'Winter Chocolate' F * – 12in August to September
Raised and introduced by J. W. Sparkes. The summer foliage is green and orange, turns a chocolate colour during the winter and the young tips are red in spring.

Seven
Erica species and cultivars

Key to abbreviations, see page 85

Name and authority	*arborea* Linnaeus 1753
Syn names and authorities	—
Common name	Tree heath
Shrub, etc, height	Tall shrub or small tree up to 20ft
Habit	Erect, spreading
Stems	Young shoots hairy and branched
Leaf arrangement	Closely packed in whorls of three to four
Leaves—shape, size, description	$\frac{1}{8}$–$\frac{1}{4}$in long, smooth, grooved beneath
Inflorescence	Flowers towards ends of lateral twigs, form a panicle, 9–18in long
Fragrant	Fragrant
Corolla—shape, lobes, colour	Globular, bell shaped, greyish-white to pale pink, 1/6in long, lobes more or less spreading
Calyx—shape, colour, etc	About 1/16in long, lobes ovate
Stamens—shape, colour, exserted or included	Included, short appendages
Stigma—shape, colour	Flattened, white, exserted
Pedicel	$\frac{1}{8}$in long, smooth
Flowering time	March to April
Introduction (Great Britain)	1658
	Cultivar 'Alpina' introduced to Great Britain in 1899 from mountains of Cuenca, western Spain, where it grew at 4,500ft or more.

General

Found on poor and other siliceous soils usually on the edge of oak woods,

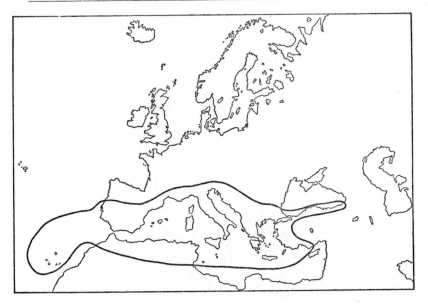

Distribution of *Erica arborea* (see also map p 128)

olives and other trees. It could be killed by a cold British winter, although it will stand 20° F of frost if only for one or two nights. It grows naturally in alkaline soil and nearly always on a very sunny site. Its bushy growth in cultivation is useful, in contrast to its tall straggly growth in the wild. A good specimen in a heather garden with its pale green foliage can be a striking feature, although not so outstanding as a plant in full flower, when it is usually smothered with white hawthorn-scented blooms. Bees like the flowers which are moderately high in nectar content. When training a specimen it is necessary to prune back by half leading shoots in the first few years.

'Alba'   –
                Similar to species, but flowers supposed to be a purer white.
'Alpina'   – * – 6–8ft   white   March to May
                Syn 'Montana'
                AGM 1933, AM 1962
                Found about 4,000ft above sea level, very hardy and will thrive in many places where *E. arborea* itself will be killed quickly. It has more upright growth, is more compact and its close clusters of pure white flowers are more sweetly scented than *E. arborea*. In the spring and early summer its very bright green

Erica arborea

young foliage, paler than *E. arborea* itself, is an added attraction.
In some sites in cultivation it will readily self-sow itself.

'Gold Tips'   F – 6–8ft   white   March to May

Raised and introduced by Maxwell and Beale. This cultivar is
identical in habit and flowers to *E. arborea* 'Alpina', but in the
spring its young growths are golden, which fade to pale green
as the season advances.

Name and authority	*australis* Linnaeus
Syn names and authorities	—
Common names	Southern Tree Heath, Spanish Heath
Shrub, etc, height	Shrub 3–4ft, sometimes 6–8ft
Habit	Ungainly, erect

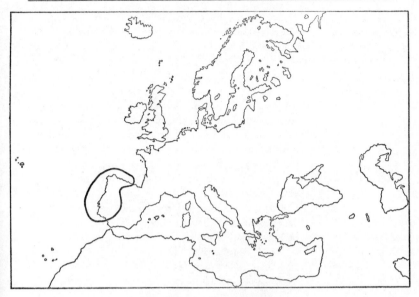

Distribution of *Erica australis*

Stems	Young shoots downy
Leaf arrangement	Whorls of fours
Leaves—shape, size, description	Linear, ¼in, glandular ciliate on margins when young, dark green above, channelled beneath
Inflorescence	Flowers on previous year's growth in umbel-like clusters of four or eight at end of shoots
Fragrant	Fragrant
Corolla—shape, lobes, colour	Cylindrical, ⅓in long, bright purplish-red with four rounded lobes at mouth
Calyx—shape, colour, etc	Less than half corolla, ⅛in, slightly downy
Stamens—shape, colour, exserted or included	Anthers slightly exserted
Pedicel	1/12in long
Flowering time	April to June
Introduction (Great Britain)	Introduced from Portugal in 1769

General

AM 1935, FCC 1962

A member of the Lusitanian flora that will stand reasonably low temperatures. In the 1962–3 winter plants subjected to 28° F had their stems split, but sprouted from lower down and grew into new plants. It stands lime to a certain degree and grows best not as individual plants but in colonies. It has very little resilience and is easily damaged by snow and wind.

'Aragonensis'   – – 4–6ft rosy-pink March to June
Very similar to *E. australis* itself but the bracts and sepals are glabrous instead of being hairy and the leaves are finer, but more dense. It would appear that this is one of the more tender forms of *E. australis*. It is more floriferous than the type although its corolla is slightly smaller.

'Mount Stewart'   – – 5–6ft bright rosy-purple April to June
AM 1936
Less hardy than the other cultivars. Its flowers are freely produced if some shelter can be given. This cultivar may be lost to cultivation.

'Mr Robert'   – * – 6–9ft white March to May
AM 1929, AGM 1945
This was named in honour of Lt Robert Williams, son of J. C. Williams of Caerhays, Cornwall, who was known by the staff as 'Mr Robert'. He found it while searching for plants at Algeciras in 1912, during ten days' leave. Its foliage is a paler green than *E. australis* itself and is more tender. When growing well it is a good garden plant, but it is not the easiest of cultivars to root from cuttings (plate, p 108).

'Riverslea'   – – 5–6ft fuchsia purple April to June
AM 1946
Arose as a chance seedling on the nursery of Maurice Pritchard & Sons Ltd, Christchurch, Hants. The flowers of this cultivar are slightly larger than *E. australis* itself, and are borne in clusters of four or five on tiny side shoots from stiff stems.

'Rosea'   – – 6ft pink April to June
Identical in habit to *E. australis*, but the flowers are slightly larger.

'Wishanger Pink'   Syn *E.* × 'Wishanger Pink'
AM 1957
A so-called hybrid raised in 1946 by Brigadier Evans and mentioned by Krussman and later by McClintock in the Heather Society Year Book in 1965. It was reputed to be a hybrid between *E. australis* and *E.* × *darleyensis* but Kew say that it was an *E. australis* cultivar. It looked like *E.* ×

Page 125   (above) Erica carnea (herbacea) 'Vivellii'; (below) Erica cinerea 'P. S. Patrick'

Page 126 (above) Erica
tetralix 'Alba Mollis';
(below) Erica terminalis

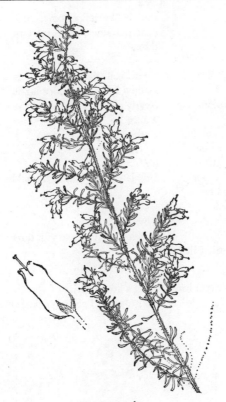

Erica australis

darleyensis, except for its flowers which were like *E. australis*. It started to flower after *E.* × *darleyensis*, but before *E. australis*. This plant is probably lost to cultivation.

Name and authority	*canaliculata* Andrews 1809
Syn names and authorities	*E. melanthera* Auctt. non Linnaeus (erroneous)
Common name	Channelled Heath
Shrub, etc, height	Shrub, 10–20ft
Habit	Erect, columnar
Stems	Densely covered with white branched hairs on young shoots
Leaf arrangement	Usually in whorls of three
Leaves—shape, size, description	Linear, 3/16–¼in long, much recurved, dark green above, paler beneath

H

Inflorescence	Panicle-like inflorescence produced by flowers clustered towards the end of twigs, often in threes
Fragrant	—
Corolla—shape, lobes, colour	Open bell shaped, $\frac{1}{8}$in long and wide with shallow lobes, white or pinkish
Calyx—shape, colour, etc	Nearly as long as corolla, lobes ovate, acute, red within
Stamens—shape, colour, exserted or included	Anthers exserted, brown
Stigma—shape, colour exserted or included	Simple stigma, long, exserted beyond anthers
Pedicel	Downy, $\frac{1}{8}$in long
Flowering time	March to May, flowers for three months or more
Introduction (Great Britain)	1802

General

It is not 100 per cent hardy, being a South African Cape Heath, although the odd specimen over 17ft has been grown at Ludgvan near Penzance and it has

Distribution of *Erica canaliculata*
and *Erica arborea* (_____)

survived at Kew outside for a few years at a time. It detests lime and is often grown in pots. The flowers change colour with temperature, remaining white with characteristic dark brown anthers when grown in a frost-free glasshouse, or a delicate pink when grown outside. Its habit is attractive, being elegantly columnar. It is regarded by some people as the most beautiful flowering shrub that can be grown outdoors in this country.

Erica canaliculata

'Boscawen Variety'   AM 1937

      The name given to plants propagated from material that originated from a good specimen of *E. canaliculata* growing at Boscawen that might be more suited to the British climate than the type. Whereas the type has pearl-white flowers this cultivar has pale rose-tinted blossoms, perhaps due to the cold.

Name and authority	*Erica carnea* Linnaeus
Syn names and authorities	*Erica herbacea* Ross 1968
Common names	Spring Heath, Mountain Heath, Winter Heath
Shrubs, etc, height	Shrub up to 12in
Habit	Low spreading decumbent
Stems	Smooth young wood
Leaf arrangement	Whorls of four, $1/12$–$\frac{1}{8}$in apart

Leaves—shape, size, description	Linear 5/16in long
Inflorescence	Terminal, leafy, one-sided raceme (plate, p 71), 1–3in long, singly or in pairs in leaf axils at end of previous summer's growth
Fragrant	—
Corolla—shape, lobes, colour	Ovoid to urn-shaped, $\frac{1}{4}$in
Calyx—shape, colour, etc	Narrow, oblong, more than half the length of corolla
Stamens—shape, colour, exserted or included	Exserted, dark red-brown, no appendages
Stigma—shape, colour, exserted or included	Exserted
Pedicel	As long as calyx
Flowering time	October to April
Introduction (Great Britain)	1763 by George Williams, Earl of Coventry

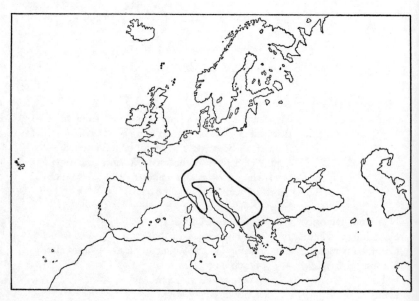

Distribution of *Erica carnea*

General

This species likes pastures, sunny slopes and the edges of pine woods, usually at a height of between 2,500 and 9,000ft. It is exceptionally hardy, being able to flower through snow and ice. It will grow in limy soils; it manages to thrive in cracks in rocks (plate, p 108). It is a useful species in that it withstands heavy shade, heavy atmospheric pollution and considerable salt spray. Its flowers are produced on the previous season's growths and fresh shoots are produced above the flowers, or from axillary buds below the inflorescence. About 1910 many of the cultivars that are grown today were collected and introduced by Messrs Backhouse of York, but many of these have become mixed and distributed under the wrong names by many nurserymen.

'Ada S. Collings'   – – 6–9in white March to April
This dwarf, white, stiff *Erica carnea* cultivar is very similar to 'White Glow' and the foliage is almost a bronzy-green.

'Alan Coates'   – * – 6–9in rose-purple February to March
AM 1965
It bears bright rose-pink flowers above deep green foliage during February to March. It is similar both in flower and habit to 'Vivellii', but its foliage does not change to purplish tints on the approach of winter.

'Alba'   – – 6in white January to April
This is one of the oldest cultivars of *E. carnea* and is a shy bloomer. Its little short white flowers are borne on top of dark green foliage. It has now been superseded by 'Cecilia M. Beale' and 'Snow Queen', although it does flower a week or two earlier than these.

'Ann Sparkes'   F * – 6–9in carmine-red February to March
Raised by J. W. Sparkes. Of recent introduction, this is a very good golden-foliaged *Erica*, resulting as a sport from 'Vivellii'. The tips of the foliage turn a rich reddish-mauve during the winter.

'Atro-Rubra'   – – 6–9in deep crimson-pink March to April
This plant of flat open growth, particularly when young, is a distinguishing feature. The foliage is dark and somewhat glaucous. Late in the season it has long racemes of deep rich crimson flowers.

'Aurea'   F * – 6–9in deep pink December to April
This cultivar has golden foliage, being stronger in colour in spring and early summer than at other times of the year. In the winter there can be little red flecks on the leaves. Under certain growing conditions, parti-

cularly partial shade, greenish tints appear in the foliage, giving the plant an appearance of suffering from chlorosis. It is very floriferous. The usual height is somewhere between 6 and 9in.

'Carnea' — — 6–9in pink January to April
Not outstanding, yet a floriferous cultivar.

'Cecilia M. Beale' — * — 6–9in white January to March
This is one of the first whites to bloom. It is relatively dwarf and compact and its large flowers are held erect on short spikes. It is a considerable improvement on 'Alba', which is more prostrate. Its habit of holding the flowers further from the soil helps the blooms to remain clean in rough weather. It is similar to 'Snow Queen' and is an old cultivar that occurred as a chance seedling at Maxwell and Beale's nursery in the 1920s. Mr Chapple reports a pink sport of this cultivar.

'C. J. Backhouse' — — 6–9in pale pink March to April.
A very late cultivar, introduced by Backhouse of York. The blooms open as intermittent little clusters up the stem. Its pale pink flowers are probably the palest of the E. *carnea*, but they deepen slightly with age. The buds are almost colourless.

'Colwall Nurseries' See E. × *darleyensis* 'Silberschmelze'
This name arose when it was seen at the RHS Gardens at Wisley, where they put this name in brackets on a label to indicate where it had come from while they waited for it to flower and re-named it. In the meantime it got misspelt as 'Galwal Nurseries'; both have been used as clonal names.

'December Red' — — 6–9in deep rose-pink December to February
Syn 'Springwood Rose'
AM 1966
Once distributed as 'Springwood Pink Dark Flowered Form'. Arose as a seedling in the nursery of C. R. Roots. It is distinguished by its spreading habit, vigorous nature and small, dark green, fat leaves. The colour of the cyclamen-purple corolla fades slightly towards its base. The sepals are mallow pink. As the name suggests it flowers in December, but often continues into February.

'Early Red' — — 8in red November to February
Good spreading habit with pleasant green leaves. Basic growth habit and colour is similar to 'Sherwoodii'.

'Eileen Porter'   – * – 6–9in rich carmine October to April
                         AM 1956

It is considered by Maxwell and Beale to be one of their
finest introductions. Seed sown by Mr J. W. Porter of
Carryduff, Northern Ireland from 'Praecox Rubra' in
1934 produced a number of seedlings. They flowered
approximately two years later and all except one from
January to February. The long-flowering plant was
divided the following spring and one division sold to
Maxwell Beale in November 1937, who named it after
Mrs Eileen Porter, the raiser's wife. This cultivar is
sterile which could be a reason for its long flowering
period, October to April at sea level, and can sometimes
be as early as September. *E. carnea* hybrids appear to be
sterile and for this reason many people believe that
'Eileen Porter' is an *E. mediterranea* and *E. carnea*
hybrid. This theory is supported by the way the buds are
affected on this cultivar in a bad winter, just like the more

Erica carnea

tender *E. mediterranea*. Its rich carmine flowers are produced in abundance on a plant that, although usually
only just over 6in tall, can become leggy if not pruned
immediately after the flowers have finished, which is
sometimes in April. It can be a little temperamental in
some situations.

'Foxhollow Fairy'   – * – 6–9in cream-pink January to March
Found on their nursery and introduced by Mr and Mrs
J. Letts, who think it is possibly a seedling from 'Springwood White' and 'Springwood Pink'. It is a vigorous
trailing plant and very much a newcomer. The white
corolla, which becomes pink with age, is held in a
cream-pink calyx.

'Furzey'   See *E.* × *darleyensis* 'Furzey'.

'Galwal Nurseries'   See *E.* × *darleyensis* 'Silberschmelze' and *E. carnea*
'Colwall Nurseries'.

'Gracilis'   – – 6–9in pale pink December to March
Introduced by Backhouse of York. A neat small plant
with small dark green foliage. Its habit is slightly prostrate and it bears numerous spikes of blooms.

'Heathwood'   – – 9in deep pink February to April
HC 1964
Introduced by J. Brummage of Taverham, Norfolk.
This is similar to 'Loughrigg' but it is more bushy and
has slightly darker foliage that is broad for an *Erica*, being similar to that of the *Phyllodoce* species. The flower
buds are yellowish and are held on deep maroon pedicels
before opening to deep rosy-pink blooms. Flowering is
often as early as Christmas, but the usual time is from
February to April.

'James Backhouse'   – – 6in pale pink March to April
Introduced by Backhouse of York. Another very large-
flowered *E. carnea* cultivar, the blooms of which tend to
be held all round the terminal raceme. The foliage is a
good green but in the winter can have a slight chlorotic
appearance. The flower buds are green.

'King George'   – * – 6–9in rich pink December to April
Syn 'King George V'
AM 1922, AGM 1932
This is an old favourite, blooming from December to
April, and always having masses of deep rose blooms.
The actual time of flowering depends on whether it is
grown in the south-west, or the later north and east. At

a maximum height of 9in, it can still remain compact, with dark green foliage. A new sport of this, 'Lesley Sparkes', makes a good foliage cultivar.

'Lesley Sparkes' F * – 6–9in rich pink December to February
Raised and introduced by J. W. Sparkes. Of recent introduction, this *Erica* has unusual foliage which is salmon blended with golden-green. The flowers are identical to those of 'King George' from which it is a sport.

'Loughrigg' – * – 6–9in rich purple February to March
HC 1964, AM 1966
Raised and introduced by Geoffrey Hayes Ltd of Grasmere. Its raisers described it as a seedling of 'Vivellii', which would account for its similarity to this cultivar. It is a taller, upright and more vigorous cultivar than 'Heathwood'. Its foliage, light green, and often glaucous, turns bronze at the tips in winter. It usually flowers from February to March with rich, soft purple blooms on growths up to 6in tall.

'March Seedling' – * 6–9in rosy-purple March to April
This is a recent introduction with a spreading habit, with dark glaucous foliage enhancing its rich rosy-purple flowers in late March and April.

'Mrs Sam Doncaster' – – 6in light pink January to April
Syn 'Mrs S. Doncaster', 'Mrs Samuel Doncaster'
Raised and introduced by Backhouse of York. An excellent carpeter with its loose and prostrate habit. Its leaves are not as dense as is normal in *E. carnea* and are a greyish-green.

'Pallida' – – 6in pale pink March to April
This little-grown heath has small dull-green foliage and its flowers open almost white and deepen to pink with age.

'Pink Beauty' See 'Pink Pearl'.
'Pink Pearl' – – 6–9in shell pink March to April
Syn 'Pink Beauty'
Raised and introduced by Backhouse Nurseries of York. It is very similar to 'Prince of Wales' which flowers a little later. It is taller than 'Thomas Kingscote' and flowers a little later, but is not as floriferous. The foliage is a pleasant light green. It can be difficult to grow in some soils.

'Pink Spangles' – * – 9–12in deep rosy-red March to April

Syn *E.* × *darleyensis* 'Pink Spangles'
Introduced by Treseders & Sons of Truro. To my mind
one of the most exciting winter-flowering *Ericas* to have
been introduced in recent years. It is a very strong
grower and makes an ideal ground-cover plant. Its
flowers are really bi-colour. The corolla is a deep rosy-
red and has sepals of a pleasant pale lilac at right angles
to it. Overall the flowers are probably the largest of all
the winter-flowering heaths. Its foliage is a pleasing
green. This plant is a 'must' for any collection.

'Pirbright Pink'   See 'Pirbright Rose'.

'Pirbright Rose'   – * – 8in red-purple December to February
Syn 'Pirbright Pink'
AM 1968
Spreading, compact and vigorous. The foliage is glau-
cous tinged red. Sepals a shade paler than corolla.

'Praecox Rubra'   – *– 6–9in deep rosy-red December to March
AM 1966, FCC 1968
Introduced by Backhouse of York. It has flowers
similar to, but darker than 'Prince of Wales'. It grows
with a trailing habit to a height of just over 6–9in and
above its dark foliage, often glaucous, are held deep,
rich red flowers. The blooms are on the small side but
last for a long period, December to March.

'Prince of Wales'   – – 6–9in pink March to April
Raised and introduced by Backhouse of York. Very
similar to 'Queen of Spain', but the flowers are a
slightly darker pink. The foliage is loose and elegant and
the whole plant can look most charming when flowering well, but in some situations it is not very floriferous.

'Queen Mary'   – – 6–9in bright pink December to February
Raised and introduced by Backhouse of York. In a good
alkaline soil the foliage is green, but in acid soils it takes
on a golden hue with coppery-orange tints, and in
winter the tips of the foliage are a reddish-mauve. In
some seasons it blooms poorly.

'Queen of Spain'   – – 6–9in pale pink February to April
Raised and introduced by Backhouse of York. It is very
similar to 'Vivellii' in growth and habit although the
tips of the leaves point downwards sometimes, up and
outwards at other times, giving a spiky appearance to
the stems. The flower buds have a slight tinge of red.

'Rosea'   – – 6–9in pale pink January to April

An old cultivar that is seldom grown these days. Compared with other varieties and cultivars it is a poor grower and a shy bloomer.

'Rosy Gem' – – 6in bright pink March to April
This is one of the later-flowering cultivars, bearing bright pink flowers in March and April, above neat and compact, good green foliage.

'Royal Gem' See 'Ruby Glow'.

'Rubra' A number of clonal stocks come under this name which appear to be either 'Praecox Rubra' or 'Vivellii'.

'Ruby Glow' – * – 6–9in rich pink March to April
Syn 'Royal Gem'
AM 1967
This is a spreading cultivar, just over 6–9in in height, and has flowers of a rich pink with a slight hint of purple in them. The blooms are brighter than 'Vivellii' and it has good dark foliage. It is also a considerable improvement on 'Atro-Rubra', although some people accuse it of not blooming prolifically.

'Sherwood Creeping' See 'Sherwoodi'.

'Sherwoodi' – – 6–9in pink February to April
Syn 'Sherwood Creeping'
Introduced from America in 1963, it is a low spreading cultivar with large green leaves. The flower buds are light green and open to an attractive pink.

'Smart's Heath' – – 6–9in pink January to March
Has been distributed under the name of 'Springwood Pink Dark Form'. It is similar to 'Springwood Pink' except that its foliage has a distinct blue-green tinge and its flowers, which are produced a little earlier, are a slightly darker pink.

'Snow Queen' – – 6in white January to March
An old cultivar distributed as early as 1934. It is similar to 'Cecilia M. Beale'. Its large pure white flowers are borne well above its foliage and it gives the better flower size and number when young.

'Springwood' See 'Springwood White'.

'Springwood Pink' – * – 6in pink January to March
AM 1964
This is one of the best vigorous carpeting heaths, ideally suited to large areas. It grows to a height of just over 6in and has good strong glaucous foliage and bright warm pink flowers from January to March (plate, p 108). It

appeared as a seedling on a Scottish nursery. There is a dwarf form on the market with slightly larger leaves. It is probably this form that is now distributed under the name 'Smart's Heath'.

'Springwood Rose'　　See 'December Red'.

'Springwood White'　　– * – 6–9in　white　January to March
Syn 'Springwood'
AM 1930, AGM 1940, FCC 1964
Found in Italy on Monte Carreggio by the late Mrs Ralph Walker of Springwood in Stirling, Scotland. This is probably the fastest-growing trailing heath, reaching a height of 6–9in (plate, p 35). It makes an ideal weed smotherer. It bears unusually long white spikes of flowers, each one having chestnut-brown anthers protruding from the corolla. The first flowers, in late December to mid-January, are greenish, and then the show continues for about two and a half months. The foliage is a useful and easily recognised apple green and remains so throughout the year. It was named at Wisley by the late Mr Chittenden as 'Springwood'. Due to these attributes, and the fact that it will stand drought better than most other heaths, it has received the above mentioned awards. Although many people report an absence of seedlings from 'Springwood White' it is still believed that it is one of the parents of 'Springwood Pink'.

'Startler'　　– – 6in　coral-pink　February to March
A useful seldom-grown cultivar with small dull-green leaves, brown buds and a bushy habit.

'Thomas Kingscote'　　– * – 6–9in　pale pink　March to April
HC 1964
Introduced by the Backhouse Nursery. Flowers from March to April, with many pale pink flowers and chestnut-brown anthers. It grows to a height of 6–9in. It is regarded as a good late cultivar, although flowers can be had as early as Christmas.

'Urville'　　– – 6–9in　carmine　February to March
The foliage is slightly darker than the bronze-green foliage of 'Vivellii', to which it is very similar in habit and flowers.

'Vivellii'　　– * – 6–9in　carmine　January to March
AM 1964, FCC 1965
It was found in Switzerland in 1906 and was first

named 'Rubra' and then because of the 'Praecox Rubra' in 1913 it was renamed 'Vivellii' (plate, p 125). It is a floriferous, 6–9in high heath, bearing carmine-red flowers from mid-January to March, and dark bronze-green foliage, particularly near its tips. The colour is intensified in the winter months, when even the buds take on bronze tints. The young foliage in summer is initially plain green.

'White Glow' – – 9–12in white February to April
This is a sport of 'Ruby Glow' and was introduced by the Alpine specialist and nurseryman, Jack Drake of Aviemore. It grows from 9 to 12in and bears pure white flowers from February to April on a neat plant and is very similar to 'Ada S. Collings' and E. × darleyensis 'Silberschmelze'. On some soils the foliage is yellowish in summer.

'Winter Beauty' – – 6–9in bright pink December to March
Raised and introduced by Backhouse of York. There is considerable controversy about this cultivar and it is mostly 'King George' which is sold under this name. It is not as robust as 'King George', its habit is weaker and it is of poor constitution and is rarely grown. When growing well its rich pink flowers are borne in profusion with prominent brown anthers. The flower buds are brown.

Name and authority	ciliaris Linnaeus 1753
Syn names and authorities	—
Common names	Dorset Heath, Fringed Heath
Shrub, etc, height	Shrub, 6–12in or more
Habit	Semi-procumbent with ascending shoots
Stems	Glandular, downy
Leaf arrangement	Leaves whorled, threes
Leaves—shape, size, description	Ovate $\frac{1}{8}$–$\frac{1}{4}$in, glandular and eglandular ciliate, under-surface white, margins somewhat revolute
Inflorescence	Flowers in threes, axillary in a terminal raceme 1–5in long
Fragrant	—
Corolla—shape, lobes, colour	Bright pink, urn to urceolate shaped, $\frac{3}{8}$in long, four short, rounded lobes, sharply contracted at mouth
Calyx—shape, colour, etc	Lobes lanceolate, glandular, ciliate

Stamens—shape, colour,   Anthers included, awnless
        exserted or
        included
Stigma—shape, colour   Smooth capsule, exserted
Pedicel   1/10in long, bracteolate about middle
Flowering time   July to November
Introduction (Great Britain)   Natural habitat

General

This was recorded in Cornwall in 1828, Dorset in 1833 and in Devon in 1911. A report in 1939 maintains a colony holding its own in an area near Manaton at a height of 1,250ft and also at Bovey Tracey. I have not found it in Devon, but this does not mean that it does not exist here. It is a member of the Lusitanian flora and is one of the most tender of the British heaths. It detests lime and prefers to grow in moist situations. Under cultivation it will however stand surprisingly dry conditions. It grows best in full sunshine, but will stand semi-shade if this is in the afternoon. It is very susceptible to atmospheric pollution and is therefore seldom grown in cities. In cultivation plants die for no apparent reason. It is damaged very easily by inclement weather, being walked on, etc and does not transplant very well.

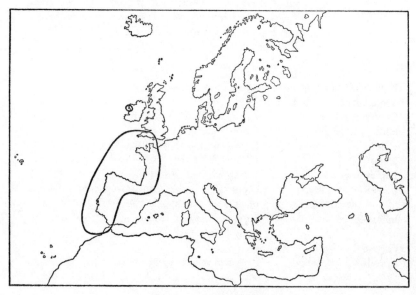

Distribution of *Erica ciliaris*

'Alba'   – – 18in white July to October
With its freely produced, globular white flowers, it was regarded as a good white *Erica*, but *E. ciliaris* 'Stoborough' has superseded it.

'Arne'   – – 15in bright pink July to October
Trehanes (Camellia), of Stapehill, Wimborne, have this plant which differs from the wild *E. ciliaris* in having a shade paler flowers.

'Aurea'   F * – 12in pink July to August
Found on the Great Heath in Dorset and introduced by Maxwell and Beale. This golden-leafed cultivar is easily recognised by its round leaves covered with fine hairs. It will reach a height of 12in, but is difficult on many soils. Although it produces a number of pink flowers in July and August, as well as a useful coloured foliage, it cannot really be recommended as an amateur's plant due to its weak constitution.

'Camla'   – – 9–12in rosy-pink July to August
It is a very good ground-cover plant and is exceptionally hardy. It bears rosy-pink bells on numerous spikes.

'Corfe Castle'   – * – 9–12in soft salmon-pink July to August
This new cultivar has the usual *E. ciliaris* green foliage which turns bronze in the winter. It will produce flowers above its compact growth often into September.

'David McClintock'   – * – 15–18in white with pink tips July to October
Found in Brittany in August 1962, introduced by Aldenham Heather Nurseries. Flowers open white with pink tips and may become pink all over. The habit is graceful but strong.

'Globosa'   – – 18in pink July to October
Raised and introduced by Maxwell and Beale. This vigorous cultivar grows into a small bush of 18in. It has greyish-green foliage and its clusters of large pink bells on erect spikes may be seen through July to October and is similar to *E. c.* 'Rotundiflora'. When finished the blooms take on pleasing chestnut tints.

'Hybrida'   See *Erica* Hybrids, Chapter Eight

'Jean Liddle'   – – 12in pale reddish-purple July to October
Typical *E. ciliaris* growth and habit. The foliage is green and grey.

'Maweana'   – * – 12in pink June to October
Discovered in 1872 by a Mr George Maw in Portugal.

Erica ciliaris

Although reputed to be the finest of the *E. ciliaris* cultivars it is not 100 per cent hardy. Its strong, stiff, upright
stems reach a height of 12in, and its rich crimson
flowers are larger than other *E. ciliaris* cultivars.

'Mrs C. H. Gill'   – – 12in   clear red   July to October

Page 143   (above) Erica
umbellata; (below) Erica vagans
'St Keverne'

Found and introduced by Maxwell and Beale and named in honour of a Mrs C. H. Gill of Thirsk in Yorkshire, who was a lover of heaths. The dark green foliage makes an ideal combination with the clear red flowers freely produced between July and October. The normal height of this plant is generally between 10 and 12in.

'Rotundiflora' – – 12in pink July to October
Syn 'Rotundifolia'
Introduced by Maxwell and Beale. Pink flowers are freely produced between July and October on this cultivar that has the added attraction of grey-green foliage and attains a maximum height of 12in. Not an outstanding cultivar.

'Rotundifolia' See 'Rotundiflora'.

'Stapehill' – – 12in pale cream/flushed purple July to October
Introduced by C. J. Marchant of Stapehill, Wimborne, Dorset. Its long spikes of creamy-white blooms are attractively flushed light purple which deepens to a darker purple towards the tips.

'Stoborough' – * – 24in white July to October
Found between the villages of Stoborough and Arne on the Great Heath in Dorset and introduced by Maxwell and Beale. This is probably the tallest cultivar of the *Erica ciliaris* group, reaching 24in quite readily. It is a very strong grower and its characteristic pearly-white pitcher-shaped flowers are freely produced between July and October above good apple-green foliage. It is generally present among the collection of *Ericas* of heather gardens on acid soil if *E. ciliaris* cultivars are grown.

'White Wings' – – 12in white July to October
A sport found by Mrs Letts on 'Mrs C. H. Gill' and introduced by Mr and Mrs John Letts. This is described as a dainty plant whose white flowers are shown up to advantage by the dark grey-green foliage.

'Wych' – – 18in creamy-white, flushed pale pink July to October
Found on Wych Heath, Dorset, and introduced by Maxwell and Beale. This very pretty cultivar has a fascinating break in colour. The long spikes are covered with numerous cream-white flowers flushed with pale pink, which from a distance appear to be an overall flesh pink.

I

Name and authority	*cinerea* Linnaeus 1753
Syn names and authorities	—
Common names	She Heath, Crimson Heath, Bell Heath, Scotch Bell, Grey Leaved Heath, Fine Leaved Heath, Twisted Heath
Shrub, etc, height	Shrub, 6–24in
Habit	Branching stiff, much divided, often rooting at base
Stems	Young wood downy
Leaf arrangement	Leaves usually in whorls of three
Leaves—shape, size, description	Linear, strongly recurved, ¼in long, margin strongly revolute, minutely ciliate
Inflorescence	Terminal umbel or short raceme 1–3in long
Fragrant	—
Corolla—shape, lobes, colour	Rosy-purple, urceolate (ovoid to urn) ¼in long, short lobes, four teeth
Calyx—shape, colour, etc	1/12in long, lobes narrow, lanceolate, semi-transparent to rosy-purple
Stamens—shape, colour, exserted or included	Anthers included and awned

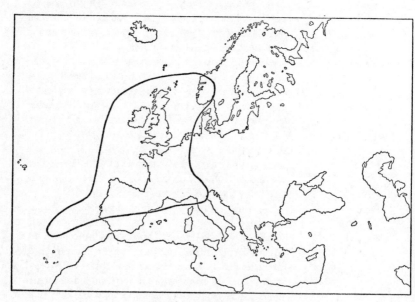

Distribution of *Erica cinerea*

Stigma—shape, colour	Ovary glabrous
Pedicel	⅛–1/6in long, puberulous bracteolate immediately below flower
Flowering time	June to September
Introduction (Great Britain)	Natural habitat

General

Erica cinerea is often found along with *Calluna vulgaris* and can also be found growing separately. It is able to bed well with *Calluna vulgaris*. It will survive in drier places than *Calluna* on hillsides and cliffs and similar dry slopes. It is very common on sea cliffs. It dislikes lime although I have seen plants growing in little pockets among limestone rocks, as for example at Berry Head, near Brixham, Devon. In these situations the pocket of soil is highly organic and also very acid, and the roots in this soil are sufficient to overcome the problems arising from the adjacent limestone. It is a sun lover and will not stand waterlogged ground. Its leaves are ovate but the edges are rolled in towards the mid-rib (revolute), which helps moisture conservation. It has less-fibrous roots than on most other heaths and heathers and therefore like *E. ciliaris* does not transplant perfectly. There are many good cultivars but unfortunately some are not worth growing, being scarcely different from the common wild forms. It has naturalised well on Nantucket Island in Massachusetts, USA. In the Hebrides, beer used to be made from it, and it grows so widely in Scotland that its flower became the emblem badge of the McAlister clan.

'Alba'	– – 9in white June to August
	It has very good white flowers on long spikes, borne to a height of 9in from June to August. Its foliage is a pleasant apple-green.
'Alba Major'	– – 9in white June to August
	Does not bloom as freely as 'Alba' and its clusters are produced in limited numbers at the ends of stems. The foliage is light green.
'Alba Minor'	– – 6in white June to October
	AM 1967, FCC 1968
	Very compact and dense pale to medium green foliage. It bears its white flowers prolifically from June to August and often into October, sometimes giving the appearance of blooming twice.
'Ann Berry'	F – 12in pink June to July
	This is a new cultivar about which I have very little knowledge. It has a loose, upright habit and bright golden-yellow foliage with a hint of pale green. During June and July it may bear one or two pink flowers.

'Apple Blossom'   − * − 12in white, flushed pink   June to August
Collected on the Corfemullen Moors and introduced by
Maxwell and Beale. This cultivar, which grows to a
height of 12in, has large white flowers with a pink flush
on long spikes from June to August. It is exceptionally
floriferous and of very neat habit, but does not appear
to be as hardy as most of the other *E. cinerea* cultivars.

'Atropurpurea'   − − 12in purple June to August
The bright purple flowers are not always freely produced on this cultivar. It has dark foliage. Sometimes it
hardly seems to grow. It has now been superseded by
'P. S. Patrick'.

'Atrorubens'   − − 6–9in bright red June to October
AM 1915
It grows to just over 6in in height and has a spreading
habit. Long sprays of bright ruby-red flowers appear
between June and October. It is exceptionally free
flowering.

'Atro-Sanguinea   − − 6in carmine-red June to August
   Reuthe's Variety'   Introduced by Reuthe of Keston. The deep carmine-red
flowers have a faint trace of purple. Except for being
larger in growth and blooming rather later, it is very
similar to 'Coccinea'.

'Atro-Sanguinea   − * − 6in scarlet June to September
   Smith's Variety'   Introduced by James Smith & Sons of Darleydale. Very
similar to 'Atrorubens', but the flowers are freely produced and have a trace of pink rather than purple. The
foliage is dark green.

'Boothii'   AM 1905
Dark purple flowers in abundance. Lost to cultivation.

'Broadstone'   See Wheatear Varieties.

'Caldy Island'   − − 9in light purple June to July
Found on Caldy Island in the Bristol Channel and introduced by Robert Hayes of Grasmere, Westmorland. It
has brilliant light purple bells from June to July on a
vigorous plant with a maximum height of 9in.

'Carnea   − − 12in, flesh pink July to August
The flesh-pink flowers are sometimes produced through
to September on stiff light green foliage.

'Carnea Under-   − − 9in silvery-pink June to September
   wood's Variety'   An extremely pleasing and useful colour, having silvery-
pink bells produced over a long period, June to Septem-
ber. It is regrettably slightly tender.

Erica cinerea (wild)

'C. D. Eason'   – * – 9in glowing pink June to September
FCC 1966
Found on the Corfemullen Moors and introduced by
Maxwell and Beale. This cultivar, with its shapely bush
of distinctive dark green foliage, making an ideal base
for its freely borne, dense spikes of glowing pink
flowers from June to August and into September, is a
firm favourite of the majority of heath and heather
fanciers. Its deep green foliage distinguishes it from
most of the other *E. cinerea* cultivars.

'C. E. Pearson'   – – 15in purple-red June to September
Similar to 'C. D. Eason' in habit but grows a little
better and the flowers are slightly smaller.

'Cevenennsis'   See 'Cevennes'.

'Cevennes'   – – 9in lavender-purple June to October
Syn 'Cevenennsis'
AM 1968
Introduced from the Cevennes Mountains in France
about 1930. It has upright growth, to a height of 9in, of
an attractive green. From June to October it bears
smallish lavender-purple bells freely. Somewhat un-
reliable, apt to die out.

'C. G. Best'   – * – 12in Salmon-pink June to August
Introduced by Maxwell and Beale from the Corfemullen Moors. A characteristic of this cultivar is the
long strong stems of flowers with a large space between
each whorl or tuft of salmon-pink bells, borne from June
to August. Its overall habit is upright and the leaves are
in small tufts.

'Cindy'   – – 12in purple July to September
Recently introduced by Mr and Mrs Letts, who found
it on a ramble in Cornwall. I have no experience of this
cultivar, but its strong upright habit and its unusual
bronze-green foliage with glowing purple flowers from
July to September, sound most interesting.

'Coccinea'   – – 4-6in bright red June to August

'Coccinea Smith's   – * – 4in bright red June to August
  Variety'   Raised and introduced by James Smith & Sons of
Darleydale. It is a most remarkable plant for its size,
often only 3in high. It bears in profusion intense bright
red flowers from June until August.

'Colligan Bridge'   – – 12in purple June to August
Syn 'Colin Bridge'
PC 1967
It was found in 1936 growing on a bank by the roadside
at Colligan Bridge in the Mourne Mountains, County
Down, Northern Ireland. Its exceptionally vivid purple
flowers are borne on long spikes.

'Colin Bridge'   See 'Colligan Bridge'.

'Cripple's Ease'   – – 9-12in pink and white June to Auguts
Found in Cornwall by Miss Waterer near the hamlet of
Cripples Ease near Penzance. The bells are pink and
white, similar to 'Eden Valley'.

'Darleydale'   – – 12in   red   June to September
'Domino'   – * –   9in   ivory-white   June to September
Found in the Corfemullen Moors and introduced by
Maxwell and Beale. Arose as a sport on a purple-
flowered plant. A very useful free-flowering cultivar. It
is one of the best whites, with long sprays of flowers and
good green foliage, not the normal pale foliage that
whites have. The white corollas contrast with the ebony-
coloured sepals and flower stalks. The stigma protrudes
slightly and is black.

'Duncan Fraser'   – * –   12in   white, tinged soft pink   July to August
AM 1968
Found on Bagshot Heath by G. D. Waterer and named
after his foreman at Knap Hill Nursery. It is of recent
introduction and is similar to 'Apple Blossom'. It is very
robust in habit and produces prolifically white flowers,
which at times have a faint tint of soft pink.

'Eden Valley'   – * –   6in   soft lilac and rose   June to September
AM 1933, confirmed in 1966
Found by Miss Gertrude Waterer on Trink Hill near
Penzance in 1926, who named it after her house near
Penzance. It was introduced by Knap Hill Nursery. It is
very floriferous with soft lilac and rose flowers, produced between June and September, which fade to
white at the base of each petal. Occasionally it reaches a
little over 7in in height. It has light green foliage and a
somewhat spreading habit.

'Foxhollow   – – 12in   mahogany   June to September
   Mahogany'   Found on the hills east of St Ives by John Letts. Recently introduced, this free-flowering heath produces
masses of tightly packed rich mahogany flowers above
dark green foliage.

'Frances'   – – 12in   cerise pink   June to August
Found on the Corfemullen Moors. Introduced by Maxwell and Beale. Somewhat similar to 'C. G. Best', but
the flowers are slightly deeper. The foliage has hints of
bronze.

'Fred Corston'   – – 12in   salmon-pink   August to September
Introduced by Knap Hill Nursery. This cultivar, al-
though semi-prostrate in habit, reaches a height of 12in.
It is very new and is still undergoing trials. From
August to September it bears good-sized salmon-pink
flowers, slightly deeper than 'Rosea'.

'Fulgida'   – – 4in purple-red August to September
Compact and flat habit with medium green foliage.

'George Ford'   See 'Mrs Ford'.

'Glasnevin Red'   – * – 14in red August to September
AM 1968
It is very compact and the flowers are a pure red that is
devoid of purple. It was found as a seedling near 'C. D.
Eason'.

'Glowbells'   – – 12in rose-carmine June to August
This cultivar is probably lost to cultivation. It should be
of bushy compact habit, have a dark green foliage and
almost glowing rose-carmine flowers between June and
August.

'Golden Drop'   F * – 4–6in pink June to August
Found by Charles Eason whose favourite jam was from
the Australian plum, 'Golden Drop'. Introduced by
Maxwell and Beale. A very characteristic *Erica* with
copper-coloured foliage that turns red in winter. It is
somewhat prostrate in habit with a maximum height of
6in (plate, p 72). It seldom bears its pink flowers. From
a cultivation point of view it can be tricky to establish,
the roots holding soil badly when transplanting, but
once settled, quickly carpets the ground. By its prostrate nature it should not get confused with the upright
and taller-growing 'Golden Hue'.

'Golden Hue'   F * – 12in pink June to August
Introduced by Maxwell and Beale, who collected it as a
sport on a green plant. Many people confuse 'Golden
Hue' with 'Golden Drop', but the confusion is more
likely to arise between 'Golden Hue' and 'John Eason',
the foliage of both being erect to a height of 12in,
whereas 'Golden Drop' seldom reaches 6in. The foliage
changes from copper-gold to red in parts during
winter, and from June to August it bears a number of
pink flowers, in greater profusion than 'Golden Drop'.

'G. Osmond'   – * – 12in very pale mauve June to September
Collected by Mr Osmond on the Corfemullen Moors.
Introduced by Maxwell and Beale. Another cultivar
with ebony-coloured sepals and flower stalks. The
corolla is a very pale mauve, produced between June
and September on a plant of a somewhat bushy and upright habit that reaches a height of approximately 12in.
This cultivar contrasts very well with deeper colours.

'Grandiflora'   – – 12in rosy-purple June to August
The flowers, slightly larger than type, are borne in long spikes.

'Gwinear'   – – dark red
Found by Miss Waterer near Gwinear Road railway station, midway between Camborne and Hayle. It was the junction station for Helston and the Lizard district of Cornwall. The dark red flowers are almost sooty. This cultivar has almost certainly died out.

'Heathfield'   – – 24–30in deep purple August to October
Found in south Devon and introduced by that well-known nurseryman and horticulturist Neil Treseder of Truro. Its growth of 24–30in is unusually tall and erect for an *E. cinerea* cultivar, and from August to October masses of deep plum-coloured bells cover its long stems.

'Honeymoon'   – – 6in white, tinged lavender July to August
Tight and compact habit bearing white flowers delicately tinged with lavender.

'Hookstone   – – 12in pale lavender June to September
   Lavender'   Introduced by Underwood Brothers. A very free-flowering cultivar with characteristic pale lavender blooms. It can be difficult to grow in some situations.

'Hookstone White'   – * – 9in white June to August
Found by Mr G. E. Underwood on Grays Spot Hill on the Cobham Ridges in 1936 and introduced by Underwood Brothers. It is an exceptionally good cultivar. Its spikes can be as long as 12in, although usually between 6 and 9in and densely covered on both the spike and many laterals with large white blossoms. Its habit is upright and its foliage bright green.

'Janet'   – – 6–12in ice pink June to August
Found by Miss Waterer on Trink Hill in Cornwall in 1941. The ice-pink blooms shading to a white edge are produced above light green foliage.

'John Eason'   F – 6in pink June to August
Introduced by Maxwell and Beale. This *Erica* has upright foliage, reaching a maximum height of 12in depending on growing conditions. It is very similar to 'Golden Hue', having golden foliage with bronze tints which are more intense in the winter. The flowers are a soft salmon-pink.

'Josephine Ross'   – – 12in deep pink July to September
Collected and introduced by Mr and Mrs Letts, found

Erica cinerea (cultivar)

in Cornwall and named after one of their lady gardeners.
A new cultivar that I know little about. Its habit is
bushy and its flowers are a dull reddish-pink.

'Joyce Burfitt'   – * – 12in   maroon   June to August
Collected by Miss Joyce Burfitt on the moors near

Sandford, Wareham, Dorset and introduced in 1958 by Maxwell and Beale, for whom she was working. It grows to a height of 12in with a rather loose habit. For as long as three months, from June to August, it will bear freely rich maroon flowers on reddish stems. In the winter its foliage darkens considerably.

'Knap Hill Pink' – * – 12in rose-red June to October
Syn 'Knap Hill Variety', 'Rosea Knap Hill Variety'
AM 1966, FCC 1967
Introduced by Knap Hill Nursery. It is very similar to 'Rosea' except that the flowers of rich rose-red are a shade deeper. These are borne on 12in long spikes with olive-green foliage.

'Knap Hill Variety' See 'Knap Hill Pink'.

'Lady Skelton' – – 6in crimson June to September
Introduced by Underwood Brothers. Slightly deeper than 'Coccinea'. It has dark green foliage and is slow growing.

'Lavender Lady' – – 12in lavender July to September
Found in Cornwall by Mr and Mrs Letts and introduced by their firm. The flowers are pale lavender.

'Lilacina' – – 12in pale lilac June to August

'Lilac Time' – – 9–12in pale lavender July to September
Light green foliage, habit upright and bushy.

'Miss Waters' – – 9in pale lilac June to September
It is a most unusual cultivar, giving a bi-colour effect. Its buds open white with pale purple tips and change to a lilac-purple with age.

'Mrs Dill' – * – 4in deep pink June to August
It is a useful companion to 'Coccinea Smith's Variety', attaining only 4in. The leaves are very minute and are hidden in a multitude of glowing pink flowers from June to August.

'Mrs Ford' – – 9in deep carmine June to July
Syn 'George Ford'
Introduced by Robert Hayes of Grasmere, Westmorland. It looks like an improved form of 'Frances'. The flowers of deep carmine are freely produced above dark green foliage, sometimes into August.

'Mulfra' – – 12in mauve June to August
Collected by Miss Waterer in 1934. Supposed to be an improvement on 'Lilacina', also with long spikes of blooms above light green foliage.

'My Love'   – – 15in strong blue-mauve September
Dark green foliage, habit erect and bushy.

'New Salmon'   – * – 15in salmon-pink July to August
Raised by Delaney-Lyle of Alloa. It is reputed to be a
seedling from 'Alba Major' and in July and August its
salmon-pink flowers are borne on long spikes. The
normal height for the plant is between 15 and 18in.

'Ninnes'   – – 9in white/pale mauve-red July to September
Found by Miss Waterer in 1942. The corolla is white
with a wine-coloured edge.

'Old Rose'   – – 6in pale rose June to July
Collected by Mr and Mrs Letts in Devon and introduced
by their nursery. A semi-prostrate habit, bearing a
moderate number of pale rose flowers.

'Pallida'   – – 6–12in pale purple June to August
This seems to be confused with 'Apple Blossom' and is
also similar to 'G. Osmond'. It has long crowded spikes
of pale pink flowers that have a tinge of purple in June
and August on robust plants with an erect habit.

'Pentreath'   – * – 9in purple July to September
HC 1966, AM 1968
Found and introduced by Knap Hill Nursery. It has a
compact, semi-prostrate habit and dark green foliage.
Its rich plum-purple flowers are borne in profusion.

'Pink Foam'   – – 12in white/tinted mauve-pink July to
September
Bushy habit, foliage mid-green.

'Pink Ice'   – * – 8in soft pink June to September
AM 1968
Found by Mr and Mrs Letts in their nursery as a seedling.
It is of new introduction and of a compact bushy habit.
It produces many soft pink flowers above a dark green
foliage that has bronze and green tints during the latter
part of winter and early spring.

'Plummer's   – * – 12in rich red July to August
 Seedling'   This cultivar was introduced by the late Mr Plummer, a
keen gardener near Burton on the Wirral in Cheshire.
It is reputed to be one of the less-robust E. cinerea culti-
vars, but its rich red flowers on 12in long stems between
July and August are outstanding in quality.

'Polypetala'   See 'Schizopetala'.

'Prostrate Lavender'   – – 4in lavender-pink July to August
A neat compact grower.

'P. S. Patrick'   – * – 12in   plum purple   June to August
                    AM 1967
                    Collected by P. S. Patrick on the Corfemullen Moors in
                    1928 and introduced by Maxwell and Beale. An excep-
                    tionally good and hardy cultivar with a strong habit.
                    All through June, July and August it bears numerous
                    long spikes of vivid purple blooms, and attains a height
                    of 12in (plate, p 125).

'Purple Beauty'   – – 12in   light purple   June to October
                    Another cultivar recently introduced by Mr and Mrs
                    Letts, who found it in Cornwall. It has a bushy habit and
                    tends to flower continuously throughout the summer
                    with many large light purple blooms. The foliage is a
                    dark green.

'Purple Robe'   – – 9in   purple   July to August
                    Similar to 'Atropurpurea', particularly in the flowers,
                    although the plant is not as tall, but it flowers more
                    profusely and for a shorter period.

'Purpurea'   – – 12in   purple   July to September
                    Not very outstanding but has numerous purple bells
                    above bushy dark green foliage.

'Pygmaea'   – – 6in   pink-purple   June to July
                    AM 1908
                    It is an old but not outstanding cultivar. It is one of the
                    earliest to flower, doing so from early June to July,
                    revealing bright pink-purple flowers.

'Rendlei'   See Wheatear Varieties
'Robert Michael'   – – 12in   bright pink   June to September
                    Similar in habit and colour to 'Rosea'.

'Romiley'   – – 9in   red   June to August
                    Of recent introduction and is similar to 'Coccinea' and
                    'Atrorubens'. It is of dwarf habit and its large flower
                    heads of red are produced prolifically.

'Rosabella'   – – 6in   salmon-pink   July to August
                    This is just like a dwarf form of 'C. G. Best', prolifically
                    producing salmon-pink flowers and having dense dark
                    green foliage.

'Rosea'   – * – 12in   bright pink   June to August
                    AGM 1928, AM 1966
                    It is an old cultivar that is still holding its own. Besides
                    being very hardy and robust, from June to August it
                    bears 12in long spikes of bright pink flowers. The Knap
                    Hill form of this variety, 'Rosea Knap Hill Variety', is

slightly deeper and the correct name for that form is 'Knap Hill Pink'.

'Rosea Knap Hill Variety' See 'Knap Hill Pink'.

'Rose Queen' – * – 12–18in rose-pink June to July
Collected by the late Mr T. Smith of Daisy Hill Nurseries Ltd, Newry, Ireland. Although this cultivar usually grows to a height of 12in, it can reach as much as 18in. It is a very free flowerer and bears 6–9in long sprays of rose-pink flowers from June to July on dense bushy growths.

'Rozanne Waterer' – – 9in maroon-purple June to August
It has had the name of 'Rozzanna Waterer'. Collected by Mr Donald Waterer in Cornwall in 1954. Its habit is very similar to 'Pentreath', being semi-prostrate. Its flowers are large and of a deep maroon-purple.

'Ruby' – – 9in purple June to August
Introduced by Maxwell and Beale, Ruby being the christian name of one of their staff. Very similar to 'P. S. Patrick', but differs from it in being slightly more bushy and dwarfer and starting to flower a little earlier. Its vivid purple flowers are also sometimes a little smaller.

'Sandpit Hill' – – 9–12in rose-pink June to August
Recently introduced by Underwood Brothers. This heath has long sprays of flowers which are large, rose-pink and turn red-pink with age, giving a bi-colour effect.

'Schizopetala' – – 12in pale purple June to July
Syn 'Polypetala', × *Ericalluna bealeani* 'Schizopetala'
The flowers are of a curious interest and not of particular beauty. The perianth segments are split and are pale purple. The green leaves are slightly edged with bronze.

'Sea Foam' – – 12in pale mauve June to September
An old cultivar which is very similar to 'G. Osmond'.

'Smith's Lawn' – – 12in shell pink June to August
A recently introduced cultivar with dark foliage. The flowers are shell pink with a hint of purple and are produced on long sprays.

'Snow Cream' F * – 9in white June to July
Syn 'Snow Queen'
Raised and introduced by J. W. Sparkes. The foliage is cream, reaching a height of 9in, and acts as an ideal foil to the cream flowers.

'Snow Queen'   See 'Snow Cream'.
'Spicata'   – – 6in pinkish-purple June to July
The flowers are on the small side in short spikes. The habit is bushy and the foliage dark.

'Splendens'   – – 12in deep rose June to July
I have no personal knowledge of this cultivar.

'Startler'   – * – 6–9in deep pink June to July
A very neat plant, the leaves being well spaced and of a fresh green. The flowers, which also occur on its laterals, are a deep glowing pink.

'Studland'   See Wheatear Varieties.

'Taranto Purple'   – * – 9in rich purple June to September
Produces large compact mats of long stems which, between June and September bear rich deep purple flowers.

'The Freak'   – – pink-red June to August
Found on Trink Hill by Miss Waterer. The pink-red flowers look a little tattered. I do not know this cultivar, which is probably lost to cultivation.

'Tilford'   – – 12–15in red-purple August to September
AM 1967
Recently introduced and raised by W. G. Slocock Ltd. Spreading habit with vigorous foliage of a glossy dark green. Large red-purple flowers in 3in long inflorescence on 3 to 9in long stems.

'Tom Waterer'   – – 12in red-pink July to August
Found by G. D. Waterer and his wife while on holiday in Cornwall and introduced by Knap Hill Nurseries. Habit upright, and foliage dark green.

'Velvet Night'   – * – 9in dark purple June to August
Found in 1957 by Mr F. J. Stevens, a director of Maxwell and Beale, near their nursery, Corfemullen. It is a most distinctive Erica as its black-purple blooms tinged with crimson are darker than any other E. cinerea cultivar and it is probably the darkest-flowered Erica.

'Victorea'   See 'Victoria'.
'Victoria'   – – 6–12in purple June to July
Syn 'Victorea'
Found on the Corfemullen Moors, Dorset, and introduced by Maxwell and Beale. It is usually 6in high, dwarf and compact. Its flowers are strong in colour, being large and a rich purple.

'Vivienne Patricia'   – * – 12in dark lavender July to September
AM 1968
Found by Letts on a Cornish moor and named in honour of Mrs Letts. It is darker than 'Hookstone Lavender' but just as floriferous.

'W. G. Notley'   – – 9in deep pink June to September
Syn 'W. T. Notley', × *Ericalluna bealeani* 'W. G. Notley'
It was found on Maxwell and Beale's own moor at Corfemullen and has deep pink flowers held like *Calluna vulgaris* above foliage similar to *Erica cinerea* itself. Each flower has a rudimentary stigma and another held within a divided corolla.

Wheatear Varieties   Some shoots are coloured and are retained until the end of the year when they fade and drop off. New shoots are produced lower down. The stems appeared to have been a substitute for flowers. There are two old cultivars, I believe no longer available: 'Broadstone', 12in, with shoots bright red; and 'Studland', 12in, a duller red and a few purple flowers.

'Winifred Whitley'   – – 12in pink June to August
Syn × *Ericalluna bealeani* 'Winifred Whitley'
Found in Dorset in 1936, similar to 'Schizopetala' and a paler shade than 'W. G. Notley'.

'Zennor'   Found in the Cornwall village of Zennor by Miss Waterer. Lost to cultivation.

Name and authority	*lusitanica* Rudolphs 1799
Syn names and authorities	*E. codonodes* Lindley
Common name	Portuguese Heath
Shrub, etc, height	Shrub 10–12ft
Habit	Erect, elegant, large plumose branches
Stems	Young shoots clothed with simple hairs
Leaf arrangement	Whorls of three to four and irregularly arranged
Leaves—shape, size, description	¼in long, linear, glabrous, setaceous, slightly grooved beneath, paler green than in *E. arborea*
Inflorescence	Axillary, clustered at ends of small lateral twigs like a pyramidal panicle
Fragrant	Slightly fragrant
Corolla—shape, lobes, colour	Cylindrical, 3/16in long, narrowly campanulate, pink in bud, white when open
Calyx—shape, colour, etc	Lobes white, triangular teeth, smooth, 1/16in
Stamens—shape, colour, exserted or included	Deep pink, included

Stigma—shape, colour, exserted or included	Deep pink, exserted
Pedicel	Smooth
Flowering time	March to April, January to February, or earlier in sheltered places
Introduction (Great Britain)	About 1800

General

It naturalises well in Cornwall on some railway embankments and grows on part of the Lytchett Heath in Dorset. In Cornwall it is grown particularly for 'Burns Night' and sent in vast quantities to Scotland as 'white heather'. It is a member of the Lusitanian flora and is moderately hardy, withstanding over 20°F frost before its stems split and shoots are killed. It grows naturally on a limy soil and it will grow just as well in any normal garden soil. It has large plumose branches which, early on in life, will be covered in pink-tinged buds which open into tubular white flowers. In South Devon particularly, plants can be had in flower many weeks before Christmas.

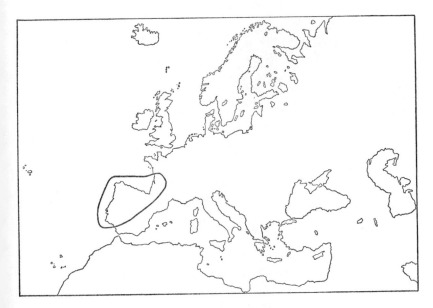

Distribution of *Erica lusitanica*

Erica lusitanica

Name and authority	*mackaiana* Bab 1836
Syn names and authorities	*mackaii* Hook, *tetralix* 'Mackaiana'
Common name	Mackay's Heath
Shrub, etc, height	Sub-shrub, 6–18in
Habit	Erect when young, spreading when old. Denser than *E. tetralix*. Will often cover a wide area and layers easily in the wild
Stems	Young stems almost hispid when young, soon glabrous
Leaf arrangement	Whorls of four forming a cross
Leaves—shape, size, description	Oblong, lanceolate, dark green and glabrous above. Margins somewhat revolute, white undersurface exposed
Inflorescence	Dense, terminal umbel-like cluster
Fragrant	—
Corolla—shape, lobes, colour	Lobes cylindrical, urceolate, $\frac{1}{4}$in, contracted at mouth, deep bright pink, usually white beneath
Calyx—shape, colour, etc	Oblong to ovate. Has glandular cilia
Stamens—shape, colour, exserted or included	Included and awned
Stigma—shape, colour, exserted or included	—
Pedicel	With scattered long hairs
Flowering time	August to September
Introduction	—

General

It is found on boggy ground in south-western Connemara between Toom-beola and Ballinaboy Bridge. It is credited, but not proved, to have come from County Clare. It is thought by some people to be an *E. tetralix* hybrid. A study of its anatomy by Miss Iris Smith, a botanist, has given weight to the theory that it is a species. It is a member of the Lusitanian flora that dislikes lime and grows in very wet spots. It is a straggly plant and its stems can be traced for many yards. While its pollen is supposed to be good enough to help form hybrids, it is not supposed to produce seedlings, although Mr D. McClintock is alleged to have checked upon some young plants he found in Ireland and discovered that they were not attached to the parent plant and so were probably seedlings.

'Dawn'	See *E.* × *watsonii* 'Dawn'.
'Dr Ronald Gray'	– – 6in white July to September

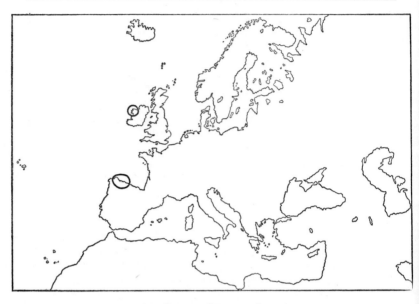

Distribution of *Erica mackaiana*

	A new cultivar propagated and introduced by Maxwell and Beale. See 'Lawsoniana'.
'Florepleno'	See 'Plena'.
'H. Maxwell'	See *E. × watsonii* 'H. Maxwell'.
'Lawsoniana'	– * – 6in pale pink July to September

Syn *E. tetralix* 'Lawsoniana'

Found in Connemara and is believed by many people to be a cultivar of *E. tetralix*. It is dwarfer and more prostrate than *E. tetralix* and the leaves are shorter and broader. The foliage is dark green. A white form of this arose in the late Dr Ronald Gray's garden in 1964. See 'Dr Ronald Gray'.

'Plena'	– * D 6in pink July to August

Syn 'Florepleno', *E. tetralix* 'Plena', 'Pleniflora', *E. tetralix* 'Crawfurdii'

A vigorous grower with two-toned double pink flowers. A prolific bloomer and a good carpeter. This is probably now the only double hardy *Erica*.

'Pleniflora'	See 'Plena'.
'Watsonii'	See *E. × watsonii* 'Truro'.

Erica mackaiana 'Plena'

Name and authority	*E. manipuliflora* Salisbury 1802
Syn names and authorities	*E. verticillata* Forsk
Common name	Whorled Heath
Shrub, etc, height	Shrub, 20in high
Habit	Stiff ascending or decumbent branches
Stems	Branches glabrous, young twigs minutely puberulent
Leaf arrangement	Whorls or three or four
Leaves—shape, size, description	Narrow, acute, $\frac{1}{3}$–$\frac{1}{2}$in long, grooved beneath, hidden by margin which is revolute and contiguous
Inflorescence	Compact, terminal clusters, three to five, forming long racemes towards ends of branches, sometimes dense, sometimes lax

Fragrant	—
Corolla—shape, lobes, colour	$\frac{1}{5}$–$\frac{1}{8}$in, rosy-pink, campanulate
Calyx—shape, colour, etc	Egg-shaped, 1/16in
Stamens—shape, colour exserted or included	Anthers purple, exserted, two lobes separate—divergent
Stigma—shape, colour, exserted or included	Exserted
Pedicel	Short pedicel, glabrous, three bracteoles at, or just below middle
Flowering time	August to October
Introduction (Great Britain)	1774

General

This Mediterranean species occurs naturally at the edges of woods. It is rarely seen in cultivation. It likes lime, growing on sandy hills or by limestone outcrops. The soil is usually very stoney. It has an upright growth and small pink flowers similar to *E. vagans*. Bentham and Hooker were two botanists among many that confused *E. manipuliflora* with *E. vagans*.

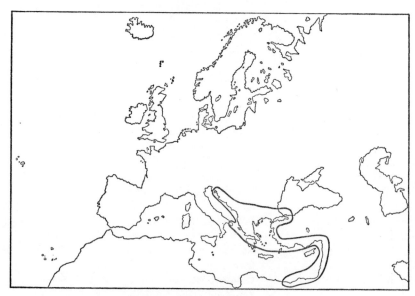

Distribution of *Erica manipuliflora*

Erica manipuliflora

Name and authority	*E. mediterranea* Auctt non Linnaeus
Syn names and authorities	*E. erigena* R. Ross, *E. hibernica* Hook and Arn. Syme non Utinet, *E. purpurascens* Auctt non Linnaeus. *E. hibernica* was once considered a separate species as it flowers three to four months after *E. mediterranea* and is 2–5ft high
Common names	Irish Heath, Mediterranean Heath
Shrub, etc, height	Shrub, 4–8ft
Habit	Stems erect, dense
Stems	Stems glabrous, young shoots glabrous
Leaf arrangement	Whorls of four or five
Leaves—shape, size, description	¼in, linear, dark green, margins strongly revolute

Inflorescence	Solitary or in pairs, axillary, nodding, forming dense, unilateral leafy racemes at end of branches
Fragrant	Honey scent
Corolla—shape, lobes, colour	¼in, ovoid to urn shaped, lobes broad, obtuse, erect, dull purple-pink
Calyx—shape, colour, etc	Lobes lanceolate, ⅛–⅙in
Stamens—shape, colour, exserted or included	Anthers half exserted, awnless, deep purple, divided into two lobes
Stigma—shape, colour, exserted or included	Exserted
Pedicel	Much shorter than flower, bracteolate about middle
Flowering time	March to May
Introduction (Great Britain)	Natural in Ireland

General

The species is rare in southern France and northern Spain, and scarce in Portugal. There is a school of thought that believes that *E. mediterranea* and *E. carnea* (Syn *E. herbacea*) are just geographical forms of the same species. Mr

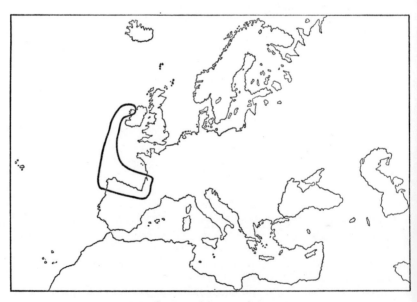

Distribution of *Erica mediterranea*

Ross has worked on this problem of nomenclature and this was reported in the Journal of the Linnean Society of February 1967. The Irish form *E. mediterranea* 'Hibernica' grows in the bogs with *E. tetralix*, some plants actually getting washed by the sea at very high tides. The plants are reasonably hardy, but like other members of the Lusitanian flora suffer damage at 20° of frost or more. The plants are somewhat brittle and can be affected severely by snow. This species with its varieties and cultivars is known for growing in limy soil although it will stand an incredibly wide range of other soils. It will stand moist spots, particularly the Irish form. The generally accepted reason for plants being found in an isolated spot on the west coast of Ireland and on the Iberian penin- sular is that this species was almost obliterated and pushed into the sea during the Great Ice Age and these two isolated areas are all that remain.

See Appendix, 'Naming of plants—developments'.

Erica mediterranea

'Alba'   – – 3–4ft white March to May
                  A rounded, dense shrub with rich green foliage which
                  can be covered in pure white blooms.

'Bohlje'   – – 18in March to May
                  A Dutch cultivar with a loose habit and medium green
                  foliage.

'Brightness'   – – 3ft purple-red March to May
                  It has dark green foliage with bronze tips in the winter.
                  The leaves are not uniform, becoming smaller near the
                  top of the plant, and also more numerous, this making it
                  noticeably different. The flower buds are deep bronze,
                  and are close to the tips in clusters, giving an appearance
                  of overcrowding. The flowers are produced from March
                  to May, although an odd shoot can open very early as is
                  typical with the cultivars of *E. mediterranea*. The blooms
                  are bright red—similar in colour to *E. carnea* 'Vivellii'. Its
                  rate of growth is rather poor when compared with the
                  other *E. mediterranea* cultivars. It is probably the toughest,
                  but may take a number of years to reach its maximum
                  height of 3ft.

'Coccinea'   – – 3ft rose-purple March to May
                  Very similar to 'Brightness' but the blooms are a brighter
                  rose-purple and are darker in bud than 'Brightness'.

'Erecta'   See *E.* × *darleyensis* 'Erecta'.

'Golden Dome'   F 2ft white February to April
                  A new cultivar introduced by Mr and Mrs Letts. It ori-
                  ginated as a sport on a plant of 'W. T. Rackliff' at their
                  nursery. Its foliage is a pale yellow to gold. It promised
                  to be a good grower but is failing in the majority of
                  situations.

'Hibernica'   – – 4ft pale pink March to May
                  Syn *E. hibernica*, *E. erigena* 'Glauca'.
                  It comes from County Clare, Ireland, and is distinguished
                  by blue-green foliage. It does not bloom so freely as the
                  majority of other heaths. The flowers are a very pale
                  pink, looking somewhat faded, and the anthers are a very
                  deep purple.

'Hibernica   – – 4ft pale pink March to May
  (Good Form)'   Syn *E. hibernica* (Good Form), *E. erigena* 'Glauca' (Good
                  Form)
                  The foliage is more glaucous than in 'Glauca'.

'Hibernica Alba' – – 4ft white March to May
                  Syn *E. erigena* (White Form), *E. hibernica* 'Alba'.

'Maxima'   – – 20in   March to May
                  A Dutch cultivar with medium green foliage.
'Nana'   – – 18in   pale pink   March to April
                  It is very compact and bushy. The foliage, which is a
                  dull greyish-green, acts as a good background for the
                  pale pink flowers.
'Nana Alba'   – – 18in   white   March to April
                  The white flowers are freely produced above a pleasing
                  red-green foliage. It sometimes reaches 2ft. The flowers
                  are slightly smaller than 'W. T. Rackliff'.
'Rosea'   – – 2ft   pink   March to May
                  This is probably a seedling of 'Brightness' as its habit and
                  foliage is so similar to it. However its flowers are a clear
                  pink.
'Rubra'   – – 18in   ruby-red   March to June
                  A slightly later-flowering cultivar, sometimes continuing
                  into early June. It has a good compact habit and dark
                  green foliage.
'Silver Beads'   See E. × darleyensis 'Silberschmelze'.
'Superba'   – – 6ft   rosy-pink   March to May
                  A very free-flowering cultivar with larger flowers than
                  type. In certain seasons and in sites where it does well, it
                  can be smothered with honey-scented flowers. The
                  flower buds are pale green and form clusters in the leaf
                  axils. The foliage is a dark green, paler in the spring.
'W. T. Rackliff' – – 2ft   white   January to April
                  This is a considerable improvement on 'Alba'. It grows
                  to 24in and has numerous large pure white flowers held
                  close to and at the tips of the compact growths. When
                  young, these growths are a very pale green and when
                  older the foliage is dark green. It is a very hardy plant and
                  can flower from January to April. However some
                  gardeners have reported this cultivar being damaged in
                  their gardens in most winters.

Name and authority	E. multiflora Linnaeus 1753
Syn names and authorities	E. peduncularis
Common name	Many-flowered Heath
Shrubs, etc, height	Shrub 12–24in high usually, but can reach 6ft
Habit	Erect, but like a small tree in the wild
Stems	Young stems smooth
Leaf arrangement	In whorls of four or five

Leaves—shape, size, description	$\frac{1}{4}$–$\frac{3}{8}$in, glabrous, sulcate beneath, grey, slightly hairy at base
Inflorescence	Terminal heads—erect raceme 2–4in without a tuft of leaves on top
Fragrant	—
Corolla—shape, lobes, colour	$\frac{1}{2}$in long, ovate to urn (bell shaped). Pink, lobes narrow, acute
Calyx—shape, colour, etc	1/12–1/15in oblong—lanceolate, white lobes
Stamens—shape, colour, exserted or included	Exserted. Anther lobes joined for most of their length
Stigma—shape, colour, exserted or included	Exserted
Pedicel	Long, $\frac{1}{4}$–$\frac{1}{3}$in
Flowering time	November to February
Introduction (Great Britain)	1731

General

It occurs naturally on the edge of woods, on hillsides and in limestone crevices and is not often found in gardens of Great Britain, perhaps because it is not 100 per cent hardy. It naturally occurs in limy soils. It is very similar to

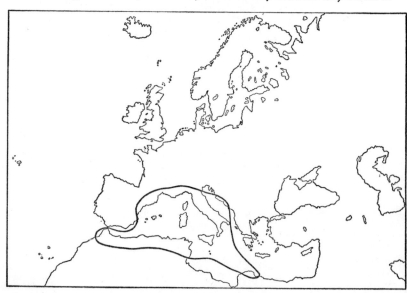

Distribution of *Erica multiflora*

Erica multiflora

E. vagans in appearance but its growth is more compact and the racemes shorter. *E. vagans* 'Multiflora' is often distributed as *E. multiflora*. There are some taller and reasonably hardy forms of *E. multiflora* now grown in England.

Name and authority	*pageana* Linnaeus
Syn names and authorities	—
Common name	—
Shrub, etc, height	Shrub 1–3ft
Habit	Erect, bushy
Stems	Young shoots downy
Leaf arrangement	Whorls of four
Leaves—shape, size, description	Linear $\frac{1}{4}$in, ciliate downy at first
Inflorescence	Terminal to lateral, making an irregular panicle
Fragrant	—

Erica pageana

Corolla—shape, lobes, colour	Bell-shaped, rich yellow, $\frac{1}{4}$in long, $\frac{1}{4}$in across, lobes four, broad, rounded
Calyx—shape, colour, etc	Pale green, lobes ovate to lanceolate, ciliate
Stamens—shape, colour, exserted or included	Included
Stigma—shape, colour	Dark brown, included
Pedicel	—
Flowering time	April to June
Introduced (Great Britain)	About 1920

General

A South African Cape Heath that is seldom seen (plate, p 71). It is usually confined to sheltered gardens in the south-west as it is of doubtful hardiness, or grown as a pot plant for Christmas. Sometimes it is grown in pots for a number of years under glass and then planted out when moderately mature. It dislikes lime.

Name and authority	*scoparia* Linnaeus 1753
Syn names and authorities	—
Common name	Besom Heath
Shrub, etc, height	Shrub, 9–10ft, occasionally 15ft
Habit	Loose erect, uneven growth
Stems	Young wood free from down, smooth
Leaf arrangement	Three or four, scattered
Leaves—shape, size, description	Linear, pointed, $\frac{1}{8}$in, glossy, glabrous, dark green
Inflorescence	Clusters one to five, axillary, over almost the whole of the preceding year's growth
Fragrant	—
Corolla—shape, lobes, colour	Greenish, 1/12in long, globular, almost insignificant
Calyx—shape, colour, etc	Smooth 1/20–1/24in, lobes ovate
Stamens—shape, colour, exserted or included	Without appendages, included
Stigma—shape, colour, exserted or included	Capsule glabrous
Pedicel	Smooth
Flowering time	May to June, sometimes into August
Introduction (Great Britain)	1770

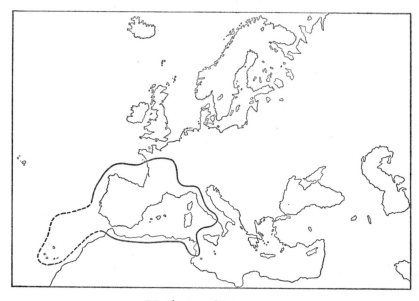

Distribution of *Erica scoparia*

General

It is a very hardy heath that grows well in lime-free soil. Its flowers are not much used in the garden since, despite being very numerous, they are a greenish-brown and crowded in the axils of the leaves. It has a very untidy habit of growth when old. It is often bald at the base and leafy at the top. It is used for making besoms in France. Very similar to *E. scoparia* is *E. azorica* Hochst, with a smaller corolla and very exserted style; perhaps so similar as to be a sub-species of *E. scoparia*. Investigation on this problem is being carried out by Dr Webb of the University of Dublin.

'Compacta'	See 'Pumila'.
'Minima'	See 'Pumila'.
'Nana'	See 'Pumila'.
'Pumila'	– – 24in greenish-white May to June
	Syn 'Compacta', 'Minima', 'Nana'
	Foliage light glossy green. Crammed into the leaf axils are numerous greenish-white flowers identical to *E. scoparia*.

Erica scoparia

Name and authority	*terminalis* Salisbury 1796
Syn names and authorities	*stricta* Andrews, *corsica* de Candelle, *ramulosa* Viviani
Common name	Corsican Heath
Shrub, etc, height	Shrub, 3–8ft
Habit	Erect, bushy, rigid
Stems	Branches covered with scarcely perceptible down, particularly when young
Leaf arrangement	Whorls of four, sometimes five or six
Leaves—shape, size, description	Linear, $\frac{1}{4}$–$\frac{1}{3}$in, dark glossy green, very finely ciliate
Inflorescence	Terminal umbels of three to eight blossoms on current season's growth

Fragrant	—
Corolla—shape, lobes, colour	Cylindrical, urceolate ovoid narrowing towards mouth, with four recurved lobes 3/16–¼in long, pale rose
Calyx—shape, colour, etc	Four lanceolate lobes, smooth ⅛in long
Stamens—shape, colour, exserted or included	Included, with appendages, brownish
Stigma—shape, colour, exserted or included	Capsule silky, half exserted
Pedicel	—
Flowering time	June to September or October
Introduction (Great Britain)	1765

General

Not a native of Great Britain although it has naturalised well on the Magilligan Dunes in Derry, Northern Ireland, for about half a century. It withstands the average British winters very well, plants standing 28° F frost without harm. As it flowers late in the year its buds are not so liable to be damaged. It will grow well in limy soil, as well as in general garden soils. It quickly forms well-

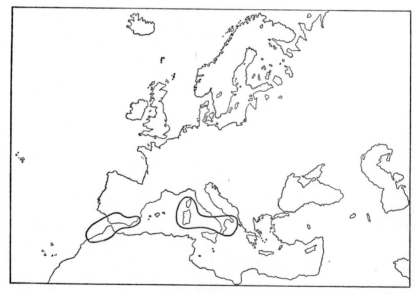

Distribution of *Erica terminalis*

Erica terminalis

shaped bushes with characteristic upright stems (plate, p 126). Unfortunately these stems are very brittle and are easily damaged by snow in some parts of the country. The russeting dead flowers give extra attraction to these plants in winter.

Name and authority	*tetralix* Linnaeus 1753
Syn names and authorities	—
Common names	Cross-leaved Heath, Bog Heath, Marsh Heath, Bell Heath, Father of the Heath, Ringe Heather, Heather Bell
Shrub, etc, height	Sub-shrub, 6–18in
Habit	Young stems erect, older stems spreading to prostrate, often rooting at base

Stems	Young shoots glandular, hirsute
Leaf arrangement	Whorls of four form a cross
Leaves—shape, size, description	Narrower than in *E. ciliaris*, ⅛in long, dark green above, white beneath, glandular and eglandular ciliate particularly at margins
Inflorescence	Flowers from terminal leaf axils in a dense head of four to twelve in an umbel-like cluster
Fragrant	—
Corolla—shape, lobes, colour	Cylindrical, urceolate, ¼in long, contracted at mouth, four shallow recurved lobes, rose-coloured
Calyx—shape, colour, etc	Lobes ovate to lanceolate, downy ciliate, sepals like leaves, more hairy, 1/10in
Stamens—shape, colour, exserted or included	Anthers included, awned
Stigma—shape, colour, exserted or included	Exserted, honey ring at base of pubescent ovary, capsule downy
Pedicel	Flower stalk bracteolate about middle
Flowering time	June to October
Introduction (Great Britain)	Natural habitat

General

A British native found all over Great Britain. It is often found where *Calluna vulgaris* grows but is not so extensive. It is very hardy and detests lime. The slightest hint of lime stunts the plants. It likes wet places, particularly wet peat bogs or other moist acid places. It is found up to a height of 2,400ft. It crosses and hybridises in the wild as well as in cultivation and in this species albino forms are less rare than in any other *Erica* in Great Britain. It is a useful species having most varieties and cultivars with grey foliage. It used to be burnt on the eve of All Saints' Day on a bonfire. The flower is the emblem on the badge of the MacDonald clan.

alba	– – 9in white June to August A very variable form that can be often found in the wild. Its clear white flowers are borne above a pale green foliage.
'Alba Mollis'	F * – 9in white June to October AM 1927 This is a very striking plant, having silver-grey foliage, silver being more effective in spring and summer (plate, p 126). With age the silver changes to green, usually

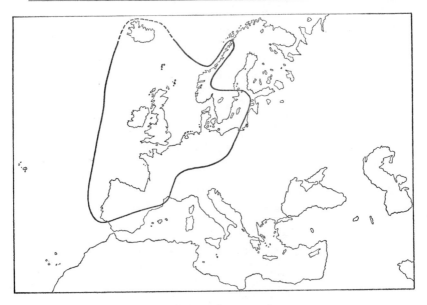

Distribution of *Erica tetralix*

taking a year or so. In the older portions of the plant the green deepens, the silver sheen coming from the new foliage in the spring and early summer. This silver sheen is uncommon in heaths. It can often look effective in the early part of the year when the faded blooms are still on the plant. Cilia on the leaves are eglandular.

'Alba Praecox'   – – 9in   white   July to August
Syn 'Praecox Alba'
As its name implies it is an early-flowering white culti-var. Its foliage is grey-green.

'Alba Whitehouse'   – – 6in   white   September
This is a cultivar I am not familiar with, but its habit is supposed to be compact and its foliage grey-green. It is an unusual member of the *E. tetralix* group in that its flowering period is so short.

'Bicolor'   – – 9in   pink-white   June to August
Introduced by James Smith & Sons, Darleydale, Derby-shire. This is more of a novelty than an attractive plant, having both pink and white flowers separately on the same plant.

'Canescens'   See 'Martinesii'.

'Con Underwood'   – * – 9in crimson June to October
                   Syn 'Constance Underwood', 'Connie Underwood'
                   Found in 1938 and nearly lost during the war, being
                   found again in 1945 on the introducers', G. Under-
                   woods', nursery when it was propagated and redistri-
                   buted. It is one of the best *E. tetralix* cultivars, having
                   large crimson flowers at any time from June to October.
                   Its foliage is a grey-green.

'Crawfurdii'   See *E. mackaiana* 'Plena'.

'Daphne   – * – 9in carmine-rose June to September
  Underwood'   Found in the Cuckoo Hill Valley on the Cobham Ridges
                   in 1953 and introduced by G. Underwoods' nursery. It
                   is a relatively new cultivar with grey-green foliage. Its
                   habit is compact and the bright carmine-rose flowers
                   are freely produced.

'Darleyensis'   – – 6in salmon July to August
                   Introduced by James Smith & Sons of Matlock, Derby-
                   shire. At a maximum of 6in it has distinctive grey-green
                   foliage and salmon-coloured flowers. Its habit is loose
                   with curling stems each carrying pleasing pink bells
                   with slightly deeper bases from July to August.

'Foxhome'   – – 12in bright pink July to August
                   Found by Mr F. J. Chapple at Foxhome, near Whaley
                   Bridge, Derbyshire.

'Gratis'   – – 9in pink June to August
                   An American cultivar. The foliage is light green.

'Hookstone Pink'   – * – 12in rose-pink June to September
                   Found in 1953 near Bagshot and introduced by Under-
                   woods. The interesting terra-cotta flower buds open to
                   an attractive shade of clear rose-pink.

'Ken Underwood'   – * – 12in cerise June to August
                   Found by Ken Underwood in the Cuckoo Valley,
                   Cobham Ridge in 1951. Its foliage is probably the
                   darkest of all *E. tetralix* cultivars. Its habit is upright and
                   its long spikes of cerise flowers are freely produced.

'Lawsoniana'   See *E. mackaiana* 'Lawsoniana'.

'L. E. Underwood' – * – 9in apricot June to October
                   Found about 1937 near West End, Woking, and intro-
                   duced by Underwoods. It has, like most of the other
                   'Underwoods', silver-grey foliage. From the leaves
                   emerge terra-cotta buds which open into apricot
                   flowers.

'Mackaiana'   See *E. mackaiana*.

'Martinesii'   Syn 'Canescens', Tomentosa'
                     I do not know this cultivar at all but it comes from
                     Spain. It is described as having pink stems and its
                     whitish downy leaves give a grey appearance. Not
                     hardy, probably lost to cultivation.

'Mary Grace'   – – 6in bright pink June to October
                     Found on the Corfemullen Moors and introduced by
                     Maxwell and Beale. The bright pink flowers are held in
                     a deeply split calyx (mite induced) and give an unusual,
                     yet attractive appearance.

'Melbury White'   – * – 9in white June to October
                     Found on Melbury Common, North Devon and in-
                     troduced by Treseder & Sons of Truro. Of recent intro-
                     duction, this heath is a slow compact grower, has good
                     grey foliage and large clusters of pure white flowers. A
                     good plant.

'Mollis'   Foliage is glandular ciliate, otherwise identical to 'Alba
                     Mollis'.

'Pink Glow'   – – 9in bright pink July to August
                     Its bright pink flowers have not a great deal of glow
                     about them; the blooms are somewhat small, but are
                     very prolific and show up well above the silver-grey
                     foliage.

'Pink Star'   – – 9in bright pink June to October
                     This is a fairly new cultivar. Its flowers are held some-
                     what differently from most other *E. tetralix* cultivars,
                     being upright as opposed to the normal drooping ter-
                     minal cluster. The foliage is a soft grey and the bright
                     pink flowers are somewhat star-like in appearance.

'Plena'   See *E. mackaiana* 'Plena'.
                     So many references in Victorian times are made to a
                     double *E. tetralix* that a double form must have existed
                     once.

'Praecox Alba'   See 'Alba Praecox'.

'Praegeri'   See × *praegeri* in the hybrid section.

'Rubra'   – * – 6in red July to September
                     Syn 'Rubrum'
                     This cultivar is very similar to 'Rufus' and is of very
                     compact habit. Its fine red flowers are produced over a
                     long period.

'Rubrum'   See 'Rubra'.

Erica tetralix

'Ruby's Variety'   – – 6in white, tinged purple and pink June to
October
Found on the Corfemullen Moors after the first world
war by Ruby Beale and introduced by Maxwell and
Beale. This cultivar is characterised by its almost white
flowers with dark purple-red tips that change overall
with age to purplish-pink. It is not stable and keeps
reverting. Its foliage is a silvery-green.

'Rufus'   – – 6in dark red July to September
Found on the Corfemullen Moors and introduced by
Maxwell and Beale. A very old cultivar with grey-
green foliage and with its dark red flowers is very
similar to 'Rubra'.

'Shetland Island' – – 6in pink July to September
I do not know this Scottish cultivar at all.

'Silver Bells' – * – 6in silver-pink June to October
The silver tints in the pink bells give a most pleasing effect on a nice short plant.

'Tomentosa' See 'Martinesii'.

Name and authority	*E. umbellata* Linnaeus 1753
Syn names and authorities	–
Common names	Portuguese Heath, Umbel Heath
Shrub, etc, height	Shrub, 1–3ft
Habit	Erect, branched
Stems	Young shoots downy
Leaf arrangement	Leaves in threes
Leaves—shape, size, description	Linear, 1/6in, obtuse
Inflorescence	In umbels of three to six at ends of shoots
Fragrant	–
Corolla—shape, lobes, colour	Ovoid to globose, urn-shaped, pink or red, 1/6in, lobes broad
Calyx—shape, colour, etc	Calyx 1/10–1/12in, lobes linear, oblong

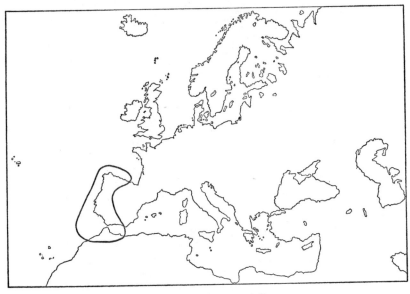

Distribution of *Erica umbellata*

Erica umbellata

Stamens—shape, colour, exserted or included	Anthers exserted, bipartite to middle
Stigma—shape, colour, exserted or included	Exserted
Pedicel	—
Flowering time	May to June
Introduction (Great Britain)	1782 by P. L. Giuseppi

It is a moderately tender species and it stands conditions very similar to *Erica australis*, although it likes them slightly drier. It has a feathery and fragile habit (plate, p 143). The late A. T. Johnson reported seeing a white-flowered form which I consider would make a useful addition to a heather collection.

It would appear that in Portugal there are at least four recognised varieties of *E. umbellata* to be found in the wild.

alba	White-flowered form.
anandra	The anthers are sterile and not exserted from the corolla, and can be found mixed with the type here and there.
major	The corolla is a little larger than the type, the anthers are longer and exserted and the leaves are larger and more thickened and found in the areas of Alentejo and Algarve.
subcampanulata	The corolla is sub-campanulate with fauces (upper part of throat) more open and anthers less exserted than in the type.

Name and authority	*E. vagans* Linnaeus 1770
Syn names and authorities	—
Common names	Cornish Heath, Wandering Heath
Shrub, etc, height	Shrub 1–2½ft
Habit	Low, spreading, straggly
Stems	Branchlets smooth, young wood glabrous
Leaf arrangement	Leaves in whorls of four or five
Leaves—shape, size, description	Linear ⅛–½in, dark green, smooth, channelled beneath, strongly revolute margins, blunt
Inflorescence	Erect, cylindrical raceme, flowering from below upwards, often terminating in leaves, 3–8in long
Fragrant	—
Corolla—shape, lobes, colour	Almost globular to urn-shaped, ⅛in long, wide, campanulate, four lobes, little recurved, deltoid, pink, purple
Calyx—shape, colour, etc	Lobes triangular-ovate, 1/20–1/24in, fringed with hairs

Stamens—shape, colour, exserted or included	Anthers exserted, awnless, split to the base, pink-red, rarely yellow
Stigma—shape, colour, exserted or included	Exserted
Pedicel	$\frac{1}{4}$–$\frac{1}{3}$in, bracteoles in middle
Flowering time	July to November
Introduction (Great Britain)	Natural habitat

General

This British species is found in Cornwall and is indigenous to parts of Europe. There is one colony growing in County Fermanagh, Ireland, which is of 50sq yd and all white. It is a member of the Lusitanian flora and is moderately hardy, very few places in the British Isles reporting plants being damaged in the winter. It does not often grow far from the coast although it is less resistant to salt spray than *Calluna vulgaris*. It grows naturally in neutral or slightly alkaline soils. It is only found in the wild above serpentine rocks, the water draining from which has a pH of 7 to 7·5. The plants usually grow very symmetrically and make attractive hummocks. In the inflorescence the lower flowers fade and change to attractive russet browns before the top blooms open.

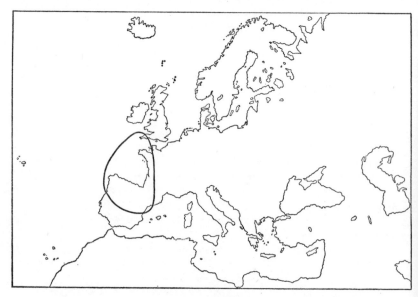

Distribution of *Erica vagans*

'Alba'   – – 24in white August to September
                         A good prolific white with its dark stamens prominent
                         and the foliage a good green. White forms can be found
                         in the wild.

'Alba Minima'   See 'Nana'.

'Alba Minor'   See 'Nana'.

'Alba Multiflora'   – – 24in white September to October
                         Very similar to 'Alba' but the foliage is more upright
                         and the flowers are a dirty white.

'Alba Superba   See 'Cream'.
   Darleyensis'

'Birch Glow'   – – 18in rosy-red August to October
                         A moderately new cultivar that is reasonably attractive.

'Carnea'   – – 18in pink August to September
                         Not an outstanding cultivar. Its flowers are smaller than
                         the type and are very numerous and tightly packed on a
                         somewhat compact plant.

'Cornish Cream'   – * – 18in cream August to October
                         Found on the Goonhilly Downs and introduced by
                         Treseder & Sons. An exciting new cultivar with very
                         fine tapering spikes of cream flowers freely produced.

'Cream'   – * – 24–36in white late July to October
                         Syn 'Alba Superba Darleyensis'
                         AM 1968
                         A vigorous grower with dark green foliage. White
                         flower buds tinged pink and reddish-brown anthers
                         give an overall cream tint.

'Diana Hornibrook'   – * – 12–15in red July to September
                         AM 1967
                         A neat, compact plant producing prolifically $1\frac{1}{2}$–2in
                         long spikes of glowing red-crimson blooms above dark
                         green foliage that is an attractive paler green when
                         young.

'Fiddlestone'   – * – 18in pink-cerise July to September
                         I believe this plant was selected by the late Mr Plummer
                         of Fiddlestone Lodge, Burton-in-the-Wirral, Cheshire.
                         It is said to be an improved form of 'Mrs D. F. Maxwell'.
                         I have found its flowers to be a slightly deeper colour
                         than 'Mrs D. F. Maxwell', while some authorities say it
                         is a shade paler. Perhaps there is a variation in colour
                         when grown under different soil conditions, but the
                         plant is a good grower and a prolific flowerer.

'George   – – 18in   pink   August to October
   Underwood'   Introduced by G. Underwood, it is a strong compact grower with long spikes of pink flowers with a slight tinge of cream.

'Grandiflora'   – * – 36in   pink   August to September
HC 1968
This is probably one of the tallest *Erica vagans* and it is a quick grower. The flower spikes, which can be from 6–9in long, are a pale pink. Its habit is loose and the flowers deepen with age and then fade. Not one of the best cultivars.

'Holden Pink'   –   – 18in   white, flushed deep pink   July to September
AM 1966
The flowers are white with a flush of deep pink to purple towards the tip. I am not altogether certain why this cultivar among many others should receive an award.

'Hookstone Rosea'   – – 18in   rose-pink   July to October
Syn 'Hookstone Rose'
Introduced by G. Underwood. It is thought to be a seedling of 'Mrs D. F. Maxwell'. It is of compact habit, freely producing its clear rose-pink spikes.

'Kevernensis'   See 'St Keverne'.
'Kevernensis Alba'   – – 12in   white   August to September
Found by the late P. D. Williams of St Keverne. A good white cultivar, far more compact than 'Lyonesse', bearing many compact flower heads of small white blooms.

'Leucantha'   – – 24in   cream   August to October
A sprawling cultivar, the flowers of which are technically called cream, but which I would call dirty white.

'Lilacina'   – – 18in   pale pink   July to September
The pale pink flowers with a hint of lilac are freely produced on a compact bushy plant.

'Lyonesse'   – * – 18in   white   August to October
AM 1928
Found by Mr and Mrs Maxwell on the Goonhilly Downs while on their honeymoon and introduced by Maxwell and Beale. An exceptionally fine heath with the pale brown anthers extending beyond the pure white corolla. The spikes are long and tapering, particularly on well-grown plants and the foliage is a good glossy green.

Erica vagans 'Lyonesse'

'Miss Waterer'   – * – 18in   shell pink   August to September
Found by Miss Waterer on the Lizard in Cornwall and
given by her to the Slieve Donard Nursery in Northern
Ireland, who were probably the first firm to catalogue
it. A good neat plant with its flowers produced abun-
dantly above foliage that is pale as opposed to most
other *E. vagans* cultivars.

'Mrs D. F. Maxwell'   – * – 18in deep rose-cerise August to October
AM 1925
Found by Mr and Mrs D. F. Maxwell while on their honeymoon, a cutting of which they sent home. A very robust, well-tried cultivar with a good dark green foliage. Its strongly-coloured flowers are held in long racemes throughout autumn. The dead flowers persist like all *Erica vagans* cultivars throughout the winter, but are of a very pleasing deep russet-brown.

'Mrs S.   – – 12–15in salmon August to October
   Donaldson'   Very similar to 'St Keverne', but slightly more compact and a little earlier flowering.

'Mrs Maxwell   – – 15in   soft creamy salmon-pink   August to
   (Doncaster)'   September
A little-known *E. vagans* cultivar that is slightly paler, shorter and less robust than 'Mrs D. F. Maxwell'. I wonder if this plant actually existed? I have not met anyone who knew or knows the clone.

'Mullion'   – – 18in rose August to September
Found near Mullion in Cornwall. Its habit is compact. I have not seen this cultivar in cultivation.

'Multiflora'   – * – 24in pale pink August to October
A fast, rampant grower with a spreading habit. The flowers are held in a long inflorescence. Very floriferous. Sometimes sold as *E. multiflora*.

'Multiflora   Probably 'Multiflora'.
   Grandiflora'

'Nana'   – – 9–12in creamy-white August to September
Syn 'Alba Minima', 'Alba Minor'.
An unusual dwarf cultivar with small racemes of creamy-white flowers, the anthers of which are chocolate.

'Pallida'   – – 18in pale pink August to September
A very fast, loose-growing cultivar with pale pink flowers in small racemes, one of the least likeable of the *E. vagans* cultivars.

'Peach Blossom'   – * – 18in peach-blossom pink August to
October
A new cultivar. Introduced by Treseders of Truro.

'Pyrenees Pink'   – * – 18in cerise-pink August to September
Very similar to 'St Keverne' and 'Mrs D. F. Maxwell', although the flower colour is intermediate. There is a paling of the flower colour with age which can give a plant a bicolour effect.

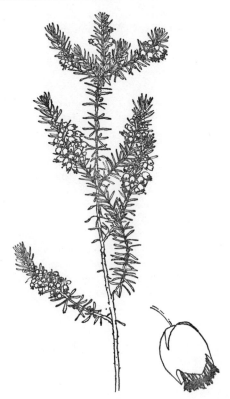

Erica vagans 'Multiflora'

'Rosea'   – – 18in   rose-pink   August to September
A vigorous form of *E. vagans* which has a sturdy, upright habit. Its flower spikes are not as long as in the best
forms of *E. vagans*.

'Rubra'   – – 18in   dark purple-red   August to October
Of a vigorous, spreading and bushy habit, freely producing its long racemes of flowers through autumn.

'St Keverne'   – * – 18in   bright pink   August to October
Syn 'Kevernensis'
AM 1914, AGM 1927
Found in the Lizard district of Cornwall. The flowers
are borne in profusion on this bushy plant of neat habit
(plate, p 143). The corolla is more bell-shaped than in

M

most *E. vagans* cultivars and the lobes are more recurved. There is a white form of this cultivar, which to date is not widely known.

'St Keverne
(White Form)'   – – 18in   white   August to September

'Summer Time'   – – 18in   very pale pink   August to September
The only plants I have seen of this could be described as awful, being of poor habit and a pathetic washed-out colour.

'Valerie Proudley'   F – 18in   white   August to September
Useful yellow foliage.

'Viridiflora'   – – 12in   sea green   August to September
This is a cultivar with fascinating green and brown flowers which are more of a botanical interest or for flower decorations than for garden beauty.

'White Rocket'   – * – 24in   pure white   August to October
Introduced by Treseder & Sons of Truro, having been found on the Goonhilly Downs in 1965. Its pure white flowers are held in long tapering spikes. The flowers tend to fade to off-white with undertones of blue before changing to the usual shade of brown.

Eight

Erica hybrids

Key to abbreviations: see page 85

E. × 'Ciliaris Hybrida'	See *E.* × *watsonii* 'Ciliaris Hybrida'.
E. × *darleyensis*	See *E.* × *darleyensis* 'Darley Dale'.
E. × *darleyensis* 'Alba'	See *E.* × *darleyensis* 'Silberschmelze'.
E. × *darleyensis* 'Arthur Johnson'	– * – 18–24in deep pink December to April

Syn *E.* × *hybrida* 'Arthur Johnson', *E.* × *darleyensis* 'A. T. Johnson'
AM 1952
Found by the late A. T. Johnson who named it after himself and believed it to be a hybrid between *E. mediterranea* (syn *E. erigena*) 'Glauca' and *E. carnea* (syn *E. herbacea*) 'Ruby Glow'. It has good green foliage and strong spikes, sometimes as long as 9in, of deep pink blooms throughout the winter into early spring.

E. × *darleyensis* 'Carryduff'	– – 18in white December to April

Raised and introduced by J. W. Porter. It was reported to have been fertile but is lost to cultivation.

E. × *darleyensis* 'Cherry Stevens'	See *E.* × *darleyensis* 'Furzey'.
E. × *darleyensis* 'Darley Dale'	– * – 18in pale pink-mauve December to March

Syn *E.* × *darleyensis*, *E. mediterranea hybrida*, *E. carnea hybrida*
AM 1905, AGM 1924
This hybrid originated at the end of the last century as a chance seedling at Darleydale in Derbyshire between *E. mediterranea* (syn *E. erigena*) and *E. carnea* (syn *E. herbacea*). It is exceptionally hardy and does not mind lime. It is a fast grower and every year will

produce in profusion masses of 2in long racemes of blooms. These blooms appear to be immune to the cold. The foliage is a medium to dark green and the general habit of the plant makes it ideal as an edging plant, dwarf hedge or, better still, as ground cover. It is surprisingly tolerant of a wide range of soils. Since the original cross was found many cultivars have resulted.

E. × darleyensis 'Erecta'
— — 15in rosy-purple December to May
Syn *E. mediterranea* 'Erecta'
Bushy, loose, open habit with upright-growing twigs. The foliage is a fresh green. Not a good cultivar despite its long and late flowering season.

E. × darleyensis 'Furzey'
— * — 14–18in deep rosy-pink December to April
Syn *E. × darleyensis* 'Cherry Stevens', *E. carnea* (syn *E. herbacea*) 'Furzey'
It arose as a seedling in a garden at Furzey in the New Forest and was then introduced into cultivation by two different firms, who each gave it a different name. It is of spreading habit but will eventually reach 18in high. Its deep rosy-pink flowers are produced in great profusion.

E. × darleyensis 'George Rendall'
— * — 18in deep pink November to March
Syn *E. × hybrida* 'George Rendall'
Raised and introduced by Maxwell & Beale. This cultivar will often have a maximum height of 18in. It is easily recognised in its similarity to *E. × darleyensis* 'Darley Dale', but in the spring and early summer it has slight yellowish tints which later turn to dark green, like the rest of the foliage.

E. × darleyensis 'Ghost Hills'
— — 18in deep rose-pink December to April
Raised by J. H. Brummage. It is thought to be a sport of *E. × darleyensis* 'Darley Dale'. Its flower buds are a pale green in early autumn and eventually open into a deep rose, which is almost red with very protruding stigmas and stamens. A number of times I have recorded the odd flowers open in early September.

E. × darleyensis 'Hybrida Alba'
See *E. × darleyensis* 'Silberschmelze'.

E. × darleyensis 'Jack H. Brummage'
F — 18in pink February to March
Yellow foliage.

E. × darleyensis 'James Smith'
— * — 18in rich mauve-pink December to April

Named and introduced by Treseder & Sons of Truro, who in turn received it from a keen amateur, Mrs Louis Reid, who herself received the plant from its raiser, the late James Smith, that famous nurseryman from Derbyshire. The foliage is a good deep green and the flowers, which are deeper than *E.* × *darleyensis* 'Darley Dale', are closely packed in good spikes and have very large brown anthers protruding from the tips of each bloom.

E. × *darleyensis*
'Jenny Porter'

– – 18in pale purple-rose December to April
A newcomer raised by the late James W. Porter from Carryduff, near Belfast.

E. × *darleyensis*
'John Wynne'

– – 18in purple December to April
Raised by the late J. W. Porter from a plant on the Hazelwood Estate of the late J. Wynne in County Sligo. J.Wynne was the first person to record finding *E. mediterranea* (syn *E. erigena*) in Ireland in 1830. This cultivar has flower spikes often as long as 9in, freely produced with many small flowers with reddish-brown anthers.

E. × *darleyensis*
'Knockomie'

See *E.* × *darleyensis* 'Norman R. Webster'
This plant has also been called 'Knocknowne'. It was given by the late Norman Webster to the Royal Botanic Gardens, Edinburgh, and was named after Mr Webster's house in Morayshire. It appears to be identical with the plants under the name of *E.* × *darleyensis* 'Silberschmelze'.

E. × *darleyensis*
'Molten Silver'

See *E.* × *darleyensis* 'Silberschmelze'.

E. × *darleyensis*
'Norman R.
Webster'

– – 18in white November to April
Syn *E.* × *darleyensis* 'Knockomie'
Introduced by Slieve Donard Nursery, Co Down. Found as a chance seedling by the late N. R. Webster in a garden at Glencairn Elgin, Scotland. It is very vigorous and just as free flowering as *E.* × *darleyensis* 'Darley Dale', although the flower spikes are not as long. A useful identification feature is that on some occasions the ends of the foliage turn bronze. So similar to *E.* × *darleyensis* 'Silberschmelze' are these whites of different origin that they might just as well all be labelled 'Silberschmelze'.

E. × *darleyensis*
'Pink Spangles'

See *E. carnea* (syn *E. herbacea*) 'Pink Spangles'.

E. × *darleyensis*   – – 36in   rose   December to April
'Rosslare'

E. × *darleyensis*   See *E.* × *darleyensis* 'Silberschmelze'.
'Silberlachs'

E. × *darleyensis*   – * –   18in   white   December to March
'Silberschmelze'   Syn *E.* × *darleyensis* hybrida 'Alba', 'Molten Silver',
                              'Silberlachs', 'Silver Beads', 'Silver Bells', 'Silver
                              Flower', 'Silver Mist', 'Silver Star', 'Snowflake',
                              'White Form', *E. carnea* (syn *E. herbacea*) 'Colwall
                              Nurseries'
                              AM 1968
                              Of German origin. Raised and introduced by Messrs
                              Arands of Wuppertal. Its flower spikes are very long
                              and are of silvery-white, probably appearing so
                              white because of the dark green foliage. It is not un-
                              usual to find a plant still in flower in May.

E. × *darleyensis*   See *E.* × *darleyensis* 'Silberschmelze'.
'Silver Beads'

E. × *darleyensis*   See *E.* × *darleyensis* 'Silberschmelze'.
'Silver Bells'

E. × *darleyensis*   See *E.* × *darleyensis* 'Silberschmelze'.
'Silver Flower'

E. × *darleyensis*   See *E.* × *darleyensis* 'Silberschmelze'.
'Silver Mist'

E. × *darleyensis*   See *E.* × *darleyensis* 'Silberschmelze'.
'Silver Star'

E. × *darleyensis*   See *E.* × *darleyensis* 'Silberschmelze'.
'Snowflake'

E. × *darleyensis*   – * –   18in   rosy-purple   December to April
'W. G. Pine'   A hybrid raised by Mr Porter about 1945. Its tubula
                              rosy-purple flowers are tipped by deep chocolate
                              anthers and the young shoots which follow the
                              flowers are red tipped.

E. × *darleyensis*   See *E.* × *darleyensis* 'Silberschmelze'.
'White Form'

E. × 'Dawn'   See *E.* × *watsonii* 'Dawn'.

E. × 'F. White'   See *E.* × *watsonii* 'F. White'.

E. × 'Gwavas'   See *E.* × *williamsii* 'Gwavas'.

E. × 'Gwen'   See *E.* × *watsonii* 'Gwen'.

E. × 'H. Maxwell'   See *E.* × *watsonii* 'H. Maxwell'.

E. × 'Hybrida'   See *E.* × *watsonii* 'Ciliaris Hybrida'.

E. × *praegeri* 'Connemara'	– * – 6in bright pink June to October Syn *E.* × *hybrida* 'Praegeri', *E.* × *praegeri*, *E. tetralix* 'Praegeri' Named after R. L. Praeger. It is sterile and believed to be a hybrid between *E. mackaiana* and *E. tetralix*, and found in Connemara and Donegal, western Ireland. It is identified from *E. mackaiana* by pubescence on at least part of the sepals and the upper part of the ovary. A close-growing cultivar which bears numerous clusters of bright pink bells. The forms from the different sites in Ireland vary. Some should make very good garden plants.
E. × 'Rachel'	See *E.* × *watsonii* 'Rachel'.
E. × *stuartii*	– – 9–12in pink June to September Syn *E.* × *hybrida* 'Stuartii' Found on 9 August 1890 by Dr Charles Stuart in County Galway, Ireland, and named after him in 1902. There is some confusion in the parentage of this taxa: *E. mackaiana* × *E. mediterranea* has been suggested, but there is no satisfactory answer to its parentage at present. It differs from *E.* × *praegeri* in its flowers which are bi-coloured, being a pale pink with deep rose tips, and the corolla is slightly pinched.
E. × 'Truro'	See *E.* × *watsonii* 'Truro'.
E. × *veitchii* 'Exeter'	– * – 6ft white December to May AM 1905 An accidental hybrid which arose as a chance seedling at Veitch's Nursery, Exeter, before 1905 between *E. arborea* and *E. lusitanica*. It is very similar to *E. lusitanica* both in habit, foliage and blossom, although it does seem to be more sweetly scented and far more floriferous, to such an extent the branches can be bent right over by the weight of the flowers (plate, p 144). It tends to be hardier and more vigorous than its parents. Identification features are simple—branched hairs and a pale pink flattened stigma.
E × *watsonii*	This hybrid and its cultivars have resulted from *E. ciliaris* and *E. tetralix*.
E. × *watsonii* 'Ciliaris Hybrida'	F – 6–8in rosy pink June to October Syn *E. ciliaris* 'Hybrida', *E.* × 'Ciliaris Hybrida' A very useful and attractive dwarf cultivar with bright yellow tips to the growths in spring. Similar to 'Dawn'.

E. × *watsonii* 'Dawn'   F * – 8in rose-pink June to October
Syn *E.* × *hybrida* 'Dawn', *E.* × 'Dawn'
Found on the Great Heath, Dorset, and introduced by
Maxwell & Beale. Its foliage resembles *E. ciliaris* but
is a little darker. In the spring and early summer it has
beautiful yellow-orange tips to its growth and its
large rich rose-pink flowers are borne from June to
October above what is a fairly dense plant that makes
a useful ground-cover plant.

E. × *watsonii*   – – 8in white tinted pink, June to October
'F. White'   Syn *E.* × *hybrida* 'F. White', *E.* × 'F. White'
Another hybrid which is very similar to 'Dawn' in
habit, but its flowers are smaller and are white with a
pink flush. It is very free flowering and also makes a
good ground-cover plant. It is very similar to *E.
ciliaris* 'Wych'.

E. × *watsonii* 'Gwen'   – – 6–8in pale pink June to October
Syn *E.* × *hybrida* 'Gwen', *E.* × 'Gwen'. 'Owen' =
'Gwen' misspelt
Found by Maxwell & Beale on the Great Heath,
Dorset, and named after Mr Beale's niece. Its habit is
similar to 'Dawn', but a little shorter. The pale pink
flowers have a slight tinge of mauve.

E. × *watsonii*   F – 12in bright pink June to October
'H. Maxwell'   Syn *E.* × *hybrida* 'H. Maxwell', *E.* × 'H. Maxwell'
Named after the father of the late D. Fyfe Maxwell
of Maxwell & Beale. This hybrid has foliage and a
habit similar to *E. ciliaris* and large bright pink
flowers as in *E. tetralix*. It is very similar to 'Dawn',
but its flowers are a shade paler pink. Its growth is
probably a little more upright and bushy and in the
spring the tips of the growth are a golden-brown as
opposed to 'Dawn's' golden-yellow.

E. × *watsonii* 'Rachel'   – – 9–12in deep pink August to October
Syn *E.* × 'Rachel', *E.* × 'Rachael'
A hybrid with deep pink flowers held above dark
green foliage.

E. × *watsonii* 'Truro'   – – 6–9in pink to crimson July to October
Syn *E.* × *hybrida* 'Watsonii', *E.* × 'Truro
Found in 1839 near Truro and named after H. C.
Watson, a pioneer plant geographer. It is partially
fertile and therefore hybridises reasonably easily. It is
also found in Dorset. In overall appearance it is

nearer to *E. tetralix* than *E. ciliaris*. It is almost prostrate in habit and will bear large pink to crimson bells in terminal umbels.

E. × *williamsii* 'Gwavas'

F * – 12in pale pink July to October

Syn *E.* × 'Gwavas'

A hybrid between *E. tetralix* and *E. vagans* found by Miss Waterer in 1924 near Gwavas Farm on the Lizard, Cornwall. It is an attractive spring-foliage plant, having golden-yellow tips to the shoots; but these rapidly turn green as summer approaches, when it loses its appeal, despite its pale pink flowers.

E. × *williamsii* 'P. D. Williams'

– * – 8–12in pink June to September

Syn *E.* × *hybrida* 'Williamsiana', *E.* × 'Williamsiana', *E.* × *williamsii* 'Percy Williams'

HC 1966

This is a natural hybrid between *E. tetralix* and *E. vagans* and is probably our rarest native heath. It was found and recorded in the 1860s and was overlooked until 1910 when a horticulturist, Mr P. D. Williams, was out partridge shooting near Lanark Farm on the Lizard. It produces orchid-purple to rose-pink bell-shaped flowers from June to September and sometimes into October in dense leafy racemes. Inside the corolla are the brown anthers and the style just protrudes. The tips of the new foliage in the spring are a yellowish-green and change to dark green in the summer and even a slight brownish tinge in the winter. It is very similar to 'Gwavas', which has slightly paler flowers.

E. × 'Wishanger Pink' See *E. australis* 'Wishanger Pink'.

× Ericalluna bealeani

This is the name published in *Deutsche Baumschile*, given by Herr Krüssman of Dortmund, Germany, as a Grex name for three hybrids of *E. cinerea*. Like many people I believe these freaks are forms of *Erica cinerea* and should really be named as *E. cinerea* cultivars. They have the habit of the *Bell Heather*, but the corolla is four-parted instead of the usual bell.

'Schizopetala' See *E. cinerea* 'Schizopetala'.

'W. G. Notley' See *E. cinerea* 'W. G. Notley'.

'Winifred Whitley' See *E. cinerea* 'Winifred Whitley'.

Erica australis × darleyensis Herr Krüssman records this cross, which he says is very like *E.* × *darleyensis*, and has flowers arranged like *E. australis*.

Nine
The Daboecias

Key to abbreviations, see page 85

Name and authority	*Daboecia azorica* Tutin and Warburg 1932
Syn names and authorities	*D. cantabrica azorica*
Common name	Azores Heath
Shrub, etc, height	Shrub
Habit	Small, 6–10in, evergreen, heath-like, shoot at first erect, later procumbent
Stems	Young shoots glandular, hairy
Leaf arrangement	—
Leaves—shape, size, description	Ovate, lanceolate, subacute, callus tipped more recurved than *D. cantabrica*. Dark green, hairy, glandular above, white tomentose beneath, 3/16–¼in long, ⅛in wide
Inflorescence	Flower upright, terminal, glandular, hairy raceme, 4–8in
Fragrant	—
Corolla—shape, lobes, colour	Ovate, urceolate, 5/16in long, four short, broad reflexed lobes, ruby-crimson
Calyx—shape, colour, etc	Sepals ovate, pointed, 1/10in, glandular, ciliate
Stamens—shape, colour, exserted or included	Included
Stigma—shape, colour, exserted or included	Included
Pedicel	—
Flowering time	June to July
Introduction (Great Britain)	1929

Daboecia azorica

General

This species from the Azores is found growing naturally on the islands of Foyal and Pico up to a height of 3,500ft. Young plants are hardier than mature specimens which can be damaged in a normal British winter. They do not like lime, preferring to grow in a peaty soil which, while being moist, must be well drained. It can be propagated from cuttings and is often grown from seed, when the flower colour and floriferousness vary. There is increasing evidence that the hardy forms of this species now being grown are hybrids and not the pure species.

Name and authority	*Daboecia cantabrica* (Huds) C. Koch 1872
Syn names and authorities	*Menziesia polifolia* Juss, *Boretta cantabrica* Ktze, *D. andromeda*, *D. polifolia* Don, *Erica daboecii* Linnaeus
Common names	St Dabeoc's Heath, Cantabrian Heath, Irish Wrarts
Shrub, etc, height	Shrub 18–24in
Habit	Heath-like
Stems	Branches glandular, pubescent when young
Leaf arrangement	Alternate

Leaves—shape, size, description	Dark green, lustrous and sparsely glandular, hairy above, white tomentose beneath, fat, evergreen, elliptic, 3/10–¼in, narrowed at end, callus tipped, mucronate
Inflorescence	Long, erect, leafless spikes (racemes), glandular, pubescent, 3–6in
Fragrant	—
Corolla—shape, lobes, colour	Egg-shaped to urceolate, 2/5in, four small lobes, reflexed, purple, deciduous
Calyx—shape, colour, etc	Small, sepals ovate to acute, glandular, ciliate, 1/6–1/5in
Stamens—shape, colour, exserted or included	Eight, included without appendages, flattened filament
Stigma—shape, colour	Style slender, ovaries four segmented, just exserted
Pedicel	Short, nodding
Flowering time	June to October
Introduction (Great Britain)	Natural habitat in S Ireland

General

This species is not 100 per cent hardy and is often damaged by a British

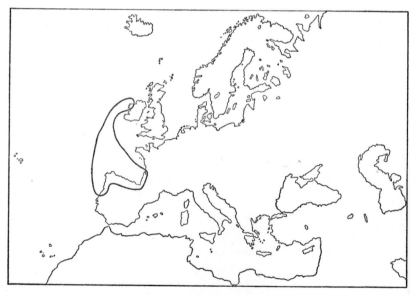

Distribution of *Daboecia cantabrica*

winter. As it prefers a moist soil it will suffer badly under drought conditions. The leaves are large and not modified with revolute margins to conserve moisture. It dislikes lime. After flowering, plants should be trimmed to remove the flowered shoots. While this operation is best carried out in November, it is often left until the early spring when any damaged shoots can be trimmed back at the same time. Propagation may be by seed in the early spring, cuttings of

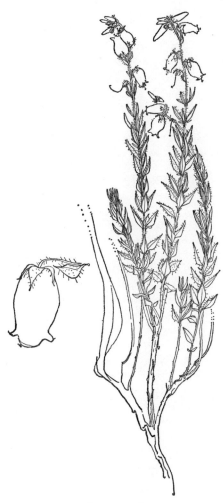

Daboecia cantabrica

1–1½in long tips in July and August, or layering in September. Women once used to carry around sprigs of this species as a talisman against incontinence.

'Alba'   – – 24in white July to October
                          Found and first recorded in the Connemara district
                          about 1820. Very large white bells which are larger than
                          the type are freely borne on 8–12in long spikes above a
                          light green foliage (plate, p 144). Sometimes the season
                          of flowering is from May through to October.

'Alba Globosa'   – * – 24in white June to October
                          The flowers are larger and rounder than 'Alba' and a
                          very pure white.

'Atropurpurea'   – – 24in purple June to October
                          Its lovely rich reddish-purple bells harmonise well with
                          dark foliage (plate, p 71). Many of the plants under this
                          name are inferior seedlings with smaller corollas. See
                          also 'Purpurea'.

'Azorica'   See *Daboecia azorica.*

'Bearsden'   Named in honour of the late Mr William Buchanan,
                          Bearsden being the name of his house. The original
                          clone was raised from seed by Miss Logan Home,
                          Edrom Nurseries, Berwickshire and taken from *D.
                          azorica.*

'Bicolor'   – * – 24in pink-purple and white June to
                          October
                          Syn 'Striata', 'Versicolor'
                          This cultivar is as free flowering as the others. It can
                          have pinkish-purple, white and some bicolour flowers
                          on the same plant. The foliage is a rich green and the
                          young stems are light green. Care should be taken in the
                          propagation of this, or the bicolour form can be lost.

'Calycina'   A cultivar recorded in 1891 in which the white and red
                          flowers were so constructed as to appear double.

'David Moss'   – * – 15in white, July to October
                          AM 1968
                          A good, compact, erect and vigorous grower with dark
                          glossy green foliage. The flowering stems are a good
                          length, from 7–12in, with a profusion of average-size
                          white blooms.

'Donard Pink'   – * – 24in white-pink June to September
                          A good grower that readily produces a good display of
                          white-pink flowers.

'Globosa Pink'   – * – 24in silvery-purple June to October
A vigorous erect grower with what are probably the largest flowers of any *Daboecia* cultivar. Under the name 'Globosa', erroneously, a white cultivar has been grown which is 'Alba Globosa'.

'Hookstone Purple' – – 24in purple June to October
A very strong grower with bright purple bells larger than the type.

'Nana'   Syn 'Pygmaea'
I do not know if this cultivar exists anymore. It is described by the Royal Horticultural Society as being dwarfer than the type with smaller, narrower leaves.

'Pallida'   See 'Rosea'.

'Pink'   – – 18in pale pink July to September
This is probably the result of propagating a pink-flowering shoot of 'Bicolor', as it is a shy bloomer and sometimes reverts to give a bicolor effect. The delicate pink flowers are borne above light green foliage.

'Polifolia'   – – 24in soft purple June to October
This cultivar is described by one of Britain's leading heath and heather growers as a good form of the species, having long spikes of soft purple blooms.

'Porter's Variety' – – 12in deep crimson July to September
A small, erect, compact plant with slender and upright leaves in good growing conditions (plenty of moisture in the growing season). It is covered with deep crimson small tubular bells and in most garden soils with a shortage of moisture during the summer it seldom exceeds 6in in height and is a sparse bloomer.

'Praegerae'   – * – 15in salmon-pink June to October
It was found near Connemara by Mrs Praeger, wife of the famous Irish botanist. It is a vigorous grower and produces long arching spikes of large bright salmon-pink bells, devoid of any shade of purple, throughout the summer and early autumn. It is more tender than the species and is easily damaged in exposed positions during the winter. It is not as vigorous as the type.

'Purpurea'   – – 24in bright purple June to October
With its long spikes of bright purple flowers above dark green foliage, it is so similar to 'Atropurpurea' that although some catalogues have it as a separate cultivar, I believe it is the same plant.

'Pygmaea'   See 'Nana'.

'R. D. Broomfield'   – – 12in rosy-purple July to September
                         A cultivar raised by Fyfe Maxwell who named it after a
                         helper in his garden. It is supposed to be very free
                         flowering with rosy-purple flowers.

'Rosea'   – – 18–24in rose-pink June to October
                         Syn 'Pallida'
                         An old cultivar having rose-pink flowers.

'Striata'   See 'Bicolor'.

'Versicolor'   See 'Bicolor'.

'William Buchanan'   – * – 10in rosy-crimson June to October
                         AM 1968
                         This is 'Seedling No 1' of three hybrids self-sown,
                         which appeared in the garden of the late Mr William
                         Buchanan of Bearsden, Glasgow, a great gardener and
                         friend of Jack Drake of Aviemore. These three seedlings
                         are possibly hybrids between *D. azorica* and *D. canta-
                         brica*. 'William Buchanan' is vigorous and in the Royal
                         Horticultural Society's trials at a height of 10in had a
                         spread of nearly 18in, with dark, glossy green foliage. It
                         flowers almost continuously from June until the frost on
                         7–9in spikes and, to quote Jack Drake, 'It is every bit as
                         hardy as *D. cantabrica*.' The flowers are a deep rosy-
                         crimson.

'Seedling No 2'   Because it was so similar to 'Seedling No 1', yet inferior,
                         it was discouraged.

'Seedling No 3'   The other hybrid seedling of the late Mr William
                         Buchanan. It is at the RHS Garden, Wisley, where it is
                         hoped it might yet receive an AM because of its more
                         dwarf stature, varying from 4 to 6in high, and its
                         crimson flowers with a touch of garnet-red. Mr Jack
                         Drake also reports that his 'No 3 Seedling' had attractive
                         little seed pods which he thought would interest some
                         flower arrangers.

Appendix

Calendar of heaths and heathers

JANUARY

Erica carnea (syn *E. herbacea*)
  'Alba'
  'Aurea'
  'Carnea'
  'Cecilia M. Beale'
  'December Red'
  'Early Red'
  'Eileen Porter'
  'Foxhollow Fairy'
  'Gracilis'
  'King George'
  'Lesley Sparkes'
  'Mrs Sam Doncaster'
  'Pirbright Rose'
  'Praecox Rubra'
  'Queen Mary'
  'Rosea'
  'Smart's Heath'
  'Snow Queen'
  'Springwood Pink'
  'Springwood White'
  'Vivellii'

  'Winter Beauty'
× *darleyensis*
  'Arthur Johnson'
  'Carryduff'
  'Darley Dale'
  'Erecta'
  'Furzey'
  'George Rendall'
  'Ghost Hills'
  'James Smith'
  'Jenny Porter'
  'John Wynne'
  'Rosslare'
  'W. G. Pine'
  'Silberschmelze'
lusitanica
mediterranea (syn *E. erigena*)
  'W. T. Rackliff'
multiflora
× *veitchii*
  'Exeter'

FEBRUARY

Erica carnea (syn *E. herbacea*)
  'Alan Coates'
  'Alba'
  'Ann Sparkes'
  'Aurea'
  'Carnea'
  'Cecilia M. Beale'
  'December Red'
  'Early Red'
  'Eileen Porter'
  'Foxhollow Fairy'
  'Gracilis'
  'Heathwood'
  'King George'
  'Lesley Sparkes'
  'Loughrigg'
  'Mrs Sam Doncaster'
  'Pink Spangles'
  'Pirbright Rose'
  'Praecox Rubra'
  'Queen Mary'
  'Queen of Spain'
  'Rosea'
  'Sherwoodi'
  'Smart's Heath'
  'Snow Queen'
  'Springwood Pink'
  'Springwood White'

  'Startler'
  'Urville'
  'Vivellii'
  'White Glow'
  'Winter Beauty'
× *darleyensis*
  'Arthur Johnson'
  'Carryduff'
  'Darley Dale'
  'Erecta'
  'Furzey'
  'George Rendall'
  'Ghost Hills'
  'Jack H. Brummage'
  'James Smith'
  'Jenny Porter'
  'John Wynne'
  'Rosslare'
  'W. G. Pine'
  'Silberschmelze'
lusitanica
mediterranea (syn *E. erigena*)
  'Golden Dome'
  'W. T. Rackliff'
multiflora
× *veitchii*
  'Exeter'

MARCH

Erica arborea
  'Alba'
  'Alpina'
  'Gold Tips'
australis
  'Aragonensis'
  'Mr Robert'
canaliculata
carnea (syn *E. herbacea*)

  'Ada S. Collings'
  'Alan Coates'
  'Alba'
  'Ann Sparkes'
  'Atro-Rubra'
  'Aurea'
  'Carnea'
  'Cecilia M. Beale'
  'C. J. Backhouse'

MARCH—CONT.

'Eileen Porter'
'Foxhollow Fairy'
'Gracilis'
'Heathwood'
'James Backhouse'
'King George'
'Loughrigg'
'March Seedling'
'Mrs Sam Doncaster'
'Pallida'
'Pink Pearl'
'Pink Spangles'
'Praecox Rubra'
'Prince of Wales'
'Queen of Spain'
'Rosea'
'Rosy Gem'
'Ruby Glow'
'Sherwoodi'
'Smart's Heath'
'Snow Queen'
'Springwood Pink'
'Springwood White'
'Startler'
'Thomas Kingscote'
'Urville'
'Vivellii'
'White Glow'
'Winter Beauty'
× *darleyensis*
'Arthur Johnson'
'Carryduff'

'Darley Dale'
'Erecta'
'Furzey'
'George Rendall'
'Ghost Hills'
'Jack H. Brummage'
'James Smith'
'Jenny Porter'
'John Wynne'
'Rosslare'
'W. G. Pine'
'Silberschmelze'
lusitanica
mediterranea (syn *E. erigena*)
'Alba'
'Bohlje'
'Brightness'
'Coccinea'
'Golden Dome'
'Hibernica'
'Hibernica (Good Form)'
'Hibernica Alba'
'Maxima'
'Nana'
'Nana Alba'
'Rosea'
'Rubra'
'Superba'
'W. T. Rackliff'
× *veitchii*
'Exeter'

APRIL

Erica arborea
'Alba'
'Alpina'
'Gold Tips'
australis
'Aragonensis'
'Mr Robert'

'Mr Stewart'
'Riverslea'
'Rosea'
canaliculata
carnea (syn *E. herbacea*)
'Ada S. Collings'
'Alba'

APRIL—CONT.

'Atro-Rubra'
'Aurea'
'Carnea'
'C. J. Backhouse'
'Eileen Porter'
'Heathwood'
'James Backhouse'
'King George'
'March Seedling'
'Mrs Sam Doncaster'
'Pallida'
'Pink Pearl'
'Pink Spangles'
'Prince of Wales'
'Queen of Spain'
'Rosea'
'Rosy Gem'
'Ruby Glow'
'Sherwoodi'
'Thomas Kingscote'
'White Glow'
× *darleyensis*
'Arthur Johnson'
'Carryduff'
'Erecta'
'Furzey'

'Ghost Hills'
'James Smith'
'Jenny Porter'
'John Wynne'
'Rosslare'
'W. G. Pine'
lusitanica
mediterranea (syn *E. erigena*)
'Alba'
'Bohlje'
'Brightness'
'Coccinea'
'Golden Dome'
'Hibernica'
'Hibernica (Good Form)'
'Hibernica Alba'
'Maxima'
'Nana'
'Nana Alba'
'Rosea'
'Rubra'
'Superba'
'W. T. Rackliff'
pageana
× *veitchii*
'Exeter'

MAY

Erica arborea
'Alba'
'Alpina'
'Gold Tips'
australis
'Aragonensis'
'Mr Robert'
'Mt Stewart'
'Riverslea'
'Rosea'
canaliculata
mediterranea (syn *E. erigena*)
'Alba'

'Bohlje'
'Brightness'
'Coccinea'
'Hibernica'
'Hibernica (Good Form)'
'Hibernica Alba'
'Maxima'
'Rosea'
'Rubra'
'Superba'
pageana
scoparia
'Pumila'

MAY—CONT.

umbellata
  anandra
  major

subcampanulata
× veitchii
  'Exeter'

JUNE

Calluna vulgaris
  'Caerketton White'
Daboecia azorica
  cantabrica
    'Alba Globosa'
    'Atropurpurea'
    'Bicolor'
    'Donard Pink'
    'Globosa'
    'Hookstone Purple'
    'Polifolia' —
    'Praegerae'
    'Purpurea'
    'Rosea'
    'Seedling No 3'
    'William Buchanan'
Erica australis
    'Aragonensis'
    'Mt Stewart'
  ciliaris
    'Maweana'
  cinerea
    'Alba'
    'Alba Major'
    'Alba Minor'
    'Ann Berry'
    'Apple Blossom'
    'Atropurpurea'
    'Atrorubens'
    'Atrosanguinea Reuthe's
      Variety'
    'Atrosanguinea Smith's Variety'
    'Caldy Island'
    'Carnea Underwood's Variety'
    'C. D. Eason'
    'C. E. Pearson'

'Cevennes'
'C. G. Best'
'Coccinea'
'Coccinea Smith's Variety'
'Colligan Bridge'
'Cripples Ease'
'Darleydale'
'Domino'
'Eden Valley'
'Foxhollow Mahogany'
'Frances'
'Glow Bells'
'Golden Drop'
'Golden Hue'
'G. Osmond'
'Grandiflora'
'Hookstone Lavender'
'Hookstone White'
'Janet'
'John Eason'
'Joyce Burfitt'
'Knap Hill Pink'
'Lady Skelton'
'Lilacina'
'Miss Waters'
'Mrs Dill'
'Mrs Ford'
'Mulfra'
'Old Rose'
'Pallida'
'Pink Ice'
'P. S. Patrick'
'Purple Beauty'
'Pygmaea'
'Robert Michael'

JUNE—CONT.

'Romiley'
'Rosea'
'Rose Queen'
'Rozanne Waterer'
'Ruby'
'Sandpit Hill'
'Schizopetala'
'Sea Foam'
'Smith's Lawn'
'Snow Cream'
'Spicata'
'Splendens'
'Startler'
'Taranto Purple'
'The Freak'
'Velvet Night'
'Victoria'
'W. G. Notley'
'Winifred Whitley'
mediterranea (syn *E. erigena*)
   'Rubra'
× *praegeri*
   'Connemara'
pageana
scoparia
   'Pumila'

× *stuartii*
tetralix
   alba
   'Alba Mollis'
   'Bicolor'
   'Con Underwood'
   'Daphne Underwood'
   'Gratis'
   'Hookstone Pink'
   'Ken Underwood'
   'L. E. Underwood'
   'Mary Grace'
   'Melbury White'
   'Pink Star'
   'Ruby's Variety'
   'Silver Bells'
umbellata
   anandra
   major
   subcampanulata
× *watsonii*
   'Ciliaris Hybrida'
   'Dawn'
   'F. White'
   'Gwen'
   'H. Maxwell'

JULY

Calluna vulgaris
   'Alba Erecta'
   'Alba Minor'
   'Alba Praecox'
   'Alba Pumila'
   'Alportii Praecox'
   'Bransdale White'
   'Caerketton White'
   'Dumosa'
   'Elkstone White'
   'French Grey'
   'Pumila'

   'Rigida'
   'Tenuis'
   'Tib'
   'White Bouquet'
   'White Mite'
Daboecia azorica
cantabrica
   'Alba'
   'Alba Globosa'
   'Atropurpurea'
   'Bicolor'
   'David Moss'

JULY—CONT.

'Donard Pink'
'Globosa'
'Hookstone Purple'
'Pink'
'Polifolia'
'Porter's Variety'
'Praegerae'
'Purpurea'
'R. D. Broomfield'
'Rosea'
'Seedling No 3'
'William Buchanan'
Erica ciliaris
'Alba'
'Aurea'
'Camla'
'Corfe Castle'
'David McClintock'
'Globosa'
'Jean Liddle'
'Maweana'
'Mrs C. H. Gill'
'Nana'
'Rotundiflora'
'Stapehill'
'Stoborough'
'White Wings'
'Wych'
Erica cinerea
'Alba'
'Alba Major'
'Alba Minor'
'Ann Berry'
'Apple Blossom'
'Atropurpurea'
'Atrorubens'
'Atrosanguinea Reuthe's
    Variety'
'Atrosanguinea Smith's Variety'
'Caldy Island'
'Carnea'

'Carnea Underwood's Variety'
'C. D. Eason'
'C. E. Pearson'
'Cevennes'
'C. G. Best'
'Cindy'
'Coccinea'
'Coccinea Smith's Variety'
'Colligan Bridge'
'Cripples Ease'
'Darleydale'
'Domino'
'Duncan Fraser'
'Eden Valley'
'Foxhollow Mahogany'
'Frances'
'Glow Bells'
'Golden Drop'
'Golden Hue'
'G. Osmond'
'Grandiflora'
'Honeymoon'
'Hookstone Lavender'
'Hookstone White'
'Janet'
'John Eason'
'Josephine Ross'
'Joyce Burfitt'
'Knap Hill Pink'
'Lady Skelton'
'Lavender Lady'
'Lilacina'
'Lilac Time'
'Miss Waters'
'Mrs Dill'
'Mrs Ford'
'Mulfra'
'New Salmon'
'Old Rose'
'Pallida'
'Pentreath'

JULY—CONT.

'Pink Foam'
'Pink Ice'
'Plummer's Seedling'
'Prostrate Lavender'
'P. S. Patrick'
'Purple Beauty'
'Purple Robe'
'Purpurea'
'Pygmaea'
'Robert Michael'
'Romiley'
'Rosabella'
'Rosea'
'Rose Queen'
'Rozanne Waterer'
'Ruby'
'Sandpit Hill'
'Schizopetala'
'Sea Foam'
'Smith's Lawn'
'Snow Cream'
'Spicata'
'Splendens'
'Startler'
'Taranto Purple'
'The Freak'
'Tom Waterer'
'Velvet Night'
'Victoria'
'Vivienne Patricia'
'W. G. Notley'
'Winifred Whitley'
mackaiana
  'Dr Ronald Gray'
  'Lawsoniana'
  'Plena'
× *praegeri*
  'Connemara'
× *stuartii*
terminalis

tetralix
alba
  'Alba Mollis'
  'Alba Praecox'
  'Bicolor'
  'Con Underwood'
  'Daphne Underwood'
  'Darleyensis'
  'Foxhome'
  'Gratis'
  'Hookstone Pink'
  'Ken Underwood'
  'L. E. Underwood'
  'Mary Grace'
  'Melbury White'
  'Pink Glow'
  'Pink Star'
  'Rubra'
  'Ruby's Variety'
  'Rufus'
  'Shetland Island'
  'Silver Bells'
vagans
  'Cream'
  'Diana Hornibrook'
  'Fiddlestone'
  'Holden Pink'
  'Hookstone Rosea'
  'Lilacina'
× *watsonii*
  'Ciliaris Hybrida'
  'Dawn'
  'F. White'
  'Gwen'
  'H. Maxwell'
  'Truro'
× *williamsii*
  'Gwavas'
  'P. D. Williams'

AUGUST

Calluna vulgaris
  alba
    'Alba Carlton'
    'Alba Compacta'
    'Alba Elegans'
    'Alba Erecta'
    'Alba Jae'
    'Alba Minor'
    'Alba Pilosa'
    'Alba Praecox'
    'Alba Pumila'
    'Alboviolacea'
    'Alportii'
    'Alportii Praecox'
    'Argentea'
    'August Beauty'
    'Aurea'
    'Barnett Anley'
    'Beechwood Crimson'
    'Beoley Elegance'
    'Beoley Gold'
    'Blazeaway'
    'Bognie'
    'Brachysepala Densa'
    'Bransdale White'
    'Californian Midge'
    'Camla'
    'Coccinea'
    'Coccinea Smith's Variety'
    'County Wicklow'
    'Crispa'
    'Cunneryensis'
    'Cuprea'
    'C. W. Nix'
    'Dainty Bess'
    'Darkness'
    'Darleyensis'
    'Decumbens alba'
    'Drum-ra'
    'Dumosa'

'E. Hoare'
'Elkstone White'
'Else Frye'
'Fairy'
'Flore Pleno'
'Foxhollow Wanderer'
'Foxii'
'Foxii Floribunda'
'Foxii Nana'
'Fred J. Chapple'
'Frances Grey'
'Goblin'
'Golden Carpet'
'Golden Feather'
'Gold Haze'
'Gold Pat'
'Goldsworth Pink'
'Gotteborg'
'Grasmeriensis'
'Hammondii'
'Hammondii Aureifolia'
'Hammondii Rubrifolia'
'Hayesensis'
'Hirsuta Albiflora'
'Hirsuta Typica'
'Hookstone'
'Humpty Dumpty'
'Hypnoides'
'Janice Chapman'
'J. F. Letts'
'J. H. Hamilton'
'Joan Sparkes'
'Joy Vanstone'
'Kit Hill'
'Kirby White'
'Kuphaldtii'
'Kynance'
'Lambs Tails'
'Loch-na-seil'
'Lyle's Surprise'

AUGUST—CONT.

'Mair's Variety'
'Minima'
'Minima Smith's Variety'
'Molecule'
'Mousehole'
'Mrs Alf'
'Mrs Dunlop'
'Mrs Pat'
'Mrs Ronald Gray'
'Mullion'
'Multicolor'
'Multiplex'
'Nana'
'Nana Compacta'
'Orange Queen'
'Oxshott Common'
'Pallida'
'Penhale'
'Peter Sparkes'
'Prostrate Orange'
'Pubescens'
'Pumila'
'Pygmaea'
'Pyramidalis'
'Pyrenaica'
'Radnor'
'Ralph Purnell'
'Rigida'
'Robert Chapman'
'Roma'
'Rosalind Crastock Heath
   Variety'
'Rosalind Underwood's Variety'
'Rosea'
'Ruby Slinger'
'Ruth Sparkes'
'Ruth Sparkes Improved Form'
'Sally Anne Proudley'
'Salmonoides'
'Serlei'
'Serlei Aurea'
'Serlei Rubra'

'Silver Knight'
'Silver Queen'
'Sir John Charrington'
'Sister Anne'
'Spicata'
'Spicata Nana'
'Spring Cream'
'Spring Torch'
'Spitfire'
'Startler'
'Stricta Nana'
'Summer Elegance'
'Summer Orange'
'Sunset'
'Tenella'
'Tenuis'
'The Pygmy'
'Tib'
'Tom Thumb'
'Torulosa'
'Tricolorifolia Smith's Variety'
'White Bouquet'
'White Mite'
'White Queen'
'Winter Chocolate'

Daboecia cantabrica
'Alba'
'Alba Globosa'
'Atropurpurea'
'Bicolor'
'David Moss'
'Donard Pink'
'Globosa'
'Hookstone Purple'
'Pink'
'Polifolia'
'Porter's Variety'
'Praegerae'
'Purpurea'
'R. D. Broomfield'
'Rosea'
'Seedling No 3'

AUGUST—CONT.

'William Buchanan'
Erica ciliaris
  'Alba'
  'Aurea'
  'Camla'
  'Corfe Castle'
  'David McClintock'
  'Globosa'
  'Jean Liddle'
  'Maweana'
  'Mrs C. H. Gill'
  'Rotundiflora'
  'Stapehill'
  'Stoborough'
  'White Wings'
  'Wych'
  cinerea
  'Alba Major'
  'Alba Minor'
  'Apple Blossom'
  'Atropurpurea'
  'Atrorubens'
  'Atrosanguinea Reuthe's Variety'
  'Atrosanguinea Smith's Variety'
  'Carnea'
  'Carnea Underwood's Variety'
  'C. D. Eason'
  'C. E. Pearson'
  'Cevennes'
  'C. G. Best'
  'Cindy'
  'Coccinea'
  'Coccinea Smith's Variety'
  'Colligan Bridge'
  'Cripple's Ease'
  'Darleydale'
  'Domino'
  'Duncan Fraser'
  'Eden Valley'
  'Foxhollow Mahogany'
  'Frances'

'Fred Corston'
'Fulgida'
'Glasnevin Red'
'Glow Bells'
'Golden Drop'
'Golden Hue'
'G. Osmond'
'Grandiflora'
'Heathfield'
'Honeymoon'
'Hookstone Lavender'
'Hookstone White'
'Janet'
'John Eason'
'Josephine Ross'
'Knap Hill Pink'
'Lady Skelton'
'Lavender Lady'
'Lilacina'
'Lilac Time'
'Miss Waters'
'Mrs Dill'
'Mulfra'
'New Salmon'
'Pallida'
'Pentreath'
'Pink Foam'
'Pink Ice'
'Plummer's Seedling'
'Prostrate Lavender'
'P. S. Patrick'
'Purple Beauty'
'Purple Robe'
'Purpurea'
'Robert Michael'
'Romiley'
'Rosabella'
'Rosea'
'Rozanne Waterer'
'Ruby'
'Sandpit Hill'
'Sea Foam'

AUGUST—CONT.

'Smith's Lawn'
'Taranto Purple'
'Tilford'
'The Freak'
'W. G. Notley'
'Winifred Whitley'
'Tom Waterer'
'Velvet Night'
'Vivienne Patricia'
mackaiana
  'Dr Ronald Gray'
  'Lawsoniana'
  'Plena'
manipuliflora
× *praegeri*
  'Connemara'
× *stuartii*
terminalis
tetralix
  alba
  'Alba Mollis'
  'Alba Praecox'
  'Bicolor'
  'Con Underwood'
  'Daphne Underwood',
  'Darleyensis'
  'Foxhome'
  'Gratis'
  'Hookstone Pink'
  'Ken Underwood'
  'L. E. Underwood'
  'Mary Grace'
  'Melbury White'
  'Pink Glow'
  'Pink Star'
  'Rubra'
  'Ruby's Variety'
  'Rufus'
  'Shetland Island'
  'Silver Bells'

vagans
  'Alba'
  'Birch Glow'
  'Cream'
  'Diana Hornibrook'
  'Fiddlestone'
  'George Underwood'
  'Grandiflora'
  'Holden Pink'
  'Hookstone Rosea
  'Kevernensis Alba'
  'Leucantha'
  'Lilacina'
  'Lyonesse'
  'Miss Waterer'
  'Mrs S. Donaldson'
  'Mrs Maxwell (Doncaster)
  'Mrs D. F. Maxwell'
  'Mullion'
  'Multiflora'
  'Nana'
  'Pallida'
  'Peach Bloosom'
  'Pyrenees Pink'
  'Rosea'
  'Rubra'
  'St Keverne'
  'St Keverne White Form'
  'Valerie Proudley'
  'Viridiflora'
  'White Rocket'
× *watsonii*
  'Ciliaris Hybrida'
  'Dawn'
  'F. White'
  'Gwen'
  'H. Maxwell'
  'Rachel'
× *williamsii*
  'Gwavas'
  'P. D. Williams'

SEPTEMBER

Calluna vulgaris
  alba
    'Alba Aurea'
    'Alba Carlton'
    'Alba Compacta'
    'Alba Elata'
    'Alba Elegans'
    'Alba Minima'
    'Alba Multiflora'
    'Alba Pilosa'
    'Alba Plena'
    'Alba Pumila'
    'Alboviolacea'
    'Alportii'
    'Argentea'
    'August Beauty'
    'Aurea'
    'Barnet Anley'
    'Beechwood Crimson'
    'Beoley Elegance'
    'Beoley Gold'
    'Betty Baum'
    'Blazeaway'
    'Bognie'
    'Brachysepala Densa'
    'Californian Midge'
    'Camla'
    'Carole Chapman'
    'Coccinea Smith's Variety'
    'County Wicklow'
    'Cramond'
    'Crispa'
    'Cunneryensis'
    'Cuprea'
    'C. W. Nix'
    'Dainty Bess'
    'Darkness'
    'Darleyensis'
    'Decumbens Alba
    'Drum-ra'

'Dumosa'
'E. F. Brown'
'E. Hoare'
'Elegantissima'
'Elegantissima Walter
  Ingwersen'
'Else Frye'
'Elsie Purnell'
'Fairy'
'Flore Pleno'
'Foxhollow Wanderer'
'Foxii'
'Foxii Floribunda'
'Foxii Nana'
'Fred J. Chapple'
'Frances Grey'
'Gnome'
'Gnome (Pink Form)'
'Goblin'
'Golden Carpet'
'Golden Feather'
'Gold Haze'
'Gold Pat'
'Goldsworth Crimson'
'Goldsworth Crimson Variegata'
'Goldsworth Pink'
'Gotteborg'
'Grasmeriensis'
'Gregor's Variety'
'Hammondii'
'Hammondii Aureifolia'
'Hammondii Rubrifolia'
'Hayesensis'
'H. E. Beale'
'Hirsuta Albiflora'
'Hirsuta Typica'
'Hookstone'
'Humpty Dumpty'
'Hypnoides'
'Janice Chapman'

SEPTEMBER—CONT.

'J. F. Letts'
'J. H. Hamilton'
'Joan Sparkes'
'Joy Vanstone'
'Kit Hill'
'Kirby White'
'Kuphaldtii'
'Kynance'
'Lambs Tails'
'Late Crimson Gold'
'Loch-Na-Seil'
'Long White'
'Lyle's Surprise'
'Mair's Variety'
'Minima'
'Minima Smith's Variety'
'Molecule'
'Mousehole'
'Mrs Alf'
'Mrs Dunlop'
'Mrs Pat'
'Mrs Ronald Gray'
'Mullion'
'Multicolor'
'Multiplex'
'Nana'
'Nana Compacta'
'Orange Queen'
'Oxshott Common'
'Pallida'
'Penhale'
'Peter Sparkes'
'Pilosa'
'Prostrate Orange'
'Pubescens'
'Pygmaea'
'Pyramidalis'
'Pyrenaica'
'Radnor'
'Ralph Purnell'
'Rigida'

'Robert Chapman'
'Roma'
'Rosalind Crastock Heath Variety'
'Rosalind Underwood's Variety'
'Rosea'
'Ruby Slinger'
'Ruth Sparkes'
'Ruth Sparkes Improved Form'
'Sally Anne Proudley'
'Salmonoides'
'September Pink'
'Serlei'
'Serlei Aurea'
'Serlei Purpurea'
'Serlei Rubra'
'Silver Knight'
'Silver Queen'
'Silver Spire'
'Sir John Charrington'
'Sister Anne'
'Spicata'
'Spicata Nana'
'Spring Cream'
'Spring Torch'
'Spitfire'
'Startler'
'Stricta Nana'
'Summer Elegance'
'Summer Orange'
'Sunset'
'Tenella'
'Tenuis'
'The Pygmy'
'Tib'
'Tomentosa'
'Tom Thumb'
'Torulosa'
'Tricolorifolia Smith's Variety'
'Underwoodii'

SEPTEMBER—CONT.

'White Gown'
'White Queen'
'Winter Chocolate'
Daboecia cantabrica
   'Alba'
   'Alba Globosa'
   'Atropurpurea'
   'Bicolor'
   'David Moss'
   'Donard Pink'
   'Globosa'
   'Hookstone Purple'
   'Pink'
   'Polifolia'
   'Porter's Variety'
   'Praegerae'
   'Purpurea'
   'R. D. Broomfield'
   'Rosea'
   'Seedling No 3'
   'William Buchanan'
Erica ciliaris
   'Alba'
   'David McClintock'
   'Globosa'
   'Jean Liddle'
   'Maweana'
   'Mrs C. H. Gill'
   'Nana'
   'Rotundiflora'
   'Stapehill'
   'Stoborough'
   'White Wings'
   'Wych'
  cinerea
   'Alba Minor'
   'Atrorubens'
   'Atrosanguinea Smith's Variety'
   'Carnea Underwood's Variety'
   'C. D. Eason'
   'C. E. Pearson'

'Cevennes'
'Cindy'
'Darleydale'
'Domino'
'Eden Valley'
'Foxhollow Mahogany'
'Fred Corston'
'Fulgida'
'Glasnevin Red'
'G. Osmond'
'Heathfield'
'Hookstone Lavender'
'Josephine Ross'
'Knap Hill Pink'
'Lady Skelton'
'Lavender Lady'
'Lilac Time'
'My Love'
'Pentreath'
'Pink Foam'
'Pink Ice'
'Purple Beauty'
'Purpurea'
'Robert Michael'
'Sandpit Hill'
'Sea Foam'
'Taranto Purple'
'Tilford'
'Vivienne Patricia'
'W. G. Notley'
mackaiana
   'Dr Ronald Gray'
   'Lawsoniana'
manipuliflora
× *praegeri*
   'Connemara'
× *stuartii*
terminalis
tetralix
   'Alba Mollis'
   'Alba Whitehouse'

'Con Underwood'
'Daphne Underwood'
'Hookstone Pink'
'L. E. Underwood'
'Mary Grace'
'Melbury White'
'Pink Star'
'Rubrum'
'Ruby's Variety'
'Rufus'
'Shetland Island'
'Silver Bells'
vagans
   'Alba'
   'Alba Multiflora'
   'Birch Glow'
   'Cream'
   'Diana Hornibrook'
   'Fiddlestone'
   'George Underwood'
   'Grandiflora'
   'Holden Pink'
   'Hookstone Rosea'
   'Kevernensis Alba'
   'Leucantha'
   'Lilacina'
   'Lyonesse'

'Miss Waterer'
'Mrs S. Donaldson'
'Mrs Maxwell (Doncaster)'
'Mrs D. F. Maxwell'
'Mullion'
'Multiflora'
'Nana'
'Pallida'
'Peach Blossom'
'Pyrenees Pink'
'Rosea'
'Rubra'
'St Keverne'
'St Keverne White Form'
'Valerie Proudley'
'Viridiflora'
'White Rocket'
× *watsonii*
   'Ciliaris Hybrida'
   'Dawn'
   'F. White'
   'Gwen'
   'H. Maxwell'
   'Rachel'
× *williamsii*
   'Gwavas'
   'P. D. Williams'

OCTOBER

Calluna vulgaris
   'Alba Aurea'
   'Alba Elata'
   'Alba Multiflora'
   'Alba Pilosa'
   'Alba Plena'
   'Betty Baum'
   'Cramond'
   'Cunneryensis'
   'C. W. Nix'
   'David Eason'
   'Durfordii'

'E. F. Brown'
'Elegantissima'
'Elegantissima Walter
   Ingwersen'
'Elsie Purnell'
'Gnome'
'Gnome (Pink Form)'
'Golden Feather'
'Goldsworth Crimson'
'Goldsworth Crimson Variegata'
'Goldsworth Pink'
'Gregor's Variety'

OCTOBER—CONT.

'H. E. Beale'
'Hibernica'
'Hiemalis'
'Joan Sparkes'
'Johnson's Variety'
'Kit Hill'
'Long White'
'Mrs Alf'
'October Crimson'
'Penhale'
'Peter Sparkes'
'September Pink'
'Serlei'
'Serlei Aurea'
'Serlei Purpurea'
'Serlei Rubra'
'Silver Spire'
'Tib'
'Tomentosa'
'Underwoodii'
'White Gown'
'White Queen'
Daboecia cantabrica
'Alba'
'Alba Globosa'
'Atropurpurea'
'Bicolor'
'David Moss'
'Globosa'
'Hookstone Purple'
'Polifolia'
'Praegerae'
'Purpurea'
'Rosea'
'Seedling No 3'
'William Buchanan'
Erica carnea (syn *E. herbacea*)
'Eileen Porter'
ciliaris
'Alba'
'David McClintock'

'Globosa'
'Jean Liddle'
'Maweana'
'Mrs C. H. Gill'
'Rotundiflora'
'Stapehill'
'Stoborough'
'White Wings'
'Wych'
cinerea
'Atrorubens'
'Cevennes'
'Heathfield'
'Knap Hill Pink'
'Purple Beauty'
manipuliflora
× *praegeri*
'Connemara'
tetralix
'Alba Mollis'
'Con Underwood'
'Daphne Underwood'
'L. E. Underwood'
'Mary Grace'
'Melbury White'
'Pink Star'
tetralix
'Ruby's Variety'
'Silver Bells'
vagans
'Alba Multiflora'
'Birch Glow'
'Cream'
'George Underwood'
'Hookstone Rosea'
'Leucantha'
'Lyonesse'
'Mrs S. Donaldson'
'Mrs D. F. Maxwell'
'Multiflora'
'Peach Blossom'

o

OCTOBER—CONT.

'Rubra'
'St Keverne'
'White Rocket'
× *watsonii*
'Ciliaris Hybrida'
'Dawn'

'F. White'
'Gwen'
'H. Maxwell'
'Rachel'
× *williamsii*
'Gwavas'

NOVEMBER

Calluna vulgaris
   'David Eason'
   'Durfordii'
   'Elegantissima'
   'Elegantissima Walter
     Ingwersen'
   'Goldsworth Crimson'
   'Goldsworth Crimson Variegata'
   'Goldsworth Pink'
   'H. E. Beale'
   'Hibernica'
   'Hiemalis'
   'Johnson's Variety'
   'Penhale'

   'Serlei'
   'Serlei Aurea'
   'Serleu Rubra'
   'Underwoodii'
Erica carnea (syn *E. herbacea*)
   'Eileen Porter'
   'Early Red'
× *darleyensis*
   'Darley Dale'
   'George Rendall'
multiflora
vagans
   'Cream'

DECEMBER

Calluna vulgaris
   'Durfordii'
   'Elegantissima'
Erica carnea (syn *E. herbacea*)
   'Aurea'
   'December Red'
   'Early Red'
   'Eileen Porter'
   'Gracilis'
   'King George'
   'Lesley Sparkes'
   'Pirbright Rose'
   'Praecox Rubra'

   'Queen Mary'
   'Winter Beauty'
× *darleyensis*
   'Arthur Johnson'
   'Carryduff'
   'Darley Dale'
   'Erecta'
   'Furzey'
   'George Rendall'
   'Ghost Hills'
   'James Smith'
   'Jennie Porter'
   'John Wynne'

DECEMBER—CONT.

'Rosslare'
'W. G. Pine'
'Silberschmelze'

multiflora
× *veitchii*
    'Exeter'

Heaths and heathers for foliage effect

CALLUNAS

S=Spring effect only.

'Alba Aurea' (S)
'Argentea'
'Aurea'
'Beoley Gold'
'Blazeaway'
'Bognie'
'Carole Chapman'
'Cuprea'
'Fairy'
'Fred J. Chapple' (S)
'Golden Carpet'
'Golden Feather'
'Gold Haze'
'Goldsworth Crimson Variegata'
'Hammondii Aureifolia'
'Hirsuta Typica'
'Hugh Nicholson'
'J. F. Letts'
'Joy Vanstone'
'Kirby White'
'Lambs Tails'
'Late Crimson Gold'

'Mrs Pat'
'Multicolor'
'Orange Queen'
'Prostrate Orange'
'Pubescens'
'Robert Chapman'
'Rubrifolia'
'Ruby Slinger'
'Ruth Sparkes'
'Ruth Sparkes Improved Form'
'Sally Anne Proudley' (S)
'Serlei Aurea'
'Silver Queen'
'Sir John Charrington'
'Spring Cream'
'Spring Torch' (S)
'Spitfire'
'Summer Orange'
'Sunset'
'Tricolorifolia Smith's Variety'
'Winter Chocolate'

ERICAS

Erica arborea
    'Gold Tips'
    carnea (syn *E. herbacea*)
        'Ann Sparkes'
        'Aurea'
    ciliaris
        'Aurea'

cinerea
    'Ann Berry'
    'Golden Drop'
    'Golden Hue'
    'John Eason'
    'Snow Cream'

ERICAS—CONT.

mediterranea (syn *E. erigena*)
  'Golden Dome'
  'Lesley Sparkes'
vagans
  'Valerie Proudley'

× *watsonii*
  'Ciliaris Hybrida' (S)
  'Dawn' (S)
  'H. Maxwell' (S)
× *williamsii*
  'Gwavas' (S)

Plant collecting

Horticulturists or gardeners who have been fortunate enough to go abroad for their holidays have probably at some time brought back plants or propagating material (if they have already obtained a Certificate for Plant Importation from the Ministry of Agriculture, Fisheries and Food, Horseferry Road, London, SW1). If one has gone to all the trouble of getting a plant permit, which is essential if one wishes to bring material back into this country, then great care and correct treatment should be given to material, whether it be rooted or unrooted.

Cutting material should be collected as short a time as possible before journeying home. It is best collected in the early morning when it is cool and fresh, and kept until the last minute before travelling in a very cool and shady situation. Plants that are to be brought back should be small and well rooted and lifted with a reasonable amount of root and some soil attached. These too should be stored in a cool shady place until leaving. The final packing of both cuttings and plants should be left to the last minute.

I have always purchased or obtained a supply of paper handkerchiefs or soft toilet paper, and my cuttings have been carefully wrapped in a moist paper tissue, with a label, often only bearing an index number for identification. It is illegal to import plants with soil on the roots, unless the site, which of course is usually a nursery, has been visited by government officials and given a clean bill of health. Therefore all the soil must be washed off the roots. Most of my escapades have been carried out not far from a good running stream and my plants have been washed in this water. These too are wrapped tightly in slightly moist paper tissues. The whole lot is then wrapped in dry paper tissues and placed in a polythene bag, which itself is put inside a box, tin or other receptacle that will not easily get squashed. Failing this, little packages can be made up and put inside one's shoes in a case or rucksack.

One might have to declare the material at the customs, so I would advise all travellers to have their parcels where they can easily get at them. A list of all the material should be prepared and this, with the permit, should either be given to the customs official on entry into this country or sent to the ministry soon after arrival. It is a condition that all material should be kept in one place for at least three weeks during which time an official from the ministry may come to see whether it is free from pests and diseases.

Often good plants are dug up and fail to become established in cultivation. It would be better if only cuttings or other propagating material were taken from choice plants.

The plant breeders' rights

The Plant Varieties Rights Office at Murray House, Vandon Street, London, SW1 is producing, if it has not done so already, a Plant Breeders' Rights scheme for trees, shrubs and woody climbers, applying to about 100 genera and species, which would include *Ericas, Callunas* and *Daboecias*.

A person wishing to make an application for Plant Breeders' Rights has to pay a fee of £10 and when his application is accepted he has to submit plant material for trial. Clear distinctness, uniformity and stability of his variety or cultivar will be assessed every year that his plant is on trial; an annual fee of approximately £15 will be charged and when the breeding right is granted a fee of £20 has to be paid before a grant certificate can be issued. From then onwards every year that the holder wishes to keep the rights, an annual fee of £1·25 would be needed.

These were the costs of operation in 1970. The person holding the Plant Breeders' Rights of a cultivar receives royalties from plants grown and sold.

Nomenclature

It was Linnaeus in his *Species Plantarum* of 1753 who brought the system of binomial nomenclature before the world. For example with *Erica tetralix* or *Erica cinerea, Erica* is the genus or generic name and *tetralix* and *cinerea* are specific epithets.

As the interest grew in heaths and heathers so natural plant variants and those raised in the garden were selected and grown on and called varieties, but now it has been internationally agreed that the term cultivar, abbreviated to cv, should denote a plant variant raised in the garden as a seedling or sport, or introduced from the wild and maintained in cultivation just because of its garden value. The names of cultivars should be printed in roman, as in this book, beginning with a capital letter and placed between single inverted commas. This distinguishes them from botanical varieties, which are recognised by botanists as distinct sub-divisions of species occurring in the wild which are called varieties, abbreviated var, and printed in italics.

Developments in plant names

It is internationally agreed that the first name a plant is given, and that is recognisable from its accompanying description and is published in or after

1753, is to be the recognised name. Periodically, botanists looking into ancient writings find references to now well-known plants under different names. For this reason names of plants keep changing: the latest alterations to heaths and heathers as suggested by Mr R. Ross of the British Museum are: *E. mediterranea* or *E. hibernica* to be *E. erigena*, and *E. carnea* to be *E. herbacea*. But as the former names are so well known to gardeners, who are unlikely to refer to these two plants by their new names, I felt it best to use *E. mediterranea* and *E. carnea* throughout the book.

Meanings of the names (Latinised roots used in cultivar names)

alba	=	white
albiflora	=	white flowered
alpina	=	alpine
aragonensis	=	of Aragon, north-east Spain
argentea	=	silver
atro-	=	dark
aurea	=	golden
bicolor	=	two coloured
boothii	=	in honour of H. Booth, amateur gardener, 1864
canescens	=	becoming grey, greyish
cevennensis	=	from the Cevennes Mountains, southern France
coccinea	=	scarlet
compacta	=	compact, dense growth
crawfordii	=	in honour of Dr F. C. Crawford of Edinburgh
crispa	=	irregularly waved, twisted
cuprea	=	copper
darleyensis	=	from Darley Dale, Derbyshire
dumosa	=	bushy
durfordii	=	from Durford Wood, north of Petersfield, Hampshire
elata	=	tall, stately
elegans	=	elegant
elegantissima	=	most elegant
elongata	=	much lengthened
erecta	=	erect, upright
flore pleno	=	double or full flowered
floribunda	=	many flowered
fulgida	=	shiny, bright coloured
glauca	=	glaucous, bluish-green, bluish-grey
globosa	=	globe shaped
gracilis	=	slender, graceful
grandiflora	=	large flowered

grasmeriensis	=	from Grasmere, Westmorland
hayesensis	=	from Robert Hayes of Grasmere
hirsuta	=	hairy
humilis	=	lower growing than the majority of the other kindred species
hybrida	=	hybrid
hiemalis	=	of winter
hypnoides	=	moss-like
incana	=	hoary, hairy
kuphaldtii	=	in honour of Herr Kuphaldt
leucantha	=	white coloured
lilacina	=	lilac coloured
major	=	larger
martinesii	=	in honour of Spanish botanist Martines
maweana	=	in honour of George Maw, 1832–1912, druggist of London. Collected in Mediterranean. He was the author of a monograph on Crocuses
minima	=	smallest
minor	=	smaller
mollis	=	soft, tender, velvety
multicolor	=	many coloured
nana	=	dwarf
pallida	=	pale
pilosa	=	hairy
plena	=	full, double
polifolia	=	many leaves
polypetala	=	many petalled
praecox	=	early
praegeri	=	in honour of R. L. Praeger, 1865–1953, librarian and botanist in Dublin
prostrata	=	prostrate
pumila	=	dwarf
purpurea	=	purple
pygmaea	=	pygmy
pyramidalis	=	pyramidal
pyrenaica	=	from the Pyrenees
rendlei	=	in honour of Dr A. B. Rendle, British Museum
rigida	=	rigid, stiff
rosea	=	rose coloured
rotundiflora	=	round flowered
rotundifolia	=	round leaved
rubra	=	red
rubens	=	red
rubrifolia	=	red leaved

salmonoides	=	salmon coloured
schizopetala	=	split petalled
serotina	=	produced late in the season or year
sherwoodi	=	of Sherwood Nurseries, Oregon
spicata	=	spine-like
splendens	=	splendid, brilliant
stricta	=	upright
stuartii	=	in honour of Dr Charles Stuart, 1825–1902
superba	=	superb
tenella	=	frail
tenuis	=	slender
terminalis	=	terminal, at the end
tomentosa	=	closely covered with down
torulosa	=	having small swellings at intervals
tricolorifolia	=	having three colours in foliage
typica	=	the type, or original
underwoodii	=	after Underwoods of Woking
variegata	=	variegated
veitchii	=	in honour of Veitch of Exeter
viridiflora	=	green flowered
vivellii	=	in honour of A. Vivell a garden architect
violacea	=	violet
watsonii	=	in honour of H. C. Watson, 1804–81

Meanings of names (specific epithets)

arborea	=	tree-like
australis	=	southern, no connection with Australia
azorica	=	from the Azores
canaliculata	=	grooved, referring to the leaves
cantabrica	=	from the Latin *cantabricus*—region of Spain, formerly inhabited by the Cantabric tribe
carnea	=	flesh coloured, from the Latin *caro*—flesh, from the corolla colour
ciliaris	=	fringed with hairs; *cilium*—an eyelash, hair fringe on leaves
cinerea	=	ashen grey; *cinis*—ashes, probably referring to the stem colour
codonodes	=	bell-bearing
corsica	=	of Corsica
erigena	=	Irish-born, medieval designation from the Old Irish *eriu*
herbacea	=	herbaceous, thin, green, having the characteristics of a herb
hibernica	=	Irish—from Ireland
lusitanica	=	Portuguese

mackaiana	=	in honour of MacKay, late curator of the Botanic Garden, Trinity College, Dublin
manipuliflora	=	with few-flowered clusters, from the Latin *manipulus* (handful)
mediterranea	=	calm, Mediterranean, inland, remote from the sea, opposite to *maritimus*
multiflorus	=	many flowered; *multus*—much, *flos*—flower
occidentalis	=	western
pageana	=	in honour of Mrs Mary Page, botanist at the Bolus Herborium, Cape Town (1914-24)
peduncularis	=	having a flower stalk
ramulosa	=	twiggy
scoparis	=	broom-like, thin branched
stricta	=	very straight, erect
terminalis	=	at end of, short, not axillary
tetralix	=	*tetra*—four, *helix*—a spiral, from the leaf arrangement
umbellata	=	flower in umbels; *umbella*—a parasol
vagans	=	Latin meaning—wandering
verticillata	=	whorled, forming a ring around a common axis
vulgaris	=	common

Glossary of botanical terms

acute	=	distinctly and sharply pointed, but not drawn out
alternate	=	placed on opposite sides of a stem on a different line
androecium	=	male part of a flower, filament and anther
anther	=	male part of a flower, containing the pollen
anther exserted	=	anther protrudes beyond corolla
anther included	=	anther does not protrude beyond corolla
ascending	=	directed upwards
awn	=	bristle-like appendage, bearded, found on many filaments of *Erica* stamens
awnless	=	not having awns
axillary	=	growing in an axil
bell shaped	=	campanulate
bract	=	modified leaves intermediate between calyx and true leaves
bracteolate	=	having bracts
callus	=	a hard-skinned abnormally thick part, as at the base of a cutting
calyx	=	from the Greek—*calyx*, covering of a flower or fruit. Made of sepals, usually the outside whorl of floral segments

campanulate	=	bell shaped
canaliculate	=	long, concave, like a gutter or channel
capsule	=	dry dehiscent seed vessel
chlorophyll	=	green colour in leaves concerned with the manufacture (photosynthesis) of sugars from carbon dioxide, water and light
chlorosis	=	disorder showing a loss of green colour or chlorophyll
chlorotic	=	showing loss of green colour or chlorophyll
cilia	=	a short hair like an eyelash
ciliate	=	fringed with cilia
clonal	=	vegetatively produced from one original stock
clusters	=	compactly gathered together, eg *E. mackaiana*, *E. tetralix* raceme
contiguous	=	when neighbouring parts are in contact as in some leaves
corolla	=	made of petals—usually the second whorl of floral segments
corymb	=	an inflorescence arrangement in which the pedicels are lengthened so that the flowers are at one level
cylindrical	=	tubular, long, round, round as in *E. lusitanica*, *E. australis*
deciduous	=	falling in a season, eg autumn leaf fall or petal fall in a flower
decumbent	=	reclining but with the ends ascending
decussate	=	in pairs alternatively at right-angles
dehiscent	=	splits open as in fruit
divergent	=	the angle between the succeeding organs in the same spiral or whorl (as in stamens)
downy	=	pubescent with fine soft hairs
eglandular	=	not glandular
epidermis	=	true cellular skin of a plant
exserted	=	protruded beyond the surrounding organs
fauces	=	upper part of throat
filament	=	stem of stamen
gamopetalous	=	petals are united, not separate
glabrous	=	smooth, without pubescence
glandular	=	possessing glands
glandular ciliate	=	possessing glands at end of an epidermal hair-like appendage
globular	=	nearly in a true sphere—eg *E. vagans*
gynoecium	=	female part of a flower
hirsute	=	with long distinct hairs
hispid	=	covered with coarse, rigid, erect hairs, harsh to the touch

hybrid	=	a mongrel plant obtained by the pollen of one variant fertilising the stigma of another
included	=	not protruding beyond the surrounding organs
inflorescence	=	the disposition of the flower on the floral axis, often used as the name for the flowering cluster
lamina	=	leaf blade
lanceolate	=	narrow, tapering at each end
lax	=	loose, distant
linear	=	narrow, several times larger than wide
mucronate	=	possessing a short and straight point
obtuse	=	blunt or rounded at the end
opposite	=	refers to leaves—two at each node or stem joint, one on either side of stem or one part before another, eg stamens in front of petals
oval	=	egg shaped, eg *Daboecia*
ovoid—urn	=	see urceolate ovoid
ovary	=	part of a pistil containing the ovules (seed), the immature fruit
panicle	=	loose flower clusters, as a branched raceme or corymb
pedicel	=	flower stalk
peduncle	=	general flower stalks
perianth	=	calyx and/or corolla segments together
petals	=	segments making the corolla of a flower
petiole	=	leaf stalk
photosynthesis	=	see chlorophyll
pistil	=	entire female organ of a flower, comprising stigma, style and ovary
plumose	=	plume-like inflorescence, eg *E. lusitanica*
pollen	=	fertilising micro-spore produced from anthers
polypetalous	=	having several distinct petals
prostrate	=	lying flat
puberulous	=	slightly hairy
pubescent	=	clothed with soft hair or down
raceme	=	a type of inflorescence, central axis has peduncles off at intervals (plate, p 71)
recurved	=	curved backwards or downwards
revolute	=	rolled back from the margin or apex
sepals	=	segments making the calyx of the flower
septicidal	=	when a capsule dehisces through lines or junctions
sessile	=	sitting close, destitute of a stalk
setaceous	=	bristle-like, when applied to a stem it means slender
simple	=	of one part or series, not compound
sparse	=	scattered

spike	=	flowers sessile on a common elongated axis
sport	=	a variant from type produced by bud or seed
stamen	=	male organ of a flower comprising filament and anther
stigma	=	top of the pistil—receives the pollen
style	=	stem of a pistil
subacute	=	somewhat acute
sulcate	=	grooved; usually leaves when rolled back and furrowed
taxa	=	a taxonomic group of any rank
tomentose	=	densely pubescent with matted wool or short hairs
tubular	=	cylindrical
umbel	=	inflorescence in which the pedicels are all arranged from one point on the peduncle
urceolate	=	pitcher-like, contracted at mouth like an urn or pitcher
urceolate ovoid	=	rounder than urceolate
urceolate narrow	=	more tubular than urceolate
whorled	=	the arrangement of organs in a circle from a common axis

The Heather Society

Sir John Charrington, an ardent heath and heather enthusiast, realising the developing interest among professional and amateur horticulturists in this group of plants, sent a letter to the Royal Horticultural Society, which was published in their Journal late in 1962, suggesting that all those interested in the subject should attend a meeting on the 20 February 1963, at the RHS buildings in Vincent Square, London.

From this meeting the Heather Society was formed. The aim of this society is to stimulate interest in heaths and heathers, as many people do not realise what a rewarding addition they can be to a garden. The society also makes a contribution in the following way:

1. To arrange visits to private and famous heather gardens.
2. To provide a source of information on cultural methods.
3. To arrange displays and competitions at the RHS and local shows.
4. To form a collection of slides to be loaned to lecturers.
5. To co-operate with the trade in expanding the *Erica* market.

The first *Annual Year Book* appeared in 1963 and now, together with this, three bulletins are produced annually. These are full of information submitted by the wide membership, which in 1969 totalled approximately 700. A good proportion come from abroad and many of these are regular contributors. The society is now developing a collection of species and cultivars at the northern Horticultural Society's gardens at Harlow Car.

Sir John Charrington is the present chairman and that eminent heather specialist Mr F. J. Chapple is president. The secretary is Mrs C. I. McLeod of Yew Trees, Horley Row, Horley, Surrey.

Conversion table—fahrenheit and centigrade

$^\circ F$	$^\circ C$	Correct to one decimal place
120°	48·88r	48·9°
115°	47·11r	47·1°
110°	43·33r	43·3°
105°	40·55r	40·6°
100°	37·77r	37·8°
95°	35·0	35·0°
90°	33·33r	33·3°
85°	29·44r	29·4°
80°	26·66r	26·7°
75°	23·088r	23·09°
70°	22·22r	22·2°
65°	18·33r	18·3°
60°	15·55r	15·6°
55°	12·77r	12·8°
50°	10·0	10·0°
45°	7·022r	7·02°
40°	4·044r	4·04°
35°	1·066r	1·07°
32°	0·0	0·0

Conversion table—inches and millimetres

Inches	Millimetres	Millimetres	Inches
1/32	0·8	1	1/25
1/16	1·5	2	1/12
$\frac{1}{8}$	3·0	3	$\frac{1}{8}$
$\frac{1}{4}$	6·0	4	1/6
$\frac{1}{2}$	13·0	5	1/5
$\frac{3}{4}$	19·0	6	$\frac{1}{4}$
1	25	10	2/5

Acknowledgements

Appreciation is expressed to:
Ardron, J. P., Fulwood Heights, Harrison Lane, Sheffield S10 4PA

Bartlett, Mrs M., Dartington, Devon
Benjamin, Ruth, Post Rupin, Institute of Agriculture, Israel
Brander, Paul Eric, Statens Forsogsstation, Denmark
Brickell, C. D., Royal Horticultural Society's Garden, Wisley, Surrey
Bucharest University, Romania (director)
Burfitt, Joyce, Aldersyde Cottage, Lychett Matravers, Poole, Dorset

Caen Botanic Gardens, France (professor of botany)
Colourful Gardens Ltd, Criccieth, North Wales
Copeland, H. W., Chatham, Massachusetts, USA
Cullen, J., Liverpool University Botanic Gardens, Cheshire

Dorrien-Smith, T. M., Lt-Commander, Tresco, Scilly Isles
Drake, J., Inshriach Alpine Plant Nursery, Aviemore, Inverness-shire, Scotland

Edinburgh Royal Botanic Gardens
Elliot, Roy, Handsworth, Birmingham

Fisons Ltd, Cambridge Division
Fulcher, Dick, Dartington, Devon

Gartner, G., University of Innsbruck, Botanic Gardens, Austria
Gillet, L., Kings Heath Park, Birmingham
Gilmour, J. S. L., Cambridge University Botanic Gardens (director)

Gordon, Mrs M., Zeal, South Brent, Devon
Gray, the late Dr R., and Mrs R. E., Southcote, Hindhead, Surrey
Griffith, J. L., Slapton Ley Field Centre, Devon

Hall, N. T., Forestry Commission
Hancock, Weed Research Organisation, Kidlington, Oxford
Heywood, V. H., Department of Botany, Reading
Hulme, J. K., Liverpool University Botanic Gardens (director)
Humphrey, B. E., Hillier & Sons, Winchester

Janssen, W. J. M., Wageningen, Holland

Keesing, J. S., Royal Botanic Gardens, Kew, Richmond, Surrey
Knight, F., Royal Horticultural Society's Garden, Wisley, Surrey
  (retired director)
Knuckey, D., Treseders of Truro, Cornwall

Larouse, Mme, A. de, Gurf-sur-Yvette, France
Leach, C. C. J., Ministry of Agriculture, Fisheries & Food
Letts, J. F., Westwood Rd, Windlesham, Surrey
Lima, Mrs Ingrid, Madlalia, Stavanger, Norway
Little, D. A. J., Somerset Farm Institute, Cannington

McLeod, Mrs C. I., The Heather Society
Maxwell & Beale, Corfe Mullen, Wimborne, Dorset
Ministry of Agriculture, Fisheries & Food, Plant Health Branch
Murphy Chemical Co Ltd

O'Hare, P. J., Peatland Experimental Station, Ballina, County Mayo,
  Ireland

Pearce, S. A., Royal Botanic Gardens, Kew, Surrey.
Primrose Hill Nursery, Haslemere, Surrey
Putiles, L., Botanic Gardens, Zurich, Switzerland

Ross, Dr R., British Museum (Natural History), London
Royal Horticultural Society, Vincent Square, London SW1
Rozeira, Prof Arnaldo, Porto, Portugal
Rushdi, A. H., University of Ibaden, Nigeria

Shaw, R., Royal Botanic Gardens, Kew, Richmond, Surrey
Slieve Donard Nursery Co Ltd, Newcastle, County Down, Northern
    Ireland
Smith, G. D., Harlow Car Gardens, Harrogate, Yorkshire
Smith, J. D. H., Tresco Abbey Gardens, Tresco, Isles of Scilly
Solli, L., Torino Botanic Gardens, Italy
Sparkes, J. W., The Heather Nursery, Beoley, Nr Redditch, Worc
Staples, Miss D. M., Royal Horticultural Society's Garden, Wisley,
    Surrey
Stearn, Dr W., British Museum (Natural History)
Stevens, F. J., Maxwell & Beale, Corfe Mullen, Wimborne, Dorset

Taylor, Sir George, Royal Botanic Gardens, Kew, Richmond, Surrey
Thornton, Miss E. V., Plant Variety Rights Office, London, SW1
Todd, Alan, Microslides (Oxford) Ltd, 7 Little Clarendon Street,
    Oxford
Treseder, Neil, Truro

Upward, E. M., Alpine Garden Society

Van de Laar, H. J., Experimental Station, Boskoop, Holland
Webb, D. A., University of Dublin
Witt, Joseph A., assistant director, University of Washington Arbore-
    tum, Seattle, USA
Wyman, Donald, The Arnold Arboretum, Harvard University,
    Massachusetts, USA

Yates, G., Tabramhill Gardens Ltd, Newstead Abbey Park, Notts

Bibliography

Baker, H. A., and Oliver, E. G. H., *Ericas in South Africa*, 1967
Beijernick, W., *Callunavulgaris—Monograph*, 1940
Chapple, Fred J., *The Heather Garden*, 1952
Johnson, A. T., *Hardy Heaths*, 1952
Letts, J. F., *Handbook of Heathers*, 1965
Maxwell, D. F., *The Low Road*, 1927
Maxwell, D. F., and Patrick, P. S., *English Heather Garden*, 1966
McClintock, David, *A Guide to the Naming of Plants*, 1969

Index